Regrowth

How organizations can overcome stalling
by unlocking their people's potential

Ernesto J.Gómez

Regrowth: How Organizations Can Overcome Stalling by Unlocking Their People's Potential by Ernesto J. Gómez

Library of Congress Number: 2024917547

eBook - 978-1-959009-16-0
Paperback- 978-1-959009-17-7
Hardcover - 978-1-959009-18-4

Published in the United States by AM1 Austin, Texas

Outside the United States - Published by Aspen Mindset 1 Monterrey, Mexico

The author has made every effort to credit all sources accurately. After over 30 years in the industry, some information may have been absorbed over time and unintentionally treated as common knowledge or not attributed to the correct individual. Any oversights are unintentional.

To my wife, Thelma, whose love and support have been vital in my personal and professional life and in making this book happen. I could not have done it without you.

To my daughters Andrea, Fernanda, and Cordelia, and my granddaughters Raquel, Mariel, and Lorenza, I am blessed by the joy you bring to my life, and I am so happy because girls rule at our house!

To my sons-in-law, Andres, Juan Pablo, and Joaquin, who engage with me in great conversations and provide points of view that I greatly value.

I am very fortunate; this is the best family I could ever wish for and my source of strength and inspiration. I will be forever grateful to all of you.

Table of Contents

Foreword

Over the past two decades, I've had the privilege of designing and leading executive education programs to drive business outcomes through leadership development, organizational learning, and enterprise-wide transformation. As a Senior Lecturer at the MIT Sloan School of Management, I've collaborated with leaders from some of the world's largest organizations, helping them navigate complex change while enhancing both individual and organizational capabilities.

In this capacity, in 2015, I had the pleasure of meeting Ernesto Gomez, who at the time represented a major Mexican conglomerate seeking to develop the leadership potential of its technical experts. This project presented an exciting challenge: integrating critical topics like technology readiness and the management of complex technical projects with the development of leadership skills. We were able to debunk the myth that technical experts are only interested in specialized knowledge and discovered their eagerness to grow as leaders, provided we could equip them with the right tools. Over 300 executives participated in these programs, and their success was so significant that they were featured as a case study on the MIT Executive Education website.

When Ernesto approached me to write this foreword, I immediately said yes. We share a deep passion for developing individuals and empowering them to make meaningful contributions to their organizations and communities. I'm also thrilled by the idea of a book allowing leaders to tap into Ernesto's decades of experience designing transformational journeys for companies—a blend of academic rigor and hands-on practical application. Ernesto offers a rare combination as a professional and book writer: a strategic, conceptually sound approach to managing organizational transformation and real-world execution in the trenches. This makes his insights uniquely valuable for leaders who want to make things happen and drive lasting and impactful organizational transformation.

The book *Regrowth* addresses a critical challenge many organizations face today: sustaining growth in an environment of constant change. The rapid pace of technological advancement and the velocity at which the world is changing demands that companies ensure their people continuously upgrade their skills. Failure to do so leads to stagnation and eventual obsolescence. This is why companies seek to develop their talent base and rely on institutions like MIT to provide their leaders with the knowledge and skills needed to stay relevant and competitive.

The core message of this book is clear: now, more than ever, organizations must unlock the full potential of their people day in and day out, as standing still in a dynamic environment is a recipe for failure. Achieving this goal requires a systemic approach, where the entire organization can be sustainable in the long run. Investing in only senior managers or developing leaders in emerging capabilities is not enough.

While talent development is crucial to delivering products and services that meet or exceed customer expectations, my experience as a coach to senior management and an expert in organizational learning shows that today's fast-paced business environment demands even more. Agile leadership, cohesive teams, and the ability to innovate both quickly and rigorously are essential qualities that must be embedded throughout the company. Large organizations, especially, function as complex systems that require transformation on multiple levels to remain nimble, resilient, and competitive.

That's why I'm truly excited about Ernesto's book, *Regrowth*. It delivers a powerful, actionable framework for reigniting growth in a business landscape where many companies are stagnating or facing constant setbacks. This book is more than just a guide—it's a playbook for navigating the complexities of modern business. You'll learn how to build talent density in key roles, foster a culture of collective decision-making, and create a shared mindset that drives adaptability, enabling organizations to pivot when needed. Ernesto's insights will equip you to confidently reclaim your growth trajectory, even in the face of challenging and uncertain conditions that have become the new normal.

Regrowth is not just a book; it's a tool for transformation. By applying its principles, you'll be better prepared to unlock your organization's full potential and achieve results that exceed expectations. I encourage you to read it with an open mind and be ready to act.

Court Chilton
Senior Lecturer, Work and Organization Studies at MIT Sloan
School of Management, MIT Leadership Center

Introduction

"As long as you're green you are growing,
as soon as you're ripe you begin to rot."
—RAY KROC (purchased a local hamburger chain from
the McDonald brothers and expanded McDonald's
restaurants to become a global powerhouse)

I f you are leading a business, you can be certain that growth is one of the indicators that will be used to evaluate your performance. It may be growth of the top line, the bottom line, return on investment, stock price, customer satisfaction, market share, the launch of innovative products, or all of the above. It could be realized growth or potential growth. You can pick any indicator or group of indicators that best measure your progress for the stage of your business or your industry, but I'll bet you will not get away from addressing growth in one form or another. Growth is critical in assessing the success or failure of your work and is a sanity check for the business. In organizations, for better or worse, it is difficult to leave growth out of the equation, even if you are a sole owner and you only answer to yourself. It is only natural to aspire to generate more value. We humans are always in a permanent race of escalating expectations.

Your staying power as a company depends on your ability to continue growing despite changes in the environment, fierce competition, or volatility in the market. But brutal reality shows us that growth is difficult to come by. For the average company, it is the exception, not the rule. Most companies grow slowly: "A typical company grew at a measly 2.8 percent per year during the ten years preceding COVID-19, and only one in eight recorded growth rates of more than 10 percent per year". (McKinsey & Co, "The Ten Rules of Growth.", August 12, 2022). Think about it for a moment: according to this McKinsey finding, the typical company's compounded growth rate will require 25 years to double its size. Under this scenario, the prospects do not look promising for stakeholders involved in developing businesses and pursuing value creation, for their dreams and aspirations are probably to become outliers in their industries and the success stories of their generation.

When growth is in short supply, competition becomes uglier. It turns into a zero-sum game with the looming possibility of being commoditized or pulled into price wars. Add to this that it is not easy to differentiate in a rowdy market, and you can tell that a perfect storm is in the making. Unless companies transform themselves and innovate their way out of a growth slump, their livelihood will be threatened. And this is not only a problem for established, legacy businesses. Both insurgent and incumbent companies are vulnerable, making it even more concerning: "Of the roughly one in five companies that managed to make it through insurgency to incumbency in a recent fifteen-year period, two-thirds face stall-out.. Moreover, of the large companies that hit stall-out, fewer than one in seven will recover its market power and prior momentum."[1]

Conventional wisdom offers a multitude of solutions to deal with the growth challenge, like product diversification, sales initiatives, strategic alliances, innovation methodologies, and agile tools, among many others. In his book Change by Design, Tim Brown introduced the "ways to grow" matrix, which summarizes the available growth options for businesses in four categories:

- Selling existing products to existing users (incremental)
- Selling existing products to new users (evolutionary)
- Selling new offerings to existing users (evolutionary)
- Selling new offerings to new users (revolutionary)[2]

These four spaces are helpful in instrumenting activities that may lead to growth. They represent the "what to do" problem, which is a necessary condition but not sufficient. It falls short of solving the crux of the growth problem, the "how to make it happen" problem, which is the "make it or break it" challenge for all organizations.

In this book, I suggest a perspective that leverages the organizational core, the soft-wiring of the company, to make growth a reality. This stems from my own professional experience in managing internal barriers in organizations that prevent growth from happening and enabling organizations to develop the capabilities to pursue their ever-ambitious goals. I have been tested in the business world. I have launched a dozen of small businesses and worked for large organizations, including leading a unit with 1.3 billion dollars in revenue per year. I know what it means to be on the "business end," delivering economic results.

On the other hand, I also know how to spearhead a talent and culture transformation. During the last ten years, I have been heading corporate positions to help the transformation of a multi-national conglomerate of 83,000 people and, lately, a CPG company with 45,000 people operating in 18 countries. My approach is more than just academic when helping organizations grow. Instead, it is grounded in the practical realities of day-to-day business operations. I have implemented mindset transformation journeys that unlock the dormant potential of organizations through practical applications.

Growing pains

As you already know, business growth is a customer-driven endeavor. Customers vote with their money and choose which product or service to buy to fulfill their needs, which defines the fate of companies competing in the market. The market system is dynamic; winners and losers often swap positions, and nothing guarantees long-term success. The cemetery of failed companies includes once-powerful organizations that could not sustain customers' preferences.

While customers are critical for growth, growth's genesis originates with actions taken inside the organization. Growing in the market is an outcome, a result, of what we do or refrain from doing inside the company. In that regard, mediocre growth or stalling out is a self-inflicted wound, dependent on how the organization works, rather than a condition in the market over which we have no control.

It's an inside job

As a rule of thumb, analysts and stockholders expect companies to achieve a permanent growth pattern resembling a 45-degree straight line or the famous hockey stick shape. However, the dynamics of the market tell us a different story. There is no such thing as a lifelong, ever-growing pattern in business. You often find some growth accompanied by irregular sequences, hits and misses, flats periods, and often regressions. Companies rarely advance at the growth pace they desire, and only a few are watchful of the perils involved in a growth path that may lead to severe problems down the road. Determining whether a company's underperformance is due to a temporary issue, like past slumps, or a more serious, long-term problem can be challenging. Bain & Company analyzed the trends of large companies experiencing stalling growth and discovered that the loss of growth momentum typically lasts a few years before rapidly declining.[3] This suggests that by the time the downturn is diagnosed, the organization may already be in a free fall and might not recover.

Despite the investor's and market's wishes, reality tells us that achieving sustainable and relevant growth is the exception, and periods of stagnation or decline are part of the journey. As Gary Hammel says, the future is indifferent to our preferences, and many variables beyond our control will impact business performance and growth. When figuring out what needs to be done to fix our problems, we naturally look outside, in the market, to gain insight and devise routes of action, but even with the proper diagnosis, implementing the appropriate solutions is not always guaranteed.

Why is that?: "We find that more than four in five problems on the outside of a business trace to problems on the inside—problems that inhibited its ability to adapt, to decide and act quickly, to embrace new ideas, to keep costs down, or to scale its ability to serve customers. The plot lines inside and outside ultimately have to converge, of course: you cannot win sustainably on the outside if you are losing internally, and vice versa...85 percent of executives perceive that the key barriers to sustained and profitable growth that they face are on the inside." Chris Zook and James Allen.[4]

We are used to assessing companies' success or failure from an external perspective, considering factors such as sales, profitability, and customer preferences to gauge their performance. However, these are just indicators of how a company is doing in the market and only reflect outcomes, not the root cause of performance. The organization's ingenuity and resources, demonstrated by how it works and its accompanying decision-making process, are the main drivers for achieving growth or lack thereof.

Since variability is inevitable and the business environment surprises us with daily challenges, the only way to jumpstart a growth path is to be ready to address downturns as soon as they arise. To achieve this, we must prepare the organization to adapt and regrow when a changing and uncertain environment stalls it out. Regrowth requires us to focus inward to wire the organization to find solutions to our problems promptly and to take a long-term perspective to evolve.

This book argues that to acheive regrowth, we must develop a malleable, adaptative organization that is resistant to any limitations the business context may bring. For the organization to keep regrowing, we must probe the "organizational atomic fusion" blueprint to release its energy and achieve its goals.

Probing into the organization's potential is the way to regrow

Within organizations, a rich source of creativity and innovation awaits release. People's collective knowledge, skills, and perspectives create a reservoir of energy that, when tapped into effectively, can drive positive change and advancement. To increase performance and achieve our goals, we must leverage the organization's capacity to rise to its potential, allowing the dormant possibilities in our people to emerge.

In recent history, several organizations have leveraged the potential of their employees to achieve success. One notable example illustrates how trusting in the ingenuity of their people can lead to remarkable results in a highly competitive market. The story of the Chobani brand, founded by Hamdi Ulukaya, exemplifies this. Ulukaya established a yogurt business that rapidly grew in just 15 years to challenge dominant competitors and currently holds approximately 20% of the US yogurt market: "If Chobani became what it became, we broke all the records because our people always found a way to make things happen. And that old factory—it is still unbelievable what we've done in that old factory, that was one small filler, four people, 70, 80 years old, no one even knew that it could be turned back on. We end up making sales almost close to a billion dollars in that factory without raising one penny of capital. And that is just not possible in any dimension that you look at it. But it only happened because people just found a way. We just found a way." (Chobani Founder Hamdi Ulukaya on the Journey from Abandoned Factory to Yogurt Powerhouse, Harvard Business Review, April 25, 2022).

Ulukaya's statement suggests that when people rise to their potential, they are able to "find a way." They apply their resourcefulness and ingenuity to solving problems and pursuing opportunities. Unlocking potential relies on activating our people's individual and collective mindsets and liberating a boundless energy source that will carry the organization forward. This source permeates everything the company does and is a lever to boost innovation, become more entrepreneurial, and attain ambitious objectives.

To unlock your organization's potential to Regrow, I will introduce a framework that leverages the collective mindset and serves as a canvas to design the journey to this transformation. The framework uses a systemic view that incorporates three dimensions: Talent Density, Culture, and Mindset, generating a reinforcing loop that not only aids the organization in its capacity to learn and adapt but also pushes forward the boundaries of what it thought was possible. I will delve into the inner workings of each dimension and lay out a plan to make it happen.

I will show that pursuing regrowth when stalling is, fundamentally, a continuous renewal exercise where the organization keeps transforming itself to become malleable, collaborative, and nimble. As Chris Zook and James Allen, the authors of the book *The Founder's Mentality,* explain: "Ninety-four percent of large-company executives cite internal dysfunction as their key barrier to continued profitable growth...As companies grow in size and complexity, they lose the dexterity and flexibility they need to sustain growth, which calls to mind what a seventy-year-old yoga teacher once told one of us about the human aging process. "You don't get old and get stiff, he said, "You get stiff and then you get old.""[5]

The underpinning of the book

Throughout the chapters of the book, you will identify key ideas that serve as a backdrop and scaffold the main message:

- Regrowth is a choice; it is rarely the result of serendipity or spontaneous generation.
- Regrowth is primarily an inner job. Although it is often assessed externally, its genesis takes place in the organization's inner workings.
- Regrowth is leveraged by a collective mindset, which is essential to unlocking potential, learning, and adapting. At its core, the organization's soft wiring is the nucleus informing the capabilities that lead to customer preference.
- Regrowth is triggered by a process of collaboration in the organization where people can contribute and build on what others think to improve decision-making. This system consists of three components: Talent Density, Culture, and Mindset. Talent Density is compounded by knowledgeable individuals exchanging ideas. Culture facilitates communication, speaking up, and experimentation without the fear of being reprimanded, and Mindset leverages a belief system, perspective-taking, and agency to make things happen.

The book's journey

Chapter I sets the stage for the context under which companies must perform today, highlighting the rapidly changing environment and the mandate for organizations to grow. There is a paradox that needs to be resolved. To compete in today's environment, we need difficult-to-build, distinctive capabilities, but in doing so, we must hard-wire ourselves for a condition that will eventually change. The capacity to learn and adapt is essential to remain relevant to our customers.

Chapter II examines how competitive advantages stem from the knowledge the company produces and the need to play both today's game and the future's game. Having a knowledge advantage is key to competing and winning in the market. Still, there is tension within the organization in the use and creation of new knowledge required to play in the future vis a vis the current knowledge used in today's business. I will visit the ambidexterity conundrum and reflect on its limitations. The late James G. March described the exploitation and exploration dichotomy in 1991. After over 30 years, there is little progress in successfully making it happen in organizations.

In Chapter III, I will reflect on what business we are in when transforming an organization. This will be the segue to discuss the two metaphors we use to understand the organization's inner workings and how these mental models limit or expand our actions to transform it. I will introduce the Talent Density, Culture, and Mindset framework, which can be used as a canvas to guide the organization's transformation to regrow and constitute the genome to unlock potential.

In Chapter IV, we will go deeper into understanding the Talent Density dimension, why having the best talent is crucial for competing in today's world, to what extent talent is portable between functions or organizations, and how the talent landscape of your company raises the bar for everybody. We will explore the Talent Density determinants; for that, I will refer to Harry L. Davis and Robin M. Hogarth's model in *Rethinking Management Education: A View from Chicago"* article and their Elements of Performance.

In Chapter V, we will examine culture and its determinants. We will discuss how culture is not what you say; it is what you do. We will also discuss the importance of having top management actively involved in culture deployment and the difficulties of sustaining the effort while battling to achieve business results. We will explore the Cultural determinants with three categories that I trust will be comprehensive and easy to understand and apply.

In Chapter VI, we will explore the Mindset dimension. We will review some of the implications of Mindset in the organization from an individual perspective, with a broader view of how it becomes a collective driver of potential and ultimately for adaptability, learning, and Regrowth. We will probe into the proposed Mindset determinants and the importance of leveraging an action and reflection cycle.

In Chapter VII, we will use a systemic approach to review how the whole system works together, including the "where to play" and "how to win" territories to unlock our people's potential and attain Regrowth. It comprehensively represents the stages necessary for transforming the organization and how each one builds into the other to create a virtuous cycle.

In Chapter VIII, I will shift from discussing organizational transformation to exploring the individual level and what it takes to undergo a self-led transformation journey. Even though this is a business-focused book, I believe it is essential to delve into what individuals can do when they encounter obstacles in their personal development. We've all faced moments when things don't go as planned, leaving us feeling stuck. I will provide a framework to kickstart our renewal process. To do this, I will reflect on eight personal transformation challenges I have encountered professionally and explain how you can take charge of your regrowth. If you feel stalled and want to revitalize your personal or professional career, consider reading this chapter first; the choice is yours.

When organizations hit a wall, the typical response is to implement best practices, new methodologies, and management systems to facilitate a turnaround. This might involve restructuring departments and bringing external talent to provide fresh perspectives. While these efforts can be valuable and effective, we must not lose sight of the fact that our people are the ultimate frontier that must be addressed when seeking to Regrow, particularly when companies aim to explore new opportunities in their industries or enter unfamiliar markets. In this book, I will explain the steps we need to take to cultivate a flexible foundation and support our employees in coping with rapid changes by unlocking their potential. The red thread touches upon our people's capacity to surpass perceived limitations. We should see the organization as a platform where our talents can flourish and break new ground. Leaders must prioritize a human-centered approach to ensure the system adjusts, learns, thrives, and stays relevant in the ever-changing market conditions.

The problem to solve for

Over the past few years, I've interviewed CEOs of multibillion-dollar companies with thousands of employees as well as leaders of much smaller organizations with just a few dozen employees about their team's performance. Specifically, I've asked them how they perceive their teams' potential. I usually phrase the question like this: "After working with your teams for some time, and based on your firsthand knowledge of what you know they are capable of accomplishing, what percentage of their potential do you think they realize relative to what you believe they could do?"

The typical response I receive is around 50%. Sometimes, the number is even lower, at around 30%. This tells me that leaders believe their organizations only tap into about half of what their people can achieve. This has always amazed me. The perceived gap in reaching full potential highlights a significant amount of untapped potential that could be harnessed by organizations. If you look at this situation as a "glass half full," in other words, as an opportunity, there is a lot we can do to help unlock our people's contribution.

Organizations that do not make an effort to untapp their people's potential not only shortchange themselves in their performance but also create an unfair situation for their people. These individuals could further develop their talents and achieve their aspirations. However, due to the organization's failure to facilitate the process, this potential is never fully realized, and they miss the opportunity to be all they can be. If we can find a solution to the problem of unrealized potential, we could significantly increase productivity—perhaps even double it—regardless of external factors such as industry challenges, government regulations, competition, or market conditions. Unrealized potential is a self-inflicted wound that we could avoid. To do so, we must figure out how to unleash all the creativity and talent that already exist within the minds and hearts of our people.

On one occasion, I interviewed a CEO who ran a large and complex organization. I knew him fairly well and liked his wittiness and sharp thinking when solving problems. I asked him this question, and he responded 50%. I inquired why he thought this was happening and wasn't leveraging his people's existing potential; I was intrigued by what he had to say about this. It took him just a couple of seconds to fire back: "I was hoping you could tell me; you are supposed to know this stuff!" Well, this book is my answer to his reply. In it, I will outline the elements that must be addressed to regrow and unlock the organization's potential and share ideas about how to design this transformation.

Realizing an organization's full potential is a never-ending quest because it is a moving target; we never quite reach our goal. Nevertheless, with this book, I want to start a conversation with people interested in the topic to shed light on this challenge and offer guidance based on my experience. I hope you will find it helpful.

CHAPTER I

Change is here to stay

"No matter how fast the growth treadmill is going,
it is not fast enough."
—Clayton Christensen

"It is precisely what made firms great in the past that
generates a sclerosis when they need to change."
—Joshua Gans

"Adapting to a changing environment isn't something a
company does—it's something people do in the multitude
of decisions they make every day."
—Adam Grant

Anybody who has been in business knows how difficult it is to keep up with the changing industry environment. The last few years have been particularly challenging due to the pandemic and the digital transformation it ushered in. Technology is now an intrinsic part of our livelihood and pushes the limits of what we thought possible. If you are old enough to remember how we used to make phone calls from a fixed line or hear music on a Walkman, you know what I am talking about. It's stunning. Thanks to technology, the rate of change in the world is accelerating, and this vortex affects all industries alike.

This wave of change does not distinguish small from large businesses, old from new, or trendy from traditional. There is no reason to believe it will slow down. On the contrary, it will continue to increase in the foreseeable future. How we pay for services, access healthcare, obtain information, enjoy entertainment, travel, shop, etc., has been fundamentally altered in just a few years, and it is difficult to predict what's next. Those who work in established, legacy companies may erroneously think they are safe from change and disruption. After all, they have faced complicated conditions before and survived. This time is different. The business environment is more challenging than ever, and nobody is safe from becoming a casualty in the digital world. This new reality demands a profound transformation in organizations, a deep re-invention that goes beyond sharing best practices or upgrading how to run a business. It involves a significant change in perspective, a new way of seizing opportunities, and a shared mindset that will help organizations adapt as conditions require.

I want to share an example of how I faced distress due to a business change. This occurred as I transitioned from being a founder in the start-up world to working in a corporate environment. By sharing my experience, I hope to illustrate how mindsets and organizational culture are closely connected to the ability to adapt.

I started as an entrepreneur many years ago. I got baptized in the demanding and uncertain world of entrepreneurship after embarking on 12 diverse businesses, ranging from ground transportation, a deli, a catering service for airplanes, Italian restaurants, cookie franchises, and toner distribution, to name a few. One of the Italian restaurants I founded, La Buca in San Antonio, became a destination for movers and shakers and won restaurant awards from a prestigious wine magazine. It also helped me earn second place as the Hispanic Entrepreneur of the Year back then. I learned a lot during those 20+ years, but the most important insight from my entrepreneurial experience was that survival entailed winning the battle within myself first. A quote attributed to Joan of Arc says, "All battles are first won or lost, in the mind," and I couldn't agree more. Making sense of the problems we face and the stories we tell ourselves creates a perspective that guides our path to achieving success or the road to demise. Like any other entrepreneur, I juggled a few good days and, more often than not, tiring days where quitting was a real and pressing possibility. I don't know how I gathered the stamina to endure the many hardships I faced, but I did. Napster founder Sean Parker has an appropriate quote to describe this experience. "Running a startup is like chewing broken glass–to succeed, you need to fall in love with the taste of your own blood."[1] Indeed, finding a viable way to stay alive was all I could think about at the time. In hindsight, that was when I developed the startup mentality I have brought to all of my endeavors.

I was used to the flexibility demands of being an entrepreneur, but that changed when I joined a large company that offered me an interesting challenge. While there, I experienced the "stability" of the corporate environment, where the longevity of the established employees creates the illusion of security. I had peace of mind because I didn't have to worry about making payroll or keeping the lights on. Still, I experienced another kind of pressure: meeting the sales quota and delivering the expected results wasn't optional. At the end of the month, my performance was judged based on two indicators, sales and profitability, with zero tolerance for excuses. There was no hidden formula to achieve my goals; I had to leverage the existing competitive advantages of the company (which meant squashing any competitors who appeared along the way) and look for new opportunities to grow. The start-up mentality was no longer necessary for survival. I just needed to let the brakes off and take care of business the old-fashioned way.

For years, life was good. I was part of a sales department that delivered above-average results, so we were recognized and collected our bonuses. Some of the corporation's practices were becoming outdated, but they worked well enough, so there was no need to change them, or so it seemed. Back then, everybody shared the "If ain't broken, don't 'fix it" mentality, and no one questioned the validity of how we worked. Suddenly, when we least expected it, things took a dramatic turn. As in Cinderella, the carriage became a pumpkin, and the competitive advantages that used to work ceased to bring the customary benefits. To everyone's surprise, old and new competitors gained customer preference and began taking our market share. Some brands felt it more than others, but the overall picture was very concerning.

As one might expect in a situation like this, the bosses applied immediate pressure to "motivate" us to find ways to deal with this situation. There was urgency among the troops in the trenches but, paradoxically, some disbelief as well. We were skeptical about the severity of the problem and could not see well through the fog of war. We went into a period of denial and thought it was temporary, that competitors would eventually run out of gas–but they didn't. Quite the opposite, they doubled down.

This episode of my life reminds me of Ernest Hemingway's famous quote about bankruptcy, "How did you go bankrupt? Two ways, gradually then suddenly." I also learned firsthand how different it is to play defense instead of offense. Although many affected brands managed to stay afloat and have done reasonably well, some never fully recovered. The main takeaway from the experience is that it's challenging to recognize the seriousness of a threat when you're in the midst of being disrupted. Old perspectives cloud your perception, and your existing beliefs make it hard to understand the situation. Nonetheless, I realized it was time to "win the battle with my mind" again, but involving the entire department in this shift was necessary. However, I didn't know how to support the team in developing an adaptable mindset, so we were in automatic pilot. Everyone was focused on forcefully defending our position, and we ended up digging a larger hole from which it was difficult to get out.

A brave new world

My experience with small competitors turning the tables on us is hardly an isolated one. The rivals we faced had a "take no prisoners' mentality (as I used to embrace in my startup life), and their products were comparable to ours if you left the brand's name aside and, in some cases, they were even better than us in critical features like flavor or texture. We were slow to react because we had profit pools to protect. We played a "not to lose" game instead of attempting to overcome the challenge with a differentiated proposition to allow us to win.

This experience happened many years ago, but it depicts a very current scenario in many industries. Today, the competition for customers' hearts and minds is fiercer than ever, and industry conditions are shifting quickly as new entrants stir things up. Many factors explain the present situation, but the one that stands out in leveling the playing field for all is the digital revolution. For more than 20 years, software has been eating the world, as the American entrepreneur and venture capital investor Marc Andreessen says, and the future looks even more challenging with Machine Learning and Artificial Intelligence." What has changed is that disruption was previously done to and through physical things, like the assembly line, the commercial jetliner, the heart transplant, flat-panel LCD screens, and so on...The power of digital disruption is that it can shake up any aspect of any product or service, including processes deep within companies focused on physical things."[2]

Let's take digital platforms. When the first ones appeared, online purchasing did not have traction for quite some time, despite years of experimentation from consumers. It gained momentum after a decade or so, but still, physical stores found a way to remain a relevant option and defend their turf. Suddenly, a "Black Swan" event boosted digital business transactions worldwide when the COVID-19 pandemic hit in 2020, making believers out of digital commerce skeptics. Digital is now becoming the standard for commercial transactions, making business activity more cumbersome for legacy companies that do not provide a digital experience. Digital-powered businesses are boundless and have added to the competition in almost every market you can imagine.

But this is only the tip of the iceberg. As a result of digital, entire industries are reshaping themselves, and new areas of competition are arising. Ron Adner, professor of strategy and entrepreneurship at the Tuck School of Business at Dartmouth College, explains it in the following terms: "The basis of competition is changing. Are you prepared? Rivalry is shifting from well-defined industries that deliver clear products and services to broader ecosystems that deliver expansive value propositions: from cars to mobility solutions, from banking to fintech platforms, from pharmacies to health management centers, from production lines to intelligent factories. Industry boundaries are collapsing everywhere you look, and the trend is accelerating."[3]

It has always fascinated me how our ability to forecast the future depends on our previous experience and is organized around a belief system of the past, a lens that inevitably falls short in anticipating the new. Thomas S. Kuhn, the American historian and philosopher, studied this phenomenon and concluded: "The transition from a paradigm in crisis to a new one from which a new tradition of normal science can emerge is far from a cumulative process, one achieved by articulation or extension of the old paradigm. Rather, it is a reconstruction of the field from new fundamentals...."[4] The new fundamentals in business disruption in this time and age have a digital signature and are a catalyst for breaking with the old paradigms. Change is market-induced, and there is no patience for companies that are slow to adapt.

The new game rules in the business world are organized under a distinctive name: "hyper-competition." This term describes a highly competitive environment where advantages are short-lived and digital capabilities set the pace of change. Despite hyper-competition's somewhat negative connotation for incumbent firms, I believe it is a positive force for change. It fires up companies to improve their offerings or lower their prices, leaving consumers to reap the benefits. This intense competition can lead to innovation and increased efficiency, driving overall progress in the marketplace.

However, there is a flipside: companies face significant consequences when engaging in intense competition. Prices and margins tend to shrink and fade relative to the cost of capital, sometimes even below the cost of capital, which is bad news for investors who expect a reward for their risk-taking. When returns are near or at the cost of capital, businesses will not deliver a premium compared to other risk-free instruments, and investors will be better off putting their hard-earned money into other alternatives, like a fixed instrument.

In public companies, the margin reduction resulting from competition generates further damage, and valuations suffer because the stock price factors in future performance expectations. Suppose investment funds or investors do not foresee a way out of margin-eroding competition. In that case, they will jump ship, selling their stock, and the company's stock price will consequently fall, generating a doomed, vicious cycle. The only alternative for the business is to adapt as quickly as possible to the new market conditions and redesign the company's capabilities and competitive advantages. This sounds great in theory, but it is not always feasible and takes much work to implement. Let's double-click on this idea.

Creating and sustaining a competitive advantage is very hard for any company, even for organizations that have been good at it throughout the years. It is difficult because you have to keep winning against emerging and evolving players who do not sit on their laurels and present a tough fight. The shorter expiration date of competitive advantages comes with a price. It reduces the higher value creation period achieved by a company relative to the standard in the industry, which puts pressure to come up with more innovative products that customarily have higher profitability due to their larger margins: "The research shows that most of an entrant's excess shareholder returns versus its industry come in the first five years. In the subsequent fifteen years, the entrant delivers total shareholder returns that are roughly in line with the industry."[5]

In layperson's terms, this means that any success attained in business is transitory; on average, the good times will last about five years. Therefore, to endure, you must be ready and willing to reinvent and differentiate yourself from the pack as a way of life. One of Andy Grove's famous books is titled "Only the Paranoid Survive." The book's premise is that "Sooner or later, something fundamental in your business world will change,"[6] and you have to be prepared to navigate that crisis point; "Business is about creating change for other businesses. Competition is about creating change; technology is about creating change…Sometimes, these changes affect only one company, other times they affect the entire industry. So, the ability to recognize that the winds have shifted and to take appropriate action before you wreck your boat is crucial to the future of an enterprise."[7] The book was written in 1996; those inflection points were only a few back then. In today's world, inflection points show up repeatedly and test the organization's capacity to adapt.

CEO's rotation is one of the most telling indicators of a highly competitive environment. When companies fail to grow and create value for stockholders, the CEO is among the first casualties to pay the ultimate price, "The probability that a CEO will crash and burn is now higher than ever," note Carolyn Dewar, Scott Keller, Vikram Malhotra, in "CEO Excellence, The Six Mindsets that Distinguish the Best Leaders from the Rest." As they point out, from 2000 through 2019, a CEO's average tenure in the U.S. shrunk from ten years to less than seven".[8]

Building a successful business in today's market requires growing and remaining profitable while creating value for all stakeholders involved. However, the challenge lies in how long a company can sustainably compete and maintain its position in the market despite margin erosion and turn it around with new offerings that could increase margins again. To shed some light on this problem, we must discuss business capabilities and how they are positioned to fulfill customers' expectations.

Capabilities and positioning: The hardwiring

When asked what the purpose of a business was, the legendary Peter Drucker explained, "The purpose of a business is to create a customer."[9] This simple but powerful statement is the reason why businesses exist. You may have long believed that the purpose of businesses is to generate profit for investors, which is true because if businesses do not generate profits, they will close their doors. But Drucker invites us to go beyond the obvious and acknowledge that businesses must first serve customers and care for their needs for profits to exist. By the way, there is a corollary to Peter Drucker's quote that is not very well known: "Because the purpose of business is to create a customer, the business enterprise has two—-and only two—-basic functions: marketing and innovation. Marketing and innovation produce results; all the rest are costs."[10]

If you run a business, you know that many things must come together right to create customers. They all must coalesce in a way that delivers value that meets or exceeds their expectations. For a business to create customers, it must develop the appropriate capabilities that enable such value delivery. These capabilities are often unknown to customers; when they decide to buy a product or a service, they are unaware of what happens behind the scenes for the company to do the job, and rightly so. They just appreciate the value they receive and how it solves their problems relative to other offerings in the market.

Let me illustrate this point with the example of cars powered by a combustion engine. You are probably unaware that "A typical car contains nearly 30,000 individual parts. Many are prebuilt—like the starter motor or the seats. Still, a typical auto manufacturing line will receive around two thousand unique parts from several hundred different suppliers, arriving from as many as seventeen different countries. The complexity of taking so many things from so many different sources and turning them into a working car is a miracle in itself."[11] When we start and drive a car, we don't care what it takes to build it. We just want it to enjoy the experience, be reliable, function properly and safely, and take us from point A to point B. The capabilities developed by companies allow customers to fulfill their expectations.

Capabilities are the means that enable a company to generate the "job to be done" on behalf of the customer. I will address the "jobs to be done" concept throughout the book, so we might as well define what this idea means. Clayton M. Christensen coined the definition: "When we buy a product, we essentially 'hire' something to get a job done. If it does the job well, when we are confronted with the same job, we hire that same product again. And if the product does a crummy job, we 'fire' it and look around for something else we might hire to solve the problem... The foundation of our thinking is the Theory of Jobs to Be Done, which focuses on deeply understanding your customer's *struggle for progress* and then creating the right solution, and attendant set of experiences to ensure you solve your customer's jobs well, every time."[12]

If an organization wants to reliably deliver the "job to be done" that its customers demand, it must make sure that it has the capabilities to do so. Capabilities constitute the abilities developed by a company to deliver its unique value proposition. Each capability is, in turn, articulated by groups of activities to accomplish a goal, like Domino's Pizza's 30-minute free pizza delivery system, for example. Many activities must be integrated into distinctive capabilities to deliver a pizza in less than 30 minutes. Once added, they are the backbone that provides coherence to the whole value delivery system. It represents the clockwork that makes the customer experience possible (the *HBR* article "What is strategy?" by Michael Porter is an excellent reference for learning about activity systems).

Many companies are known for their unique capabilities. For example, Amazon is known for its digital platform, Apple for its innovation, Coca-Cola for its branding, and Ritz-Carlton for its customer service. Developing a capability like this is not easy, as it requires a lot of work, effort, trial and error, the development of distinctive proprietary processes, and intense collaboration. A successful company may develop three, four, or five distinctive capabilities, but it's rare for companies to have more.

A notable aspect of capabilities is that companies devote valuable resources to developing and embedding them within the organization to surpass their competitors. However, this investment might not yield the desired results if they disregard existing rivals with superior capabilities or if market conditions change. Imagine you're a regional retailer aiming to compete with Walmart. Walmart has been a retail leader for decades, building solid and hard-to-replicate capabilities in its distribution center system. This system serves groups of stores within each region and has been very successful for Walmart, contributing to the impact of its low-price policy. When you shop at Walmart, you're guaranteed to find the products you want in stock and at the lowest price. To compete with Walmart, you need a distribution system that ensures product availability on shelves while offering competitive prices without Walmart's buying power. It's quite a challenge!

Walmart's capability system has developed into a self-reinforcing loop, often called a flywheel. Over the years, its competitive advantages have improved, creating a strong barrier around its business. The components of the flywheel, including bargaining power, distribution centers, store locations, product assortment, and low-price guarantee, have all become more robust over time. These components reinforce each other, creating a strong and unique system that is incredibly difficult to replicate. This is why established and new retailers find it challenging to compete with Walmart.

However, in the last decade, a new element entered the retail landscape that threw off even Walmart: digital platforms. We now take it for granted that customers can easily buy online products in an almost "frictionless experience." Amazon has become a formidable competitor to Walmart, with a that has essentially blown up the moats Walmart built out of its key competitive advantages. The same capabilities that helped Walmart win the customers' preference in the traditional retail space are no longer differentiators in a virtual space, where a different array of salient attributes is required. For instance, Amazon has neutralized Walmart's advantageous store locations by competing in a virtual, omnipresent space; it offers a much more extensive product assortment than Walmart, with a robust rating system and customer recommendations that assist shoppers in purchasing decisions. Amazon eliminates the hassle of driving to the store and finding a parking space. It offers a "no questions asked money back guarantee" policy without requiring customers to line up at a customer service department, etc. All told, Amazon brings unmatched, distinctive value to customers.

As of this writing, Amazon is advancing rapidly to become the largest retailer in the world and beats Walmart.com six to one in visits to their websites, although the contest remains. To catch up to Amazon, Walmart needs to rapidly develop best-in-class digital capabilities and leverage its physical stores to create a better omnichannel experience for the customer. If Walmart succeeds with this, will it be enough? It is difficult to say because Walmart is chasing a moving target. Amazon will still advance, innovate, and create better customer experiences, while Walmart is behind in trying to close the gap. It is an uphill battle for a company that flourished in a brick-and-mortar era and needs to renew itself to remain relevant to customers.

The lesson to be learned is that hardwiring how you position your company (particularly if it's a strong position) anchors the way you play the game. This makes sense when you have developed a distinctive competitive advantage, and the business context remains predictable. If circumstances change as they did for Walmart, which is often the case, what once was an advantage can become a liability because the new rules to play and win in the game call for a different approach, and your positioning binds you. If this ever happens to your organization, there is no choice but to reinvent yourself.

The Walmart example is interesting because it shows how a disruption in the market forces companies to change how they compete and deliver on the jobs to be done for customers. Digital platforms are disrupting not only the retail industry but many other sectors. Financial services, telecommunications, hospitality, education, etc., are also becoming prey to digital platforms and are reinventing their business models and capabilities to survive. James McQuivey, the principal analyst of Forrester Research and one who tracks the development of digital disruption, articulates this situation very well: "I find Economists talk about trends that reduce barriers to entry. The force of digital disruption doesn't just reduce these barriers, it obliterates them...and it will happen to every industry on the planet, whether that company makes digital products or not."[13] Companies must develop capabilities for today's game and be able to adapt quickly to develop capabilities for tomorrow's game, with change being the only constant. This new frame for competing reminds me of what General Eric Shinseki, an Army four-star general who served as the Chief of Staff of the Army from 1999 to 2003, said, "If you don't like change, you are going to like irrelevance even less."

The frequency at which companies need to update their capabilities is uncertain and depends on the dynamics of their industries. There is no standard formula for when it is best to carry it on. Sometimes, it is wise not to rush things up because organizations may overreact to a new business model in the market that has yet to prove its worth, but in other cases, delaying the decision will waste precious time and disrupt the organization. The sensitive thing to do is to assess the nature of the change in the market, try to read the implications for your company, and act accordingly in the right time frame.

There is a real-life example that illustrates how this process takes place, which I like very much. It is portrayed in Andy Grove's book "Only the Paranoid Survive": "It was a grim and frustrating year. During that time we worked hard without a clear notion of how things were ever going to get better. We had lost our bearings. We were wandering in the valley of death. I remember a time in the middle of 1985, after this aimless wandering had been going on for almost a year. I was in my office with Intel's chairman and CEO, Gordon Moore, and we were discussing our quandary. Our mood was downbeat. I looked out the window at the Ferris wheel of the Great America Amusement Park revolving in the distance, then I turned back to Gordon and I asked: If we got kicked out and the board brought in a new CEO, what do you think he would do? Gordon answered without hesitation he would get us out of memories (computer memory). I stared at him, numb, then said, why shouldn't you and I walk out the door, come back and do it ourselves?"[14]

The ability of a company to develop capabilities to adapt to changing market conditions is primarily a human-specific problem. It calls for a strong emphasis on teamwork, communication, and cross-functional problem-solving. This involves encouraging a culture where employees feel empowered to challenge the status quo and explore new ways of doing things. Secondly, it is a functional issue, entailing methods and practices to follow up on process improvements, resource allocation, and performance measurement to ensure efficiency and effectiveness.

When Satya Nadella became CEO of Microsoft, he highlighted the importance of the human component in developing the capabilities that would make them adapt and change to win their customer's preferences. He knew he needed to work on organizational culture to establish a strong core guiding their change process. In his book *"Hit Refresh: The Quest to Rediscover Microsoft's Soul and Imagine a Better Future for Everyone,"* Nadella describes how the system works: "Steve Ballmer helped me deeply understand (culture) with his three C's. Imagine a target with three concentric rings. The outer ring is "concepts." Microsoft, Apple, or Amazon may have an exciting product idea, but is that enough? An organization may have a conceptual vision—a dream or imagination filled with new ideas or new approaches, but do they have what's in the second ring: capabilities? Do they have the engineering and design skills required to build that concept alone? And finally, the bullseye is a culture that embraces new concepts and new capabilities and doesn't choke them out".[15]

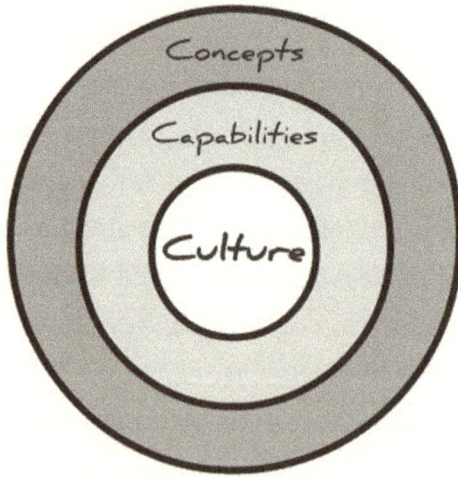

This is a simple yet powerful way to portray the interconnectedness of consumer preference, organizational capabilities, and culture. Usually, we focus on the concepts (products) and capabilities that will help us win in the market and take culture for granted. We assume culture is already there and should work by default. However, culture must seamlessly align with the other two rings to produce results. In a constantly changing environment, culture's importance cannot be ignored; it fuels the organization's value creation system, and neglecting its importance puts us at risk of failing and becoming obsolete.

I have personal experience with the impact of culture on providing products and services that meet customer wants and needs. I'd like to share a story from when I was the sales head of convenience stores at a CPG company. We were selling Franks to convenience stores nationwide for their hot dog rollers, and our product was the top seller with the largest C-Store chain. However, we were underperforming in a region in central Mexico, where the stores had below-average hot dog consumption compared to other areas. To increase hot dog consumption, my team and I created a promotion targeting construction workers in the area, as they were heavy consumers in every category except ours. I approached a contact I had who worked in marketing at the largest cement company in Mexico. I intended to print a 2-for-1 hot dog deal coupon on the cement bags, which could be cut out and redeemed at the leading C-store chain. The three parties (us, the cement company, and the C-store chain) agreed to launch the promotion for two weeks, and we all shared the associated costs.

We were confident in the success of our promotion because we knew that even though construction workers in the area were consuming other types of food, they enjoyed hotdogs. Our deal could persuade them to make the switch. Representatives from the cement company, the convenience store chain, and colleagues in my company worked together for several weeks to plan every detail, including logistics, warehousing, delivery dates, store communication, point-of-sale systems, training manuals for staff, condiments, buns, and on-call delivery trucks. We thought we were fully prepared and didn't leave any stone unturned, so we launched the project with high expectations for record-breaking sales. However, just three days in, everything started to unravel.

The teams of the three entities had different priorities and were not used to working together, especially in stressful conditions. While people in my company were used to the variability of serving the end consumer, the cement company operated with distributors with more stable replenishment cycles and demands. Their sense of urgency was very different, leading to clashes among teams. On top of that, the convenience store clerks were angry because the cut-off pieces of the cement bags handed out by construction workers were dirty and released lots of dust in the stores; they had to face the hassle of cleaning up constantly and altering their work routines. The truth was that none of the companies involved in the promotion were clear about how to address these problems, and nobody took ownership of the situation. Line workers at the three companies blamed their respective corporate offices for their problems and were right to do so. We failed to communicate the promotion's goals and establish open channels of communication and effective coordination to deal with unforeseen issues.

Despite facing numerous challenges, we achieved a 40% increase in sales during the promotion. However, resolving the resulting animosity between my team and the C-Store teams took a long time, keeping our sales flat and preventing us from pursuing other growth opportunities. This experience taught me a valuable lesson: when attempting to change established routines and working methods, people should come first, and processes should take a secondary role. Never underestimate the importance of involving people and gaining their support; without it, you are bound to fail.

Hardwiring the organization to compete in a fast-paced, changing environment will eventually get us in trouble. A company's Regrowth journey must be rooted in its ability to adapt to new conditions and fulfill the" jobs to be done" our customers demand. In the pages ahead, I will complement Nadella's cultural approach with two additional dimensions that will help us strengthen the organization's adaptation core and design a sustainable system.

CHAPTER 2

Knowledge rules!

"Every knowledge eventually becomes the wrong knowledge.
It becomes obsolete. The question should always arise: What
else do we need? Or do we need to do something different?"
—PETER DRUCKER.

"Our behavior is driven by a fundamental core belief:
The desire, and the ability of an organization to
continuously learn from any source—and to rapidly
convert this learning into action—is the ultimate
competitive advantage."
—JACK WELCH

"We don't know much relative to what we need to know."
—RAY DALIO

What makes growth possible? Customers are the driving force behind growth. A company can only achieve growth by expanding its loyal customer base, which means fulfilling customers' unmet needs better than other options available in the market (such as competitors or substitutes). Therefore, to grow, customers must be at the epicenter of everything we do as a company and should be the reason for the business's existence.

Understanding customers' wants and needs is the first step in creating a business. To accomplish this task, we must articulate those wants and needs better than customers. This requires an in-depth knowledge of the customer's root motivators and expectations.

Gathering that knowledge has never been easy because what matters from the customer's perspective is often a moving target. Companies invest lots of resources to fathom what customers want and still miss the mark: "They spend time and money compiling data-rich models that make them masters of description but failures at prediction," says Clayton M Christensen.[1] Sometimes, customers have a clear idea of what they want, and sometimes, they don't—their needs change in a way that is usually ambiguous to them, especially when technology is involved. As the pace of change accelerates, the customer's job is not to know what they might want in the future; it is the company's job serving the customer to figure it out. Therefore, to learn the customer's motivations and needs as a company, we have to explore a lot, dig and probe into what they want today, and, most importantly, why they want it so we can deliver on the job they hire the product to do. As Hubert Joly, former chairman and CEO of Best Buy, puts it, "Obsessing about competition is sort of interesting, but it's much more interesting to obsess about the customers and then what you can uniquely do for customers leveraging your unique assets."[2] So, the first step is to understand what customers want and, if possible, anticipate what they still don't know they will eventually want.

The second step in business creation entails being able to provide a solution for the customer to fulfill those wants and needs, a value proposition that exceeds our customer's expectations of their "jobs to be done" through a given product or service. It is always a "customer-based approach" since customers are the ones who "hire" the product to do a job for them. Steve Jobs referred to this in the following terms: "You've got to start with the customer experience and work backward for the technology. You can't start with the technology and try to figure out where you're going to sell it."[3] Innovation on behalf of the consumer is the only way to develop a value proposition that keeps up with change. Invent or perish. As Bill Campbell puts it, "If companies don't continue to innovate, they are going to die - and I didn't say iterate, I said innovate."[4]

In the third step of creating a business, it is essential to connect with the customer. By leveraging the customer's experience and the value proposition, we need to establish a value chain that consistently provides a unique offering to our customers efficiently and sustainably. We aim to ensure that the customer's experience is as seamless and enjoyable as possible to build loyalty and encourage repeat purchases. This step is crucial because it requires capabilities to support the value delivery system, and the company's success relies on its organizational structure performing with the highest standards.

I acknowledge that this account of events oversimplifies the process. It provides a high-level perspective of a much more complex system. However, my intention with this high-level approach is to showcase how a business must start by understanding customer needs and then reverse engineering its way back to the business capabilities and with the fundamental human core within the organization that are necessary to deliver value. It is crucial to regularly review the value chain to improve it, enhance its effectiveness, and elevate the customer experience, even during stable conditions. This is where the contributions of our people come into play, as it's an ongoing, never-ending process. When you think you've mastered a process, a new situation inevitably emerges, requiring you to start from scratch and strive to fulfill better the job customers hire the product to do: "Customers are always beautifully, wonderfully dissatisfied, even when they report being happy and business is great. Even when they don't yet know it, customers want something better, and your desire to delight customers will drive you to invent on their behalf,"[5] says Jeff Bezos.

The above description aims to convey the idea of business as a place where individuals utilize their talents to help the organization adapt and meet constantly evolving customer expectations. Market growth is no longer solely dependent on economies of scale, access to capital, or proprietary knowledge. Although these factors used to be significant, they are no longer the only determinants of success. Today, emerging companies can secure funding through venture capital and expand by forming alliances with other businesses. Additionally, readily available information allows them to access the same knowledge previously exclusive to big corporations. This has leveled the playing field for all market participants. Thriving today requires adaptability, agility, and a continuous discovery process to stay ahead in a complex environment and gain a competitive edge.

That is why intangible assets now account for most companies' value in the stock market. Creativity, innovation, and the ability to acquire and apply knowledge are more valuable than a company's fixed assets, which was a counterintuitive proposition not too long ago: "It's no wonder, then, that over the past two or three decades, intangible assets rose to become the major value drivers of business, high as well as low tech, manufacturing and services alike. Physical assets are now, by and large, commodities available to all,"[6] says Baruch Lev, the Philip Bardes Professor (Emeritus) of Accounting and Finance at New York University Stern School of Business.

Not all knowledge is created equal

The products and services companies need to grow and succeed in the market depend on the specific knowledge they possess that gives them a competitive edge. When we refer to "knowledge," we are not talking about knowledge for knowledge's sake but having a distinct understanding of what can make a difference in fulfilling our customers' needs and how we can provide them with the right solution. Organizations are entities that generate knowledge and can apply it to create value. While it may not be obvious to think of organizations as knowledge networks, it is essential to recognize them as such to understand why they hold a competitive advantage. By acknowledging that knowledge is a differentiator and attempting to develop proprietary knowledge, the organization will set a path ahead of the rest in the market and reap the benefits.

The intangible nature of knowledge can make it challenging to manage. Unlike fixed assets that are easily visible in a company's value chain, knowledge is embedded in various activities and practices. It's not always easy to pinpoint the knowledge that connects the whole system and makes it function effectively. However, whether we can spot it or not, knowledge is present, often in the shadows, ensuring that things operate smoothly.

Think about what happens when an organization places a purchase order with one of its suppliers; there are quality specifications to be met, timing, a delivery process that has been agreed upon, etc., that are part of a seamless mechanism to coordinate and ensure the outcome of creating value with your product or service. In forecasting, production, fulfillment, distribution, pricing, customer engagement, etc., thousands of processes and practices are at play, many specific to your company, based on knowledge accumulated and perfected over time. Experimenting and learning what works and what doesn't take a lot of time and effort, but once knowledge is codified and structured, it can generate the advantages that help us win in the market: "Learning is where competitive advantage comes from...the biggest risk a firm can take is to cease to learn,"[7] as organizational anthropologist Timothy R. Clark puts it.

There are many examples in our daily lives where we take for granted how organizations have learned and developed knowledge to improve our experience and gain our preference as consumers. For instance, when we watch Netflix, we expect to find a movie or series we like intuitively and hassle-free. For this to happen, they had to develop, apply, and refine knowledge to create a platform that has arguably been the golden standard of streaming. They not only provide movie suggestions based on our watching history but showcase original content that successfully competes with the big studios to fulfill our entertainment needs. Another example is Zara, the retail chain that created a new clothing category with its Fast Fashion offering. They can adjust their value proposition by capturing a customer's insights at the point of sale and immediately manufacture clothing that meets their desired style, which reaches their stores in a matter of days. They have created differentiated knowledge along their value chain, which has become an effective moat for competitors in the clothing space. Salesforce presents another interesting case: they built a Customer Relationship Management tool that supports sales and marketing teams for companies worldwide. Salesforce operates in the cloud and has developed a proprietary system that is extremely difficult to replicate.

The examples above demonstrate how these companies have used knowledge to differentiate themselves. It's important to note that this knowledge advantage isn't restricted to tech companies; it applies to all industries. All businesses should understand the significance of acquiring knowledge to stay ahead of the competition and succeed in today's rapidly changing business environment. We need to recognize the intangible nature of knowledge and create an organizational system that encourages its development. The days when traditional advantages alone were sufficient for the competition are long gone; the rules of business dynamics have changed: "Competitive advantage rarely comes from tangible assets since these assets can easily be acquired by competitors. Competitive advantage tends to be associated with unique, hard-to-duplicate intangible assets...The name organizational capital is gaining acceptance to represent both the formal and informal processes that determine how shallow or deep the firm's competitive moat is."[8]

The intangible source of competitive advantages raises a question: how can we prepare an organization to attain a knowledge advantage? There is a tendency to explain advantage creation in the business world due to a sophisticated strategy formulation effort or a thorough planning exercise. But truth be told, these exercises are often overrated. Powerful ideas are not the property of a few privileged individuals and frequently come from curious collaborators who ask "What if?" questions that help solve daily problems. For knowledge advantage to happen at the organization, leaders must have patience and a nurturing approach to test and developing new ideas since they are born fragile and require protection to attain their potential. John Ives, former Apple's Chief Design Officer, explains how careful we must be when pursuing new ideas in innovation: "Ideas are fragile. If they were resolved, they would not be ideas; they would be products."

Having a good idea is a necessary first step in generating knowledge advantage. It is said that ideas are a dime a dozen, but still, they are an essential ingredient for success. However, knowing in advance which ideas will be successful in the market is not intuitive; it is far from it. Many ideas with great potential may not see the light of day because they were not deemed feasible in the first place. It is easy to be right after the fact, like reading Monday's newspaper, but having the necessary foresight to know what will work when starting a company is challenging.

To illustrate how this works, let us try to reverse engineer the original idea or insight of the above-mentioned successful companies at the time of their inception. The insight behind Netflix is that you don't have to rent or visit a movie theater at a particular time to watch an original movie. You can stream it at your leisure in your home any day at any hour. Moreover, you can pause or change the film and watch as many movies as you want, all for a monthly fixed fee. Zara's insight stems from offering convenient, affordable, fast fashion that lets you express who you are without having to conform to the standards of style and availability set by big clothing retailers. Salesforce is based on the idea that small to medium companies can have state-of-the-art Customer Relationship Management (CRM) software equivalent to the one used by big, successful enterprises without a large investment or having to own any servers. With the benefit of hindsight, we can see that these were groundbreaking, innovative ideas that led to successful companies. But when they were first proposed, they were far from guaranteed success. Many ideas that can give an organization a knowledge advantage are bold and initially met with skepticism. By their nature, disruptive ideas are unconventional and often face resistance from well-intentioned, intelligent people. Everyone does not immediately embrace these new ideas; they are seen as improbable future visions with uncertain chances of success. In organizations, supporting and implementing daring ideas that lead to a knowledge advantage always involves taking a leap of faith. Not everyone is equally comfortable with the level of risk involved.

Within established organizations, a natural tension exists between the desire to generate new knowledge and the risks inherent in the innovation process. The farther the new idea strays from the company's core, the more reluctant the organization will be to face the inherent uncertainty and risk involved in pursuing it. Established companies, particularly those publicly traded, prioritize predictability and have little appetite for risk. As a result, their innovation efforts are expected to be more cautious and risk-averse compared to those not under intense financial scrutiny. In essence, for legacy companies, innovative endeavors are often conservative and closely aligned with existing operations. This cautious approach contradicts the imperative for growth that we have been discussing and the urgent necessity for companies to adapt swiftly to survive. Risk avoidance can impede innovation and hinder gaining a competitive advantage through new knowledge.

To show how this dynamic can be managed from an established company perspective, I would like to introduce a knowledge advantage model as a 2x2 matrix to convey the tradeoffs in pursuing new ideas for innovation and entrepreneurship in legacy organizations. As you will see, it leverages knowledge development as a way to play.

The 2x2 framework has two axes. The horizontal axis describes the consensus (or agreement) on the ideas worth pursuing from the company leader's perspective: How much agreement or disagreement is there among those who give the green light to pursue an innovative and entrepreneurial idea? The vertical axis describes the potential fit with the current company's capabilities: To what extent are the company's existing capabilities compatible and able to support the implementation of the innovative and entrepreneurial ideas to be pursued?

The framework aims to map the playing field a company is willing to leverage to generate a knowledge advantage that spearheads growth. I will label the resulting quadrants in the 2x2 with a knowledge categorization familiar to those studying human cognition. For this purpose, I will use a knowledge typology that has gained much traction in the last 20 years and is attributed to former Secretary of Defense Donald Rumsfeld under President George W. Bush. During a Department of Defense News Briefing on February 12, 2002, Rumsfeld told the media outlets: "Reports that say that something hasn't happened are always interesting to me because as we know, there are known knowns; there are things we know we know. We also know there are known unknowns: that is to say, we know there are some things we don't know. But there are also unknown unknowns—the ones we don't know we don't know."[9] I find Rumsfeld's typology helpful in defining the organization's alternatives in its quest for growth ideas.

The framework for knowledge advantage is the following:

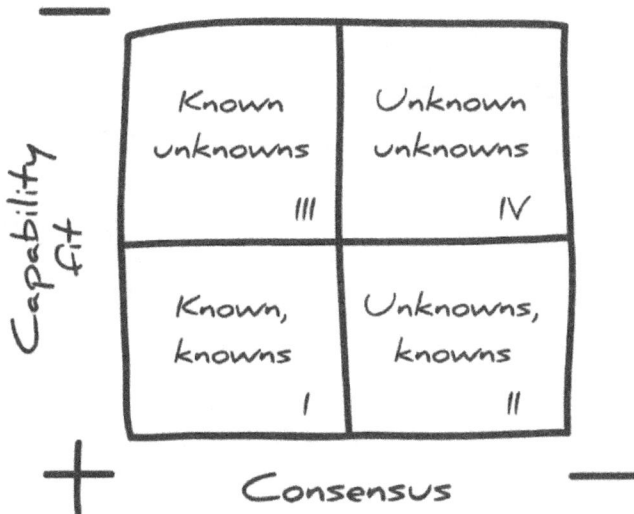

Let's now proceed to describe each of the quadrants:

Quadrant I: Known Knowns

Quadrant I describes the space where the leadership team with decision-making power has a high consensus on the ideas worth pursuing, and the organization has solid and suitable capabilities to deliver on them. In this quadrant, we find the "Known, Knowns"; we know very well what we want and can do. We feel most comfortable in this space because we don't need to reinvent the wheel; we know what to do and how to do it. In this quadrant, we find the knowledge related to the current business and all the incremental performance and continuous improvement projects that fall within the scope of our present work, all of which bring unquestionable value to the company. Some examples of projects in this space are on-time delivery initiatives, waste reduction programs, capacity increases, quality improvements, marginal product adjustments, cost efficiencies, etc. Even though these activities bring value and merit an effort, they are" safe bets" and belong to the realm of what is expected in a company. The "size of the price" in this quadrant is not as significant when compared to more disruptive, game-changing ideas.

Quadrant II: Unknown Knowns

Quadrant II describes a space best represented by the remark, "We know more than we can tell." In this quadrant, the organization's accumulated information, resulting from our employees' knowledge and experience, is more extensive and perhaps more valuable than we can assess. The technical term to describe this condition is tacit knowledge. We are discussing knowledge and ideas within the organization that could be available to implement if we can unearth it by probing, facilitating employee contributions, and asking thoughtful questions. It is not as accessible as the explicit knowledge found in manuals or procedures, but it is still there, ready to be revealed if unearthed. Since we are dealing with knowledge that has yet to be made available to decision-makers, there is no consensus on the ideas to pursue in this space. Still, it is part of the company reserve, and the organization can deliver on it. Hence the name "Unknown, Knowns." Some examples of this Quadrant are Frito Lay Flamin Hot corn chips, Amazon Prime, or 3M Post-it notes, to name a few. All of them were ideas that came from existing knowledge within the organization, contributed by employees who offered very successful solutions when given the opportunity, and their launch was compatible with existing business capabilities. Every time you visit operators in plants or sales teams, for instance, you can capture plenty of good ideas that can generate value if you make an effort to listen.

Quadrant III: Known Unknowns

Quadrant III describes the space of the "Known Unknowns," here, we can identify in general terms the areas where we don't know enough but still pinpoint the specific topics where we would need to probe deeper. In this quadrant, the organization coincides with the ideas worth pursuing but needs more depth about what is there to know and how to make it a reality. Since we are not clear on how to proceed, we likely do not possess the adequate knowledge and capabilities to deliver on it. This space is very interesting for knowledge advantage creation because the value to be captured falls within our vision, we have a consensus on the idea's worth, and the potential size of the price is attractive compared to the current business. However, there is a leap we must take to capture its value: first, understanding what must be done and then developing adequate capabilities to make it happen, which is no small feat. For example, let's say the leaders of a company want to build a digital business model to gain customer preference or develop artificial intelligence prowess to compete effectively. They are already persuaded that it is worth pursuing, but they must still generate the necessary knowledge and capabilities to accomplish the goal. Another case where you can define what you want but need more capabilities to achieve it is food companies. Market trends signal that customers demand affordable, convenient, healthy products, but many food companies still need to learn how to generate products with these characteristics. Or the case of a company that needs to significantly reduce its carbon footprint to become sustainable and remain relevant to consumers, though the required transformation is beyond its current know-how and technology. In all these examples, there is consensus among the company leaders about what to do, but the critical knowledge and the corresponding capabilities to attain the goal are missing.

Quadrant IV: Unknown Unknowns

Quadrant IV describes the space of the "Unknown, Unknowns"; the "we don't know that we don't know" territory. This is a space for possibilities, where revolutionary ideas can make a difference in customers' lives but are wild guesses yet to prove their worth. To create a knowledge advantage in this quadrant, we must explore and pursue disruptive, game-changing ideas with a low probability of success but with the potential to deliver tremendous outcomes. Concepts that originate here are mostly unplausible but hold the potential to generate extraordinary returns for the organization. Suppose an established company desires to venture into this quadrant. In that case, it must identify and select which ideas merit exploration. This will be challenging because of their outlier nature, potential controversy, lack of consensus among the company's leaders, and the internal absence of supportive capabilities. Leaders will face the reality that the business processes that steer the current organization are incompatible with the processes needed to advance these novel ideas, and this condition can derail the decision to proceed. Even if the internal barriers to executing these ideas were resolved, lack of consensus would be a significant deterrent because betting on the unknown is risky, and various opinions on what is best to do exist. Think of businesses that belonged to the "Unknown Unknowns" territory when they were created: Airbnb, Nespresso, Zipcar, Uber, GoPro, and Lynda, to name a few. Today, in hindsight, we can tell these business ideas were worth pursuing, and we can identify the distinctive capabilities needed to deliver on their value proposition. Still, it was challenging to prove their merit when conceived, even with a visionary, forward-looking vision. Intelligent and daring venture capitalists declined to invest in them because they did not believe they could be successful projects. It is only logical to conclude that from the perspective of established companies accustomed to doing business with conventional rules, this space is very uncomfortable because risk mitigation and stable, predictable processes are incompatible with the serendipity, experimentation, chaos, and entropy that come with disruption and the generation of new ideas and knowledge. Steve Jobs used to say, "It is more fun to be a pirate than to join the Navy," expressing his preference for unconventional environments. The truth is that unconventional businesses are attractive but are not for everybody. Established companies could play in this unpredictable space, but they must be willing to welcome uncertainty and commit to learning and adapting as a way of life.

Why is it that the ideas in Quadrant IV can deliver outstanding value? To illustrate the dynamics of the "Unknown, Unknowns" space, particularly with non-consensual ideas, I would like to refer to the thinking of William P. (Bill) Barnett, professor at the Graduate School of Business at Stanford University, who teaches business strategy, among other topics, and explains it in the following terms (this is my take on his explanation in his class):

Let's assume you have an idea to launch a growth initiative or new business. When you first conceive the idea, you do not know if it will work, so you can end up being right or wrong about its future success. When other people judge your idea or insight, they may also be right or wrong about their assessment of its probability of success. So, after launching the growth initiative or new business and confirming if it worked or not, you get four possible combinations from these two premises:

Alternative 1: *They Were Right* (People judging the idea thought it was not going to succeed, and it didn't) / *I Was Wrong* (I thought it was going to succeed, but it didn't)

Alternative 2: *They Were Wrong* (People judging the idea thought it was going to succeed, but it didn't) / *I Was Wrong* (I thought it was going to succeed, but it didn't)

Alternative 3: They Were Right (People judging the idea thought it was going to succeed, and it did) / *I Was Right* (I thought it was going to succeed, and it did)

Alternative 4: They Were Wrong (People judging the idea thought it was not going to succeed, and it did) / *I Was Right* (I thought it was going to succeed, and it did)

Now, let's look at the implications of the four combinations:

Alternative 1: *You are a moron.* You thought the idea would be successful, but you were wrong, and it did not work. The consensus was that it would fail: "You didn't listen, but we told you so."

Alternative 2: *Back to square one.* Although you were wrong because the idea wasn't successful, those judging you were wrong in their assessment, too. It is a neutral verdict on your performance.

Alternative 3: *No big deal.* Those judging the idea and you were both right because the idea succeeded. You do not deserve any praise.

Alternative 4: *Eureka!* Those judging the idea believed it would fail, but you succeeded. You triumphed against conventional wisdom and created value when nobody thought it was possible.

Alternative 4 represents the jackpots, the low probability of a large payback territory. To better understand what the success of a nonconsensual idea entails, let's refer to the Airbnb case. When Brian Chesky, Nathan Blecharczyk, and Joe Gebbiathe presented the original insight about the Airbnb business, there was no consensus about their chances to succeed. On the contrary, the prevailing view was that it had no chance of survival; there were many skeptics. However, those investors who believed the business had potential and jumped in to invest first capitalized most of the value. Those investors that came in late reaped some benefits, too, but much less than the first movers. There are other examples of nonconsensual insights, like Uber or Amazon, which were controversial propositions at the beginning and became very successful companies later on, capturing immense value for their founders. The lesson is that being right about an idea that most people initially doubt pays off and can be very profitable.

The idea of a massive payback for successful nonconsensual ideas is very enticing for any company, both new or established. Still, its occurrence is rare, and "the planets need to align" to make it a reality. Truth be told, it is a long-shot game, and most incumbent companies are not designed to withstand the heat of being told by everybody that the idea they want to pursue will fail. On the contrary, many established companies strive to find sure bets to invest and view failure as a flaw in the plan rather than an indispensable step in the path to winning. This is why established companies prefer pursuing consensual ideas, where the prevailing average viewpoint prevails, and opt for a safe and predictable proposition to ensure success.

The concepts expressed in the knowledge advantage framework and Professor Bill Barnett's example of nonconsensual ideas help us understand the playing field and the implications for established companies when venturing to grow with bold, innovative, and entrepreneurial propositions. Paradoxically, many companies begin their growth journey with high ambitions and out-of-the-box ideas. Once an enterprise commits to a transformative adventure to grow, it typically starts with bold, far-reaching goals, attempting to become highly innovative and entrepreneurial as soon as possible; they want to hit the quadrant IV jackpot to reap the benefits. However, down the road, what looks like an achievable goal at the beginning, when everybody has high hopes, turns into a seemingly impossible endeavor delivering meager results. *Harvard Business Review* reports that 94% of executives are dissatisfied with their firm's innovation performance.[10] This finding signals a gap between the company's aspirations and the realities of what they can effectively achieve. No wonder financial markets are cautious about buying into the fanfare regarding the growth opportunities expressed by leaders and are unforgiving when companies fail to deliver on their promises. Organizations require a clear understanding of their playing field to set the right ambition before opening the champagne; it can spare many future frustrations and finger-pointing.

Playing today's and the future's game

Most established companies have successfully gone through a process of ingenuity and resourcefulness to develop a value proposition that, at some point, was able to gain customer's preferences. They created a knowledge advantage in the past that allows them to be in business today. The question remains if they will be able to do it again, and as often as is required, to stay relevant to their customers in a changing and highly competitive landscape. As we have discussed, inventing on behalf of customers is a journey of renewal that touches the very organizational genome of the company. The organizational core operates with lagging legacy standards, which were built to enable a value delivery system that may or may not be suitable to generate the new solutions that customers demand. W. Edwards Deming put it in the following terms: "Every system is perfectly designed to get the result that it does." This begs the question: Would the ongoing system of an established business be adequate for getting results that are different from the ones it was designed to perform?

Exploitation and Exploration: Irreconcilable Differences?

Corporations typically seek to pursue new ideas by separating the teams exploring the "new" from those in charge of producing and selling the "current" products. The rationale for the separation is grounded in the belief that the inertia of the established company will kill any attempts to develop something new. There is a deep-seated belief that combining the two teams, the team in charge of explorative work (future business) and the team in charge of the exploitative work (current business), will eventually generate a dysfunction that will cancel out any innovation efforts: "The new needs protection," as former Pixar president Ed Catmull puts it. "Business-as-usual does not. Managers do not need to work hard to protect established ideas or ways of doing business. The system is tilted in favor of the incumbent. The challenger needs support to find its footing."[11]

Two options stand out when separating innovation teams. The first option consists of creating a small sibling organization, wholly separate and independent from the original company, to explore new products or technologies and later incorporate them into the mothership. This alternative is known as the "skunkworks" approach (the name skunkworks is inspired by the comic strip Li'L Abner): "A skunkworks is an independent division of a firm set up and owned by the firm but with a distinct mission to explore new technologies free of goals, presumptions, and the culture of the firm itself,"[12] explains scientist Joshua Gans, a professor of technical innovation and entrepreneurship at the Rotman School of Management at University of Toronto. For all practical purposes, it entails creating a different organization altogether to innovate. As a result, notes Gans, "Skunkworks are extremely challenging to execute."[13]

The second option implies conserving the organization but separating those people who will carry on the business as usual, the exploitation (being efficient in current capabilities), from those who will perform the exploration (creating new offerings) while keeping the business infrastructure to serve the two. This alternative is known as the "ambidextrous" organization, which aims to "leverage organizational assets to compete in both the old and new businesses."[14]

The second option is the one companies pursue more often. This idea has gained much attention, and for good reasons; the concept suggests that an organization can execute today's business while simultaneously bringing about innovation to develop the products and services that will create the business for the future; what's not to like about it? However, rarely do companies achieve this objective and balance both practices consistently. In reality, companies find it challenging to become proficient in playing these two games simultaneously, the reason being that the "ambidexterity" alternative depends heavily on the commitment and abilities of the leader supporting the endeavor: "Senior management (role) is to manage the interface between the new business and the mature one and to resolve the inevitable conflicts that occur"[15] and "when the leader moves on, there is no guarantee that the new person will have the same strategic insight or ability to execute."[16] The balance to be able to uphold both systems is highly fragile. Ambidexterity is easy to derail because it poses a contradiction of terms: "The essence of exploitation is the refinement and extension of existing competencies, technologies, and paradigms. Its returns are positive, proximate, and predictable. The essence of exploration is experimentation with new alternatives. Its returns are uncertain, distant, and often negative."[17] —as the legendary James G. March, an expert on organizational leadership, put it.

March developed the "exploitation vs. exploration" description in 1991, and I believe it has been helpful to understand the dilemma. However, it is essential to highlight that his observations on the phenomena described an organizational outcome, not the method for making exploitation and exploration possible. The truth is that most organizations struggle with ambidexterity implementation because of the enormous gravitational pull the legacy business has over the new business initiatives, inclining the system in its favor. Conventional wisdom refers to this situation with the adage, "Old dogs can't learn new tricks."

Specializing teams is generally a good idea; it is an efficient way to advance any initiative the organization desires to pursue. Whenever you allocate a group of people to focus on something, whatever it may be, they will surely make progress, and it does not have to be necessarily on innovation-related activities. If you create a task force to work on spoilage, manufacturing productivity, reducing lead times, saving on utilities, etc., you will likely improve your current performance. Therefore, it makes sense to devote people and resources to advance your exploitation and exploration initiatives so you will have a better probability of improving on them. The problem originates when attempting to harmonize both systems without a hands-on leader who constantly pushes to make the whole thing work, and even with that kind of leader, success is not guaranteed. Since the legacy organization is the one that overshadows the new due to its inertia and established ways of working, it is critical to make it an active part of the solution, more so than with the teams in charge of experimentation. Still, the challenge for the organization is developing a shared culture and mindset that permeates the legacy and exploration areas and helps remove barriers that prevent the company from balancing both.

When companies attempt to solve the challenge of balancing exploitation and exploration, they often concentrate on the functional aspects of the organization, hoping to address the ambidexterity issue with procedures, routines, or processes (which may be required, but it remains a superficial solution). Alternatively, they may propose the establishment of two separate cultures, one for the current business team and another for the new business team, to avoid interfering with the culture design of the "cash cow" that generates the current profits. Neither of these approaches is effective and sustainable, and it is a big mistake to pursue two types of cultures within the same organization; it is a recipe for antagonism and division.

To effectively address this issue, we need to tackle the underlying cause of the dysfunction. This involves creating a robust and cohesive company culture that promotes adaptability across all areas of the organization and cultivating the right mindsets within our teams. In the upcoming sections, I'll outline the elements of such an organizational framework and describe the necessary steps to achieve this equilibrium. It's evident to me that after 40 years of discussing how to balance exploitation and exploration without any practical results that can be applied across all organizations, we need to reassess our approach to this topic.

There are no pure tones

The reality that most organizations face today is that they must renew more often than they used to. Even companies that leverage solid competitive advantages cannot afford to stay still because the pace of change in their industries and fierce competition threaten their permanence. The implication for the so-called "exploitation" practices is that they must adapt too; there is no pure exploitation mode anymore. Exploration has ceased to be a transitional state to become integrated into exploitative practices.

In modern organizations, the boundaries between exploitation and exploration are blurry. Rarely will you find a "purely exploitative" function or area within a company. Continuous improvement practices and the impact of technology in business have pushed the limits of what used to be a single approach, and established businesses and functions are forced to explore to keep up. Since customers drive growth and constantly raise their expectations, no one can rest on their laurels. The ambidexterity metaphor, which implies developing the equal use of right and left hands to function, in our case, exploitative and explorative activities, must give way to a more integrative metaphor. To provide a different perspective on the ambidexterity dichotomy, consider the example of writing with a pen on paper. If you are left-handed or right-handed, your dominant hand will dictate how you hold the pen and write. Switching hands to become ambidextrous can be a big challenge for most individuals, hence the difficulty of switching back and forth. However, what happens when you type on a keyboard instead of writing with a pen on a sheet of paper; the dominant use of hands will be less of a burden, and you can perform very well using both hands under a new set of conditions. Something similar is happening to organizations nowadays; the nature of the challenges and the uncertain conditions they face require using a different platform, where they can combine their business-as-usual activities with generating and implementing new ideas for growth seamlessly. Such a platform is represented by its human system, which is the very fabric for value generation.

The organization's soft core is the way

Organizations must set a navigation path on the knowledge advantage quadrants to gain customer preference and grow profitably. They must ask themselves, do we want to remain in the "Known Knows" and operate by continuous improvement or commit to the "Known Unknowns" with the associated risks involved? Do we have what it takes to go into the "Unknown Unknowns" and withstand uncertainty as a way of life? Once an organization chooses the Quadrant it aims to be in, it must be prepared to adapt to the conditions of that Quadrant. However, regardless of the size of the stretch they want to make, organizations should become flexible enough to evolve within their chosen Quadrant and more so if they decide to move from one Quadrant to another, as the nature of its value-generation ideas and desired capabilities changes.

The main takeaway from the knowledge advantage framework is that it is inevitable for organizations to venture into the unknown at some point, and to do that, they must have enough bandwidth in place to adapt and perform. They must nurture slack and leave room to escape from the hardwiring of their current organizational processes to keep up: "The most efficient organization in the execution of programmed tasks, often thanks to sophisticated procedures and a high degree of specialization of each actor, is rarely the most capable of innovating in a turbulent environment."[18]

Picture the organization as a vessel navigating a sea of complexity and unpredictability, facing failure, launching ideas, learning, and developing capabilities to create customers that lead to profitable growth. The more you navigate into the unknown, troubled waters, the more flexible and adaptable you must be; otherwise, the vessel will capsize or sink.

As the company transitions from Quadrant to Quadrant in the Knowledge Advantage Framework, it will develop new knowledge to fulfill or exceed customer expectations. Eventually, this new knowledge will settle and become the new baseline, the "Known Knowns." space. At that point, which may happen very quickly, the organizations must transition again, using this baseline as the launching pad to continue generating new knowledge. The idea is to hardwire while you need to be until it is time to find another positioning and hardwire again. It's a fluid process driven by the new knowledge necessary to gain consumers' preferences.

Even if the organization succeeds in becoming a flexible vessel, it will have its most significant challenge when attempting to venture into Quadrant IV, the "Unknown, Unknowns." space. Suppose the organization wants to venture into this territory. In that case, it must seriously consider whether its current organizational setup is the best platform to steer this endeavor because it likely may not be. The nature of Quadrant IV is incompatible with the way established organizations operate. There is no consensus on the ideas worth exploring, and its current capabilities are inadequate to deliver the required value proposition. Add stress, risk, and ambiguity to this equation. Now, if it were your organization and you acknowledged this situation, do you believe you could still pull it off? Can you develop a knowledge advantage using the current organizational makeup under these circumstances? Remember that 90%-95% of startups fail, so the odds will not be in your company's favor. Do you still want to do it? This is why disruptive "Corporate Intrapreneurship" is so challenging to attain; the further away you set your growth ambitions from the existing core, the more you will need to have a suitable vessel to accomplish the goal, which is different from the one you have now. If you are not prepared for the hardships ahead, you will be better off playing a Venture Capitalist game, investing in startups that are 100% focused on this space.

Navigating into the unknown implies accepting that more wrong things than right things will happen, and being right will be the exception. The natural habitat of established companies is not suitable for this quadrant. As James G. March says: "(To have novelty) you have to have a kind of system that is willing to go with a process that generates mostly mistakes and an occasional good thing; that's a hard system to create."[19]

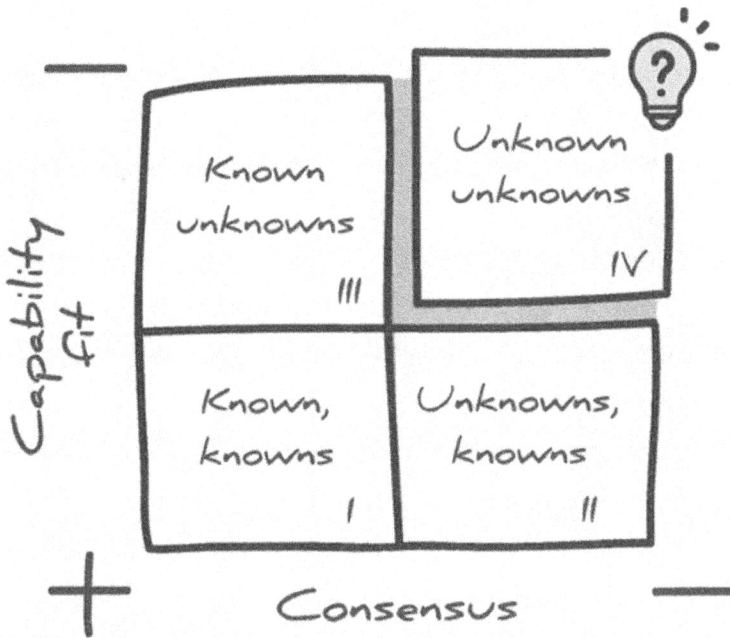

Quadrant IV is not for the faint-hearted; even if you know what you are getting into, you may be surprised by the ambiguity in this space. It is a horse of a different color, and the customary hardwiring of the company is different from what is required going forward. I encourage you to be realistic when assessing your condition and your willingness to do what it takes because casting your net too wide will only return frustration and will not be the best use of your scarce time and resources.

What you know for sure
that it just ain't so

I will shift from the organizational perspective to the individual one to demonstrate how navigating the knowledge quadrants can be challenging, and our assumptions play a significant role in the process. I will recount a personal experience from a few years ago that I still refer to as an example of our self-imposed limitations when exploring new territories.

During that time, I was responsible for the modern channel (supermarkets and convenience stores) in the northwestern region of Mexico for a Consumer Packaged Goods Company. I visited stores in the Tijuana and Rosarito areas to help them overcome their problems and opportunities to grow sales. We had a structured procedure to evaluate performance indicators at the store level, which implied reviewing data during the visit with the sales head promotor in each store (we had dedicated company employees working in stores to handle purchase orders, product displays, demonstrate products to consumers, in-store promotions, etc.). As I was checking on the purchase orders itemized product by product, in one of the stores, I noticed an anomaly; one item in particular, the one-pound package of premium beef franks, showed a purchase pattern of 50 packages per week for the last 8 to 10 weeks, but in one week, 250 packages were purchased by the store. Then, in the following weeks, it returned to ordering the 50 packages again.

I asked the head promotor responsible for the store what happened:

Me: I was reviewing the store's purchase pattern, and I noticed that four weeks ago, you ordered 250 packages of our premium one-pound franks, and then in the following week, it returned to the 50 packages per week that you normally order. Would you care to comment on this?

Head sales promotor: As you know, beef franks are premium products that sell at a high price; they are almost double compared to regular pork franks and nearly triple the cost of our value brand. We usually order 50 packages a week because it is the level that our customers can afford. The customers who buy at this store are very cost-conscious. We are located in a middle-class neighborhood, and the store assortment matches the type of products they can buy within their budget. As you can see on the shelves, we have one front for the premium beef franks, while the regular franks have four fronts, and the value franks have six fronts, which in itself tells you the story. I took a few days off three weeks ago, and another promoter covered my shift. She came from a high-end store in one of Tijuana's most expensive neighborhoods. The purchase order day coincided with her being responsible for placing orders. When she reviewed the suggested purchase order for the following week, she decided to increase the number of units ordered for beef franks. At her store, she usually orders 250 units of premium beef franks and thought the suggested 50 units was a system mistake. When I returned to the store, I adjusted the purchase order back to the 50 units I usually sell in this store.

Me: What did you do with the extra 200 units that the store received?

Head sales promoter: Well, I had to sell them. As you know, this is a perishable item, and when it reaches its expiration date, the store returns it, which will impact my performance indicators.

Me: So, you sold them. What did you do?

Head sales promoter: I took specific actions to rotate this premium product. The first thing I did was negotiate an extra display at the store for the seasonal products area; then, I took it upon myself to approach customers and explain to them the benefits of this product, the memories they would create with their family while enjoying a high-quality, flavorful beef frank, barbecuing with friends for a memorable get-together, they could watch a movie with their significant other and enjoy a perfectly cooked, tasty hot dog, enjoying life with a premium product after an intense day of work, etc.

Me: Wow, those were powerful reasons for them to buy the premium beef franks!

Head sales promoter: Indeed, they were. I also mentioned that the price difference with other regular franks was considerable, but only when evaluating it as a percentage. It's just a few bucks when you look at it in dollars. I asked them, "Arent you and your loved ones worth a few extra bucks to enjoy the best hot dog frank there is?".

Me: And what did they say?

Head sales promoter: They thought about it for a moment and said, you know, you are right. I can indulge in something like this without seriously adjusting our budget, and my family and I deserve to be rewarded for all our hard work.

Me: This is incredible! So, you sold the additional 200 packages during the week?

Head sales promoter: Yes, I did; by the end of the week, they were gone. And it was a big relief for me. Now, I could return to the store's normal sales volume.

Me: Has it occurred to you that the 50 premium beef frank packages you typically sell in this store may be a stuck number that does not reflect the store's real sales potential?

Head sales promoter: We have been selling 50 packages a week for a long time. It is just the way it is.

Me: But you proved that the store can sell more. Maybe 250 units is a long stretch, but 100 or 150 units may be possible, don't you think?

Head sales promoter: No, I don't think so. I pulled it off once, but the customers that live in this neighborhood are cost-conscious, and if we order extra product, it will go to waste.

Me: What if we run an experiment, and I authorize an increase in the waste target at this store for a few weeks to test if the potential consumption is higher?

Head sales promoter: I don't believe it is worth the try. As I told you, 50 units a week is the right number for the store.

Me: What happened during the week after you sold the 250 units when you went back to 50? Did customers return to buy more? Did you stock-out?

Head sales promoter: Some of them returned and bought the premium beef franks again; I recognized their faces. And yes, we almost ran out of inventory for a few days, but things returned to normal afterward.

Me: Well, sure, I think a week is not enough time to change a pattern; it requires more time. You must keep working with your customers to get their buy-in for the new target.

Head sales promoter: Or maybe that unusual week was just an exception that confirms the rule.

Me: Well, we will not know if we don't try, don't we? Think about it: there might be an opportunity to grow, and if you change your mind, call me. I would love to determine whether 50 packages a week is a stuck number.

Head sales promoter: I will think about it and let you know.

In the upcoming chapters, I will explain how our perception of potential can limit us and how we can achieve better results by reviewing and updating our belief system. In this case, what struck me was that her willingness to explore was restricted by her experience, even when she found a way to overcome the challenge. This restriction hinders the development of new knowledge and the ability to gain an advantage. Even when there is evidence that our assumptions limit our potential, we tend to stick with them due to habit.

If you wonder what happened in the following months with the sales of premium beef franks in this store, I am sorry to tell you that I don't have a happy ending for you. The result stayed pretty much the same. I talked to the zone supervisor, and we agreed on not forcing the hand of the head sales promoter. Instead, we tried to motivate and encourage her to go the extra mile, which she did marginally. The inertia ended up being very strong, and little progress was made. Looking at this event in hindsight, I now know she did not have a strong enough reason to change her mind and be more daring. Her internal anchors became restrictions for pushing the existing boundaries. When we enter unknown territory, we must be open-minded to adapting and learning. We need to overcome the impetus from the business as usual to venture into the new, even if it's scary and takes time to become a reality.

The anecdote might lead you to believe that this only occurs at the individual level and that organizations are immune to this situation. Companies may seem to have many intelligent individuals who would assess information and pursue the correct ideas. However, you'd be surprised to learn that numerous real-life examples demonstrate the pitfalls of organizations unwilling to explore new knowledge or that pursue the wrong ideas.

Blockbuster, Kodak, Nokia, Xerox, Blackberry, Toys R Us, and more recently, WeWork and Silicon Valley Bank are companies that arguably had systems in place that resulted in winning value propositions and capabilities that were difficult to replicate. These companies were leaders in their respective categories and commanded high market shares. We all have heard their stories; despite their success, they could not compete under changing market conditions and eventually failed. The demise of such reputable enterprises tells us that the ability to renew themselves and adapt is not intuitive. Brilliant executives at the time ran these companies. Still, for whatever reason, they could not anticipate the much-needed change, were not open to considering another way to play, or were simply incapable of adapting to the new circumstances.

I have always wondered about the mindset of those managing the "soon to fail" incumbent organization and what prevents them from adapting and renewing their business. There is an interesting story shared by Marc Randolph, one of Netflix's founders, in his book, "That Will Never Work, The Birth of NETFLIX and the Amazing Life of an Idea," on how Blockbuster's thinking drove them to take a wrong turn in building their business for the future, despite the existence of signs of a shift to an internet-based movie rental. At the time, Blockbuster executives were convinced that online business was a short-lived trend and they didn't have to worry about it. This thought was revealed to Randolph and Reed Hastings during a meeting in September 2000 with Blockbuster's CEO John Antioco, where they discussed Blockbuster's potential interest in acquiring Netflix:

"We were intimidated because Blockbuster was in a much stronger position than us. Flush with cash from their recent IPO (450 million), they weren't dependent on the good graces of VCs to keep them afloat...but the most important point in our favor was the inexorable march of progress. The world was going online. No one knew exactly how it would happen, or how long it would take, but it was inevitable that increasing numbers of Blockbuster's customers would want — no, insist on — transacting their business online. And not only was Blockbuster ill-positioned to take advantage of the trend, they didn't even see it was coming... Their objections were just what we had anticipated, the dot-com hysteria is completely overblown, Antioco said; Stead (Ed Stead, Blockbuster's general counsel) informed us, that the business models of most online ventures, Netflix included, just weren't sustainable. They would burn cash forever."[20]

Marc Randolph closes the passage, sharing a conversation he had with Reed Hastings after the meeting, in which he made the following remark; "Blockbuster doesn't want us, I said, So it's obvious what we have to do now. I smiled. Couldnt help it. It looks like now we're going to have to kick their ass."[21]

Based on Marc Randolph's description of the meeting with Blockbuster, we can tell that top management did not believe that the Internet could derail their business model. My understanding of the case is that, later on, when they realized they needed to move to online transactions, they attempted to do something, but it was too late, and they did not have the capabilities to compete with Netflix. In addition to their lack of vision, a system was in place that hardwired Blockbuster to operate with a rental model leveraged with 9,000 company-owned and franchise stores, serving around 20 million members. Their operating system was stiff, tailor-made for a brick-and-mortar chain, and their renewal muscle could not adapt to what customers wanted next. They were hardwired to a soon-to-be-disrupted business model.

Another critical misreading of a market trend occurred in 2007 with Apple's launch of the iPhone. At the time, Microsoft CEO Steve Ballmer was asked for his opinion on how the iPhone would compete with Microsoft's Zune phone.

Reporter: "Let me ask you about the iPhone and the Zune. If I may, the Zune was getting some traction, and Steve Jobs goes to Macworld and he pulls out this iPhone. What was your first reaction when you saw that?

Ballmer (laughing): A $500 dollars fully subsidized with a plan; I said that is the most expensive phone in the world, and it doesn't appeal to business customers because it doesn't have a keyboard, which makes it not a very good email machine."[22]

Zune was introduced to the market in 2006, and by 2011, it was discontinued.

The key takeaway from these examples is that it's challenging for organizations to come up with the right ideas to develop a knowledge advantage. Leaders often hold on to existing beliefs, which can hinder progress. Embracing a beginner's mindset is crucial for navigating the Quadrants of the Knowledge Advantage Framework.

The Hungry Beast and the Ugly Baby

I want to conclude this chapter with Ed Catmull's metaphor, "the hungry beast and the ugly baby." Ed Catmull was one of the co-founders of Pixar Animation Studios and the former president of Pixar Animation and Disney Animation. In his metaphor, he states that today's business is like a hungry beast, "The Beast cannot be sated. It is one of life's cruel ironies that when it comes to feeding the Beast, success only creates more pressure to hurry up and succeed again."[23] The new ventures represent the ugly baby, our exploration projects to Regrow, and our job is "to protect our babies from being judged too quickly...when there is no sufficient pushback to protect new ideas -things go wrong. The Beast takes over."[24] The legacy belief system operating in the organization is powerful and needs to be revamped to allow advancement.

CHAPTER 3

Reframing Our Perspective

*"When shall we open our minds to the conviction that the
ultimate reality of the world is neither matter nor spirit, is no
definite thing, but a perspective?"*
— JOSÉ ORTEGA Y GASSET

*"As Matisse said, When I look at a fig tree, every leaf
has a different design. They all have their own manner of
moving in space; yet in their own separate ways,
they all cry, "Fig Tree"."*
—FRANCOISE GILOT

*"If you want truly to understand something,
try to change it."*
—KURT LEWIN

W hen formulating a marketing strategy, every leader must ask one fundamental question: What business are we in? This crucial question may seem trivial, but it forces you and your team to understand the benefits your brand provides to its customers, which is why they buy from you in the first place.

Asking yourself what business you are in helps frame your activities and shifts your thinking from product-oriented to customer-oriented. For example, suppose you declare that you are in the car business. In this case, a product will define your organization, and your focus will be on the car itself, in manufacturing a better car—whatever that means to you—but producing a great car will not necessarily solve your customers' problems.

This line of thinking will lead you to build a "better mousetrap" for sure, but the question remains: "Is this what your customers want and need?" Now, let's imagine what happens when you respond to the question of what business we are in by declaring that you are in the mobility business instead of the car business. Your focus shifts from the product itself to providing a better solution to your customers' transportation needs, which is the service they "hire" the car to perform for them. It is a very different perspective to guide your actions. The competition arena shifts, too, to a different playing field. Instead of competing only with other car companies, your scope widens to include additional mobility solutions (like buses, taxis, ride-sharing, or airplanes). Being customer-centric changes the dynamics of your thinking and your role as a supplier in the market.

Why are we discussing marketing strategy and trying to define our business within the perspective of Regrowth and unlocking the potential of our people? It's a simple reason: this is a crucial question we need to ask to guide our thoughts about organizational transformation and the journey toward helping people acheive their best.

Regrowth: What business are we in?

We discussed how organizations usually concentrate on their products, capabilities, and competitive strategies to achieve Regrowth. While these are important, I stressed that more than that is necessary. I suggested that adapting and transforming in response to changing market conditions is primarily a human effort within the organization. This means that we must focus on the fundamental issue - our people - to create the right conditions for Regrowth. When striving for Regrowth, we must harness the mindsets of our people in the organization. So, when asked, "What business are we in for Regrowth?" I assert that **we are in the mindset business.**

What does it mean to be in the mindset business? Sometimes, it's helpful to define our playing field by figuring out what business we're not in and determining the territory by exclusion. Following this, I argue that we are not in the "feeling good" or "pleasing all" business. Indeed, we need our people to be satisfied with how they feel about being members of the organization; otherwise, it cannot function properly, but this is a necessary condition, not the goal. We are not in the "boosting morale" or "providing comfort" business either; again, we must achieve a necessary threshold for people to do good work, but that is not the playing field. There are plenty of "basic conditions" that allow the organization to exist and that we must fulfill to operate, but they are not the business we are in.

Being in the mindset business means engaging with our people's mind makeup, including their hearts and aspirations, and upholding a shared perspective to transform the organization. Activating a collective mindset of the organization is the core that unleashes potential and produces growth-promoting energy. In attaining this objective, we must recognize that we are facilitators of the process, but the shift must come from within the organization; it's an inside-out, not an outside-in endeavor. It can be elicited but requires the participation of our people to be embraced. We will discuss these ideas in-depth in the following chapters.

Change to Regrow

"I can't think of an example where real change was
driven from the top only. It's like pushing on a string"
—Peter Senge

Organizational change is inevitable in order to stay relevant in a fast-paced environment; companies constantly seek to transition from their current state to a desired state. For instance, leaders always want to increase revenues, volume, profitability, consumer preference, employee engagement, etc. They begin with a baseline, the status quo; from there, they set goals and ambitions; then, they allocate resources and talent to mobilize the organization to achieve the desired results. We conduct business in a never-ending transitioning cycle, from the old to the new, eventually becoming old with time, and then we aspire to the new again. This is, after all, the essence of leadership: to mobilize the organization by embracing change, unlocking its potential, and constantly reaching for ever higher and bolder goals. As Reid Hoffman, founder of LinkedIn, puts it, "You're always leading through transitions, your company is always changing around you."[1]

The perpetual change condition is not new. Business change has been studied left and right and often over-analyzed. When you Google "change management," you get more than 7 billion results! Very renowned authors have devoted their lives to developing theories, concepts, and frameworks about change and how to attain it sustainably. From my perspective, the one thing that stands out in the process is that for change to occur in the organization, its constituents must believe in it and follow through. Nothing changes in a company if they have yet to decide to move along the proposed path. As we all know, minds are anything but simple. Mobilizing change is complicated because each person's mind is different and makes sense of reality using a unique, filtered set of facts. Reality is primarily personal, never fixed, and does not necessarily correspond to hard, shared, proven evidence. It is fundamentally a perception and eventually made into the content we play in our thoughts when acting. Anais Nin famously said, "We don't see the world as it is; we see the world as we are."

Our people and the organization as a whole are minds in action. As leaders, we constantly strive for their attention and buy-in. The mind of each individual is the basic unit of analysis when attempting change, especially when navigating the path for Regrowth. Nothing in the company "exists" outside their minds. The surrounding organizational reality of a person exists insofar as a mind recognizes its existence. The company is not so much a place as it is a thought in the peoples' minds, a state of their mind. Henry Mintzberg had it right, "It's not as if the organization is a museum with that big picture on some wall. It has to be constructed in the mind of its people."[2] The collective mind of our people is our canvas for change initiatives.

Engaging our people's minds to jumpstart their willingness to change and unlock their potential is the holy grail. This task is difficult, as the human mind is complex, and our understanding of its workings is limited. Our minds are wired in a certain way, and our knowledge of its dynamic is poor, to say the least. We often fail to recognize how our minds are influenced by the particular connections of our beliefs and rarely question their usefulness. But, as we will see in the pages ahead, we must change our beliefs if they cease to help us progress; as Phillip E. Tetlock and Dan Gardner say, "Beliefs are hypotheses to be tested, not treasures to be guarded."[3]

Steering the collective mindset of the company is a complex task, and leaders have to be prepared to deal with ambiguity at every step. Achieving sustainable mindset change in an organization is a long-term journey rather than a one-time event, and it is as much of a challenge for the organization itself as it is for those leading the change. If you guide mindset change, assessing where you stand and the makeup of your beliefs is crucial since these factors will influence your actions and the course you take going forward.

Two metaphors inform our view of the organization

When an organization commits to pursuing a mindset shift, those guiding the transformation play an essential role in facilitating the process and ensuring its eventual success. They will set the goals to attain, decide on the "how to" and the pace of change, and be responsible for helping employees overcome any barriers that inevitably will arise. To fulfill their role, they will use a mental model of the organization as a backdrop when promoting the buy-in of its people, their interactions, and the unlocking of their potential. As leaders, whether consciously or unconsciously, we have a view of the organization's workings, and that understanding guides our actions to attain the collective mind-shift goal. We must be aware of our assumptions about the company because they may hinder us from achieving our objectives. However, this task proves challenging because bringing forth these assumptions to evaluate them is not intuitive. As Jennifer Riel and Roger Martin state, "We're rarely aware of the models we hold... Our models exist under the surface, and we rarely reflect on how they influence our actions. Yet they do."[4]

We will discuss mental models in Chapter 6; for now, be aware that they comprise the points of view, assumptions, biases, and beliefs that shape leaders' actions to facilitate the transformation. If you think that the mental models of leaders are not that big of a deal and will not impact the outcome, think again. The perspective of those guiding the journey constitutes the lens they will use to make sense of the situation and influence the decisions they make along the way. Its implications are essential for the transformation journey and should not be taken for granted.

Two general mental models can be used to view an organization, and they directly oppose each other. Based on my experience managing change, I have observed that employees in organizations assume these two mental models as "archetypes" or "metaphors" to make sense of how the organization works. Everyone, from the C-Suite to the entry-level, unconsciously holds and carries the logic of these archetypes when performing their jobs or making decisions. They establish how organizations should function and what can be expected from their people in the work setting. The first metaphor views the organization as a machine, while the second sees the organization as a living organism, similar to the animated beings in biology.

The machine metaphor

Let's look at the first metaphor, where the organization is compared to a machine. In this metaphor, the organization is seen as a whole composed of parts working synchronously, aiming to be effective and efficient. The overall functioning of the total depends on the efficiency of the parts. Each part of the machine has a specific task, and every part must strive for optimal work. Various functions in the organization—like operations, logistics, sales, finance, marketing, human resources, etc.—are viewed as parts of such a machine, and each must continually find ways to be more efficient and work together most effectively. Each function, in turn, comprises parts that follow the same optimization principle. The organization aims to lock the system into a virtuous cycle that increases the performance of each part and the whole at the lowest possible cost.

The central belief is that the system works best when all the parts in the machine integrate to pursue efficiency and excellent performance simultaneously. The tighter the coupled parts of the machine work with each other, the better and more efficiently they operate, with no room for idle time, rework, or waste. Roger Martin, in his book "When More is not Better," explains how this same perspective applies to the economy, which is a helpful view in light of how organizations work: "The model in question holds that the economy is a machine, a machine that can be optimized by breaking it into constituent parts, optimizing each, and adding them back together to make an optimal running whole. Further, the machine can be made even more perfect by pursuing increasing levels of efficiency, by which the desired outputs are created with the least possible inputs, in each constituent part."[5]

The machine metaphor is the prevalent mental model in many organizations; people must focus on identifying and eliminating errors and reducing wasted resources. Any sensible manager would agree that pursuing maximum efficiency is essential to increase productivity, reduce waste, and achieve higher returns on invested capital. Therefore, the machine metaphor is a practice that hardly gets questioned, even if it sometimes interferes with the freedom required for innovation or experimentation. Sports teams are widely used as an example of this metaphor. In sports, minimizing or eliminating errors is the key to improving performance and achieving better results. In fixing a problem and improving performance, the first step is to analyze the source of the error, correct it, and then practice relentlessly until achieving perfection. One of the most celebrated football coaches of all time, Bill Walsh, developed a comprehensive system to achieve excellence in the San Francisco 49ers named "The Standard of Performance," where he detailed the daily practices for the team: "Passing routes were designed down to the inch and then practiced until receivers learned how to be at the exact inch at the exact moment the ball arrived. On paper, my diagrams of plays resembled detailed architectural drawings...

Our practices were organized to the minute—like a musical score for an orchestra that shows every musician what to play and when to play it. Our coaches then drilled the team so they could "play it" better and better."[6]

When you are pursuing perfection, how do you determine that you are achieving the desired state? To assess how well you are performing, the assessment under the machine metaphor comes from the company's past performance standards or external benchmarks in the industry; these are the indicators you will compare against.

The most important feature of the optimal performing machine is the belief that optimizing the parts of the machine will improve the system as a whole. This conclusion is crucial as it justifies the efforts made in the process and supports the pursuit of perfection. However, some respected business thinkers argue that this may not be the ultimate solution that everyone believes it to be. In his last interview with Industry Magazine, industrial engineer and economist W. Edwards Deming, best known for his work on quality management, commented: "The results of a system must be managed by paying attention to the entire system. When we optimize sub-components of the system, we don't necessarily optimize the overall system." Often, that is because optimizing a company's processes and structures creates silos and negatively affects the communication flow in the organization. Fred Koffman, Ph.D. in Economics from the University of California, Berkeley, and founder and president of the Conscious Business Center, holds the same point of view about how optimizing sub-systems is detrimental to the whole and suggests the contrarian view that sub-optimizing the parts of a system is a preferred alternative: "In order to optimize the system, you must sub-optimize the sub-systems...when you evaluate people based on the performance of their sub-systems, they will optimize their sub-systems, sub-optimizing the system."[7]

The machine metaphor thrived in an era where things were predictable, and business conditions were stable; it became the preferred view for managing business. Educational institutions contributed to training executives under the optimization view, and the machine way of thinking was ingrained in their minds; they were "taught to manage machines. Most have an educational background in business administration or engineering/computer science or both."[8]

As long as this perspective helped solve problems, there was no need to change it. The question remains, however, whether, with rapid advancements in technology, shifting consumer preferences, and unpredictable market conditions, this perspective will deliver its promised benefits.

The living, breathing company

Many leaders still view their organizations as machines because of the apparent lack of another approach to making sense of them. If the machine metaphor is not an adequate resource for the adaptability required to compete, what mental model should they use instead? Let's look at the second metaphor, which views the organization as a living organism.

This metaphor comes from biology and views the organization as a living organism, much like the ones found in nature: "Our normal way of thinking cheats us. It leads us to think of wholes as made of many parts...living systems...are not mere assemblages of their parts but continually growing and changing along with their elements", write Peter M. Senge, C. Otto Scharmer, Joseph Jaworski, and Betty Sue Flowers in their book "Presence."[9] To better understand this metaphor, one can observe nature in a nearby park, paying attention to the entire system rather than individual trees or animals. Everything is alive and adapting in nature, constantly in motion and evolving in response to environmental changes. Functions are developed or dropped based on what is necessary to survive and thrive in the surrounding ecosystem.

There are several notable examples of how biology efficiently adapts to its surroundings. For instance, the chameleon can change its skin color to blend in with the environment to avoid predator detection. The giraffe has developed a long neck to reach the leaves at the top of trees. The Alaskan wood frog freezes its body during winter to survive and then thaws out and resumes its activities when the weather warms up. While these examples may seem extreme adjustments, they demonstrate the importance of adaptability in the face of constantly evolving threats. This is just as true for businesses as for the natural world. We are all familiar with the SARS-CoV-2 virus, which dramatically changed our lives not too long ago by starting a pandemic that put the world in lockdown for many months and killed millions of people. The virus constantly adapted to a challenging environment through variants and mutations, making it difficult to combat. Although the first vaccine brought hope, the virus continued to change, rendering the available resources inadequate in a matter of months.

The metaphor of biology suggests that in the face of rapidly changing business conditions, it is wise to remain flexible and build an adaptive system to survive. In the past, a set of competitive advantages allowed companies to maintain a stronghold for many years, and optimization and efficiency were the expected outcomes at every stage of the organization. However, this is no longer the case. The ability to effectively respond to constantly evolving conditions is now crucial. As we have been discussing, technology is accelerating the pace of change in all industries, and customers are willing to switch their loyalty to companies that better understand and solve their ever-evolving wants and needs. A tightly coupled organization that prioritizes cut-to-the-bone efficiency is not flexible enough to adapt. A certain level of slack among functions is necessary, just like in the biology metaphor, where flexibility is the key to renewal.

How can biology's principles influence how we manage a business? Let me suggest a few ideas. Firstly, instead of keeping only the bare minimum number of resources for each function, it is beneficial to allow some redundancy and have extra resources available to make adjustments and take action as needed. This approach helps us be proactive rather than reactive when conditions change.

Secondly, it's crucial to staff and budget for a function's future potential, not just its current state. It's important to envision what a function will look like in a few years and support its growth path.

Lastly, it's essential to reconsider investing solely in projects included in the operating plan and be open to other options. Allowing room to experiment with new ideas and ventures is a good use of resources. Even if these were not initially planned, they could keep the company flexible and innovative.

We must acknowledge that innovation and entrepreneurship rarely result from following efficient systems. To explore and invent, we need flexibility, adaptation, resilience, and the freedom to make mistakes without fear of punishment.

How the machine and the living organism metaphors stack up

The machine and biology metaphors have unique logic for how an organization should operate. They rely on managers driven by this thinking and a shared belief system enabling implementation. Here is a quick general overview of the beliefs that support each metaphor.

Beliefs sustaining the machine metaphor

- The organization is a machine made out of parts that must work efficiently.
- Any kind of waste is harmful and undesirable, and parts of the business must be optimized constantly to eliminate it.
- All the parts must be tightly coupled, hardwired, and working together efficiently, with very limited or no slack.
- There must be a specific, actionable solution for every problem you face. Cause-effect relationships among the parts are close in time, and vision is short-term.

- The main focus in the system is on first-order consequences, encompassing the very next move only.
- Optimal performance is a function of the machine being locked into a specific positioning to achieve the expected results.
- Experience is the source of knowledge, which must be extrapolated to produce solutions for dealing with the unknown.
- Business as usual and innovation must be separated from the core and optimized independently.
- Aim for perfection
- Mantra: "Measure nine times and cut once."

Beliefs sustaining the living organism

- The organization is a living organism that behaves like a system.
- The living organism is dynamic, and constant adaptation is the norm.
- Learning and adaptation are the key outcomes. They allow the organization to rise to its becoming possibilities.
- Cause-effect relationships are assessed further in time, with a systemic view, typically medium to long-term vision.
- Some slack is necessary to function correctly. System components are loosely coupled.
- The living organism learns and repositions itself as required by the circumstances.

- The source of knowledge combines experience with adventure. The discovery system is driven by shorter cycles of action and reflection.
- The living system requires us to foresee further in time, to envision first, second, and third-order consequences of our actions.
- Day-to-day business as usual and innovation can be separated but must be integrated under a shared umbrella.
- Mantra: "Done is better than perfect."

If you work in an innovation area, consider the benefits of teams adopting a "living organism metaphor" when developing ideas for customers. This perspective encourages leaving room for exploration and creativity, allowing teams to venture into new territory and avoid remaining stuck in a fixed position.

The Aspen Grove

To illustrate the concept of a business functioning like a living organism, I'd like to share a specific example that I find helpful in explaining this idea. It comes from real life and is found in nature, which not only demonstrates how an organization operates like a biological entity but also emphasizes the importance of diversity and unity in the system. The metaphorical example I'm referring to is the Aspen Grove, which forms the core of the concepts presented in this book. I want to thank Bryan Walker, partner and managing director at IDEO, who introduced me to this analogy a few years ago.

The Aspen Grove, also known as a clone, is a collection of tens, hundreds, or even thousands of trees originating from a single root. Above ground, it appears as a forest of many seemingly independent trees spanning a large area. However, a massive, interconnected root system below the surface nourishes the entire grove: "They grow quickly, create ethereal groves with white trunks backed by shimmering green, and in fall their yellow color seems to infuse the air with a dream-like glow...There's one novelty that makes aspen stand out from almost every other tree species: The trees grow roots near the surface, and the roots sprout new trees. The new trees are genetically identical to the parent tree, and a grove of aspen—often covering more than 100 acres—is literally a single living organism."[10]

The sight of an aspen grove in the fall is genuinely breathtaking. As the summer green fades away, the leaves of the aspen trees burst into brilliant shades of yellow, painting a beautiful picture against the backdrop of the forest.

Let me further explain the living organism metaphor of the organization using the Aspen Grove analogy. Think of Aspen Grove as an organization; the trees spreading throughout the terrain represent the organization's different functions, departments, or positions, such as sales, operations, marketing, finance, and legal. As Aspen Grove expands on the terrain, you will find that each tree is situated in a different location, such as on hills, in creeks, surrounded by rocks, or on flat land, representing the challenges each must face. For example, a tree surrounded by rocks will have to overcome rugged terrain conditions, while a tree in a creek or on a hill may have water resources but a different ecosystem to contend with.

Each tree appears independent but is connected by a single root, forming a living organism. To thrive, the trees must adapt to their unique challenges. Since they form a single entity, the actions and circumstances of each tree affect the entire organism. Therefore, each tree must overcome its challenges individually while also considering the well-being of the whole organism.

The Aspen Grove metaphor is a great way to explain an organization that adapts and grows. The root is essential for the well-being of the whole; the more robust the root, the better the whole system will be. While each tree must have unique attributes to cope with its surroundings, the grove depends on having a solid root, and as long as you have one, you will acheive growth as a whole.

What is the root of an organization, and how can it be strengthened? The answer is that the organization's collective mindset represents the root. It is crucial to have a robust shared mindset that can withstand the changing conditions all areas in the organization face in coping with a changing environment. I argue that the collective mindset is, in turn, informed by two other components, talent density and culture, which constitute a reinforcing system. To develop an adaptable organization, we must strengthen all three aspects: Talent density, culture, and mindset.

The Aspen Root Framework

The framework I propose constitutes the root of Aspen and is the platform for organizational Regrowth. Driving the organization's collective Mindset implies working in the three dimensions mentioned above. While there are specific conditions that we can work on to strengthen the collective Mindset specifically, we must also activate the other two for a sustainable path to Regrowth. The following three chapters will delve into these three dimensions and their determinants. All dimensions feed each other in a way that energizes the company and allows people to rise to their potential. In Chapter 4, we will cover talent density; in Chapter 5, we will address Culture; and in Chapter 6, we will discuss Mindset.

In Chapter 7, I will offer an integrative, holistic view of the concepts presented in the book as a canvas to help you design your organization's transformation journey. Without further delay, let's get started.

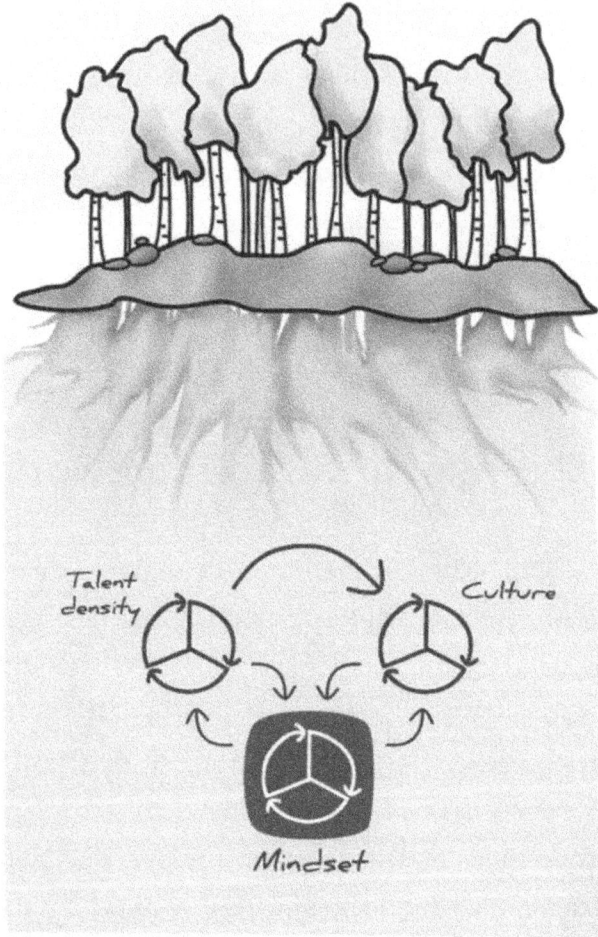

CHAPTER 4

Talent Density

"Quamplurimi et quam aptissimi—
"as many as possible of the very best".."
—JESUIT RECRUITING SLOGAN

"People are not your most important asset.
The right people are."
—JIM COLLINS

"A team is a state of mind."
—JORGE VALDANO

As the Vice President of Human Capital at an international Mexican conglomerate with a revenue of USD 16 billion and 83,000 employees across 28 countries, I overview the process for filling 120 senior positions with top-notch talent in the short term and ensuring smooth executive succession within the group. When I assumed the position, the number of senior executives retiring in the following six years equaled the number of retirees in the company's 45-year history. Therefore, my team and I organized talent development programs for 300 individuals at top universities worldwide to tackle this challenge.

One of the universities we partnered with was the Sloan School of Management at the Massachusetts Institute of Technology (MIT). Court Chilton, Senior Lecturer of Work and Organization Studies, and Steven Eppinger, Professor of Management Science and Innovation, helped us co-design a wonderful program that combined soft and hard skills for leaders. MIT is well known for its hard skills and engineering background, and it surprised me how thorough, disciplined, and effective they were in teaching soft skills as well. Once we had defined the topics to cover and interviewed dozens of renowned faculty members to select the few that were to teach classes, it was time to wrap our program up. I thought we were done, but Court and Steven introduced a new element that we needed to discuss:

Court and Steve: As you know, MIT has a motto, "Mens et Manus," which translates from Latin to "mind and hand." This motto reflects the educational ideals of MIT's founders, who promoted education for practical application. Therefore, as part of the program, we propose setting teams of participants by business unit to develop specific projects that bring value to their organizations; this must be a vital part of their work and should be conducted with the same rigor as the classes. Between cohorts, we can set up calls to guide and help them. In the final session, we will recognize the team's accomplishments, evaluating the project's impact on productivity, savings, product launches, etc.

Me: What are you talking about? Project development was not part of the original program design we agreed upon. Besides, coordinating people with different time zones in many geographies in Europe, Asia, and America will be a pain in the neck. They are swamped with work already; they have jobs, and I do not want to distract them from their responsibilities. Besides, I tried something similar in the past, and it was a complete disaster; I have never seen an idea like this work. It will waste resources and cause unnecessary stress; I am totally against it.

Court and Steve: We understand your concerns and acknowledge that it will take work. Since this is your first time working with us, you don't have evidence to help you make an informed decision. You should only know that we both know how to do projects. We are MIT, and we will make it work. We urge you to reconsider your position.

My gut reaction was to say no and finish the conversation. I was apprehensive about the idea of developing projects; it wasn't something I felt confident about. I participated in other programs where they tried to make them work, but the results were bad. However, I was impressed by Court and Steve's confidence in the project's potential for success. I respected them, and they deserved the benefit of the doubt. After some thought, I realized I didn't know how they approached projects or the value MIT could bring to my organization. I paused for a moment and then said:

Me: Well, I admit I haven't collaborated with you on executive program projects, but I hold you and MIT in high regard. I agree, so let's proceed. I hope my decision won't lead to regret.

At the end of MIT's program, the teams completed 24 projects. They generated much value in productivity, client satisfaction, energy optimization, cost reduction, absenteeism, employee motivation, etc. Court and Steve delivered with flying colors on an initiative nobody could before. Undoubtedly, there was something different about them; they were very talented at what they did, which showed in the results.

Spotting talent

We all have heard references to talent, like "That person is extremely talented," "She has a natural talent," and "She has an innate talent," etc. Talents are relatively easy to identify in areas such as music, sports, and skilled games, where individuals can be ranked based on their performance. Placing talent in these fields is easier because we can compare an individual's performance with others on the same somewhat repetitive, predictable tasks. For example, a prodigy child playing the piano, a gifted athlete in the high jump, a magician performing a disappearing act, or Picasso drawing a bull in just a few seconds are all acts of talent that only a few individuals can achieve. To determine how talented a person is, we compare their performance with others under similar conditions. We may not get a 100% consensus on the evaluation, but we can be pretty close in the ranking.

Identifying talent in an organizational setting is a far more complex process than it may seem. The process is challenging due to variables such as the influence of external forces and the quality and dynamic of team members, which are hard to isolate when assessing individual performance. I have discovered that the traditional method of singling out a "hero" for their talent is no longer effective, especially in today's work environment, where collaboration within a team and with neighboring functions is essential. Therefore, a more comprehensive approach to identifying and nurturing talent potential is necessary.

Making comparisons among individuals' performance is not always feasible; how do we evaluate the talent of knowledge workers who deal with constantly changing conditions and make difficult decisions in non-comparable circumstances? Typically, we end up judging based on their results. Still, even then, we cannot be unbiased: "Personnel decisions are noisy," write Kahneman, Sibony, and Sunstein in their book "Noise, A Flaw in Human Judgement"; "Interviewers of job candidates make widely different assessments of the same people. Performance ratings of the same employee are also highly variable and depend more on the person doing the assessment than on the performance being assessed."[1] And yet, we must persevere in our quest for spotting talent because, despite its challenges, we must find a way to identify the right talent to improve organizational performance. Without extraordinary talent, companies are doomed to fail: "If you have the wrong people, it doesn't matter whether you discover the right direction, you will still won't have a great company. Great vision without great people is irrelevant," writes Jim Collins in "Good to Great."[2]

To add another layer of complexity to this scenario, we must acknowledge the elephant in the room: The broken talent industry. The talent assessment industry is messy and difficult to navigate, to say the least. There are many different approaches to evaluating and managing talent that are not coherent and often deliver contradictory recommendations: books, papers, methodologies, assessment tools, search firms, coaching techniques, training and development programs, software tools (just the global talent management software industry is estimated to be worth ~10 billion USD by 2028 according to Expert Market Research), etc., that offer unique and "proven" methods to crack the code on talent. In the talent industry, everybody wants to sell you their secret sauce for discovering and managing talent. Vendors will play the "fear of missing out" card on you every time they have a chance, and you will likely end up giving in and buying "the flavor of the month," only to find out later that it is not worth it. I don't know how many times I have been approached by vendors telling me, "Your competitor X already has this tool," or "Between you and me, your company is the only one who is not investing in this--you are late to the game."

Those in charge of talent in organizations have to come to grips with a hard reality: there is no one-size-fits-all solution for your talent needs. You must do your homework, find out what tools can work for you, and discard the rest. And when attempting to secure top talent for your company, be prepared to embrace discomfort and ambiguity as a way of life, you will have to search long and hard before you hit the jackpot. Jack Welch used to say, "Hiring the right people is brutally hard." I cannot agree more. But, since talent identification and development are so critical for the success of a company, you can't simply leave it to chance and go with the first shiny object: "No company can grow revenues consistently faster than its ability to get enough of the right people to implement that growth and still become a great company,"[3] says Jim Collins.

When thinking about talent spotting, we must continuously ask ourselves what am I not doing? What gaps must I close in my talent practices to ensure that the right people are in place to jumpstart growth in the organization? These are complex issues; they would require a book of their own to explore them in detail. In this book, I will briefly dwell on the surface, review a few of the current hot topics in talent, and share my thoughts on the elements that will increase performance and unlock organizational potential.

Should you bet on
the horse or the jockey?

Despite the fact that the case for talent in organizations is very well supported, there are times when companies' analysts or investors put it on the backdrop as an afterthought. I find it fascinating how the weight of talent changes depending on the company's stage. When evaluating startups, investors consider the talent team at the helm and the available talent pipeline as critical factors when deciding if they want to invest in the company. Marc Randolph, Netflix co-founder, shares how startups handle talent: "You hire a bunch of brilliant people to be a jack-of-all-trades. Everyone does a little bit of everything. You're hiring a team, not a set of positions."[4] The consensus in the investment community is that the team behind a startup is a critical factor in their investment decisions, irrespective of titles and specific roles, so they get to know their profiles and, in the end, bet on the startup's collective talent. However, when the company settles and achieves a more stable position, other indicators take precedence when assessing the business, and the team's relevance often diminishes. All of a sudden, the company is a separate entity and is assessed using purely financial metrics. This means that the "show me the money" crowd, including analysts and financial market players, typically evaluate companies' performance using indicators such as ROI (return on investment), liquidity, profitability, contribution margin, EBITDA margin, debt-to-equity ratio, earnings per share, leverage, etc. and rarely address talent when evaluating quarterly or yearly results. This perspective separates the company's performance from those responsible for making decisions and implementing ideas.

Perhaps the only instance when financial institutions ponder talent directly is when a company goes public and launches an Initial Public Offering (IPO): "Investors know this—it's why they cite the quality of the top management team as the single most important nonfinancial factor in evaluating a new IPO,"[5] But other than that, the finance community customarily weighs the performance of the company using a handful of financial indicators, ROI (return on investment) being the mother of all indicators.

The markets demand predictable results and will not give you a pass on a lousy quarter just because a talented team is leading the company. The enterprise has to deliver, and everything is fine as long as it does. The "star quality" of the commanding team is merely a means to an end; the markets discount future cash flows and determine the company value based on the expectation of profitable growth. In the real world, analysts are agnostic on the CEO, the academic pedigree of the Executive Committee, and any accomplishments either has had in the past. The talent factor in a company is baked into the profit and loss statement, cash flow statement, and balance sheet. These reports are the ones that tell the story. Given these realities, it should not be surprising that the value of your "most valuable asset," your people, is nowhere to be found in any line of the balance sheet. It is just a little food for thought.

This is the context surrounding the question: "Should you bet on the horse or the jockey?" Let me explain what it refers to. Imagine If the horse is a company and its industry, and a jockey is the management team that guides the company. The dilemma to reflect upon is "What would you rather have: a strong, fast, powerful horse (a solid company in a vibrant industry) with an average jockey (ordinary leadership team at the helm) or a very talented leadership team (the jockey) trying to ride a mediocre horse (company + industry) to compete and win in a challenging race?" As an investor, I believe this dilemma poses a legitimate question. Without giving it too much consideration, it looks like having a solid horse will always beat having a good jockey because, in the end, the force of the horse will carry on the race despite the jockey's riding proficiency. The message from investors seems to be: put your money in solid horses and forget about jockeys; Horses will get you through the finish line.

If an investor thinks this way when assessing companies, what is the value of having the best talent running companies? Does this mean that talent is secondary? I acknowledge that this dilemma requires more analysis since it is a complex problem. Of course, everybody would love to have a strong company in a dynamic industry—who wouldn't?—but not at the expense of lacking as many good jockeys as we possibly can because, if the past has taught us something, is that conditions will change; all companies must be renewed at some point in time because the competitive landscape, regulatory conditions, and technology, to name a few factors, will be different in a few years and demand new approaches. Who will guide the horse into uncharted territories? Jockeys.

It's worth noting that investors are not fond of jockeys because their investment decisions tend to be focused on short-term goals and rely heavily on quarterly and yearly results. That's why they prefer a strong and predictable horse. On the other hand, the talent approach emphasizes following a process and takes time to deliver results. Even if you do everything right when managing talent, success is not guaranteed, and the risk of losing talent due to poaching is always a possibility.

What is the upshot of jockeys? Ensuring the right talent in key positions at your company is vital, even when the company seems to be doing great, and the future looks promising. "The right people choices are a key driver of organizational performance and are possibly the most important single factor for top performance."[6] writes Claudio Férnandez Araoz. And in the case of the big boss, having a great CEO will bring significantly more value than the one carried by an average CEO. According to Carolyn Dewar, Scott Keller, and Vikram Malhotra, senior partners of McKinsey & Company and authors of "CEO Excellence," a great CEO creates almost three times more total shareholder return than the rest: "CEOs who rank in the top 20 percent of financial performance generate, on average, 2.8 times more total return to shareholders (TRS) during each year of their tenure than do average performers."[7]

There is also a sin of omission, where lacking good jockeys explains the opposite of value creation: underperformance and failure. The business literature provides numerous examples of once unbeatable companies going bankrupt (Kodak, Blockbuster,

Circuit City, Pier 1, Compaq, etc.); their demise is often attributed to bad management decisions. In other words, the opportunity cost of not having the right talent is high, and there are circumstances where damage can be irreversible.

So, what do we do about the question? Should we focus on the horse or the jockey when betting on a company's success? Perhaps the best way to answer this question is the following: provided we have a reasonably good horse that can carry on the race, we should bet on the jockey. It is best to bet on the people leading the company, the "jockey," and adopt a medium to long-term view when possible. When companies face challenging situations, good leaders can turn them around or find a way out by undertaking new opportunities. In contrast, poor leaders may make bad decisions that lead to failure, even if they ride powerful horses. "Horses" are more challenged than ever in this time, when conditions change so much. However, and this is crucial, we must be capable of identifying who the right leaders are to bet on; otherwise, we risk making poor decisions and suffering the consequences.

The best of the best versus the run-of-the-mill

The talent dimension begs the question, how much better are talented individuals relative to the average? Do they really make a big difference? The answer is yes, they do. Having a larger ratio of highly talented versus average individuals throughout your organization (a concept referred to as talent density) will help you advance in ways you won't be able to imagine, and having mediocre talent will hold you back in innumerable ways. As Claudio Fernández Araoz put it, "We live in a world where the difference between the best and the rest is huge and growing fast...If you hire average Joes —that is, the type of candidate you see most often—you cannot be successful in today's business environment."[8]

Moreover, having a high talent density in the key positions of the company, meaning those positions that drive your competitive advantages or that ensure your staying power as a company, will help you get an edge to differentiate in a crowded and hyper-competitive business environment. To succeed today, you cannot afford to be behind or on par with your competitors. You have to differentiate and win with relevant attributes to your customers, and talent density is what allows you to develop your advantages. One reason why the top talent stands out is their productivity. The highest performers in a role are 800 percent more productive than average performers in the same role," according to The State of Organizations 2023, McKinsey.[9] With his characteristic ability to distill insights, Steve Jobs explained the talent differentiating factor in the following terms: "The difference between the worst taxi driver and the best taxicab driver getting you across Manhattan might be two to one...The difference between... a good software person and a great software person is 50 to one... it really pays to go after the best people in the world."[10] Companies relying on knowledge workers should recognize that the gap between exceptional talent and average individuals is much broader in higher-order abilities than in repetitive tasks: "The gap between the best and the rest depends on the nature of the job. In transactional and

repetitive tasks, a multiple of between three to five is common...
In tasks requiring more creative thinking and specialized skills,
the gap may be orders of magnitude larger."[11]

Given that talent is a scarce resource, it's crucial to focus on
improving talent density within our companies. This requires
effective management. To achieve talent density, we must shift our
perspective from absolute terms to a relative positioning approach.
This involves comparing our talent resources to a moving baseline.
Moreover, it's essential to apply analytical methods to managing
talent, as it promotes data-driven decision-making.

According to McKinsey research, a mere 5% of employees contribute to 95% of an organization's value.[12] This finding suggests
that only a small group of highly talented individuals are responsible
for driving an organization's success. In my experience, this group
can make up to 10% of an organization's workforce and rarely
exceeds that level, indicating that the talent pool is relatively
small. This select group of highly talented individuals serves as the
"catalysts" for value creation. The most skilled employees stand out
significantly from the rest of the workforce. While the remaining
employees may be competent, they cannot be considered highly
talented compared to the top performers.

To improve the quality of talent in an organization, it's essential
to recognize that talent distribution is a constantly changing system
that requires ongoing monitoring. The talent curve has an average,
which is the highest point on the curve and represents the overall
talent level in the organization. This average changes when new
talent is brought in, or individuals leave the organization. This
means that the average talent score depends on the talent levels of

those entering or leaving the organization and the development of current workers. To raise the overall talent level, it's vital to ensure that new employees entering the organization have higher talent scores than the current average or that those leaving have lower talent scores than the average. However, we need to be as objective as possible and disciplined in our approach to avoid creating any biases. As Colin Bryar and Bill Carr, authors of the book *Working Backwards: Insights, Stories, and Secrets from Inside Amazon*, say, "It takes no time to spot the superstars and to weed out the duds, but the majority of the candidates, alas, falls somewhere in between, and that is when biases tend to kick in."[13]

We must also go beyond our customary understanding of intelligence as the quintessential indicator of outstanding talent, considering emotional intelligence, creativity, social skills, adaptability, resilience, and other non-cognitive abilities that are fundamental to organizational performance. It implies a broader perspective on what constitutes excellence and recognizes the importance of diverse skills and qualities beyond intellectual capacity. Hitendra Wadhwa, a professor at Columbia Business School and the founder of the Mentora Institute, emphasizes that we have to be careful overstating intelligence as the most critical talent attribute: "By enthroning intelligence as the capstone quality of success, we have been worshiping a false god—or at least an incomplete god. We have designed our educational institutions, awards, assessments, and hiring practices around the premise that the more intelligent you are, the more value you bring to the world and the more successful you will be."[14]

Once you have identified the attributes of talent within your organization, looking beyond just intelligence - managing talent involves creating a system that brings in highly talented individuals while letting go of those with lower talents to increase the overall talent density ratio. When you bring in more talented individuals than what currently exists in your talent pool, an interesting phenomenon occurs: your overall talent profile will reorganize itself. The new, highly gifted people will occupy the upper tail of the curve, pushing down the existing talent base and potentially causing some individuals to exit the talent zone because they are now placed in a territory closer to the average. This shift happens because the updated talent distribution now includes more talented individuals than them. In simple terms, the once top-performing "A" players may become "B" players in the new bell curve of your organization due to the addition of better talent. Even if the percentage of talented individuals in the organization remains the same, the overall talent distribution improves by including new and better talent profiles.

The key benefit of adopting a statistical, dynamic approach to talent management is that consistently bringing better talent into an organization has a compounded effect, which leads to an increase in the talent density ratio. However, the real payoff comes from the company's improved overall talent distribution, which allows you to be better at problem-solving, undertaking opportunities, and, arguably, making sound decisions throughout the organization. By continually adding better talent to the existing base, the company can eventually achieve a situation where the organization's current "B" players are comparable to other organizations' "A" players, enhancing your capacity to compete and win in the market.

We can look at how this phenomenon works with our favorite sports teams. If an already good squad incorporates top players into its lineup and works as a team, the talent of the whole team improves, increasing the probability of winning. Managing talent density in an organization is a never-ending process crucial for its transformation. It involves continuous monitoring, assessment, and adaptation to the changing needs and dynamics of the organization. As businesses evolve and face new challenges, the composition and distribution of talent must also evolve to support the organization's goals and objectives.

Recruiting

This section provides a good transition from the previous one, as having a good recruiting process is the means to achieve the goal of having the best possible talent density in the organization. It is the foundation for outstanding company performance. Jim Collins wrote in "Good to Great" that "Who" questions come before "what" questions, before vision, strategy, tactics, organizational structure, and technology.[15] Yet, in most companies, recruiting is seen as a table-stakes activity, meaning that having a good enough performance, at par with everybody else, is generally considered adequate. This finding contradicts the self-evaluation that most companies make about their talent planning activities. The general agreement is that their talent pipeline needs to be stronger to fulfill the business requirements. According to Michael Mankins and Eric Garton, "CEOs with whom we work rarely feel that their talent pipeline is sufficiently robust to consistently meet their companies' future needs."[16] The relevant issue is that we must stop viewing recruiting as a table-stakes function in Human Resources. Instead, we should design and build this capability as a competitive advantage to help us strengthen our talent base to generate value and win in the market. Many administrative and back-office functions in Human Resources must work adequately to "keep the lights on" and operate, recruiting is not one of those. It should be considered a make-it-or-break-it situation for the company's survival.

Two examples come to mind when considering recruiting as a pillar for winning in the market. The first one is from Amazon, known for its expertise in recruiting: "Setting the bar high in our approach to hiring has been, and will continue to be, the single most important element of Amazon.com's success,"[17] founder and former CEO Jeff Bezos said in his 1998 letter to shareholders. Amazon's hiring program, called "Amazon Bar Raiser," is based on the following call to action: "Every new hire should "raise the bar," that is, be better in one important way (or more) than the other members of the team they join"[18] as Colin Bryar and Bill Carr, wrote in their book "Working Backwards." The main principle is quite simple, but the repercussions of the relentless practice of this program compound talent to a different level.

The second example is from Ben Horowitz, the co-founder with Marc Andreessen of the venture capital firm Andreessen Horowitz, which holds about $28 billion in assets. Ben Horowitz states the importance of recruiting practices in technology companies in the following terms: "Every good technology company needs great people. The best companies invest time, money, and sweat equity into becoming world-class recruiting machines."[19] Clearly, Ben

Horowitz's perspective underscores the contribution of recruiting in the creation of lasting value for companies in the technology sector, which can be extended to other sectors as well.

As much as I would like to delve into the specifics of how to achieve a best-in-class recruiting practice, it escapes the intent of this book. Suffice it to say that I highly encourage you to pay attention to the way you are conducting this practice today in your organization so you can take the necessary steps to improve it because chances are it may be running on automatic pilot: "When you consider the potential positive and negative impacts of an important hire, not to mention the precious time dedicated to it, it is shocking how little rigor and analysis most companies put into their hiring process."[20]

Having said this, I have four words of counsel for you regarding your recruitment approach:

Be thorough and close loops: Regardless of the methods you use for posting job openings, conducting background checks, assessing candidates, and interviewing them, it is crucial to have a consistent and thorough recruitment process. This process should be executed with discipline and rigor every time; it is the only way to develop the recruiting muscle and improve on it as we do business. One of the most critical aspects of the recruitment process is to follow up with the applicant promptly and effectively. Their experience with your company can significantly impact your employer's brand. Even if the candidate is not selected, their feedback about your recruitment process can influence others interested in working for your organization.

Hunt for biases: Being biased is part of our human condition, and awareness of its influence can help us mitigate its adverse effects. When hiring, I have always favored structured behavioral interviews (asking questions about the candidate's behavior in specific situations of their experience). Typically, conversations quickly diverge into the anecdotal, and having a systematic approach to interviews helps increase the probability of an effective outcome. In addition to having a reasonable number of different interviewers', it is also beneficial to separate topics and have interviewers explore a single trait each, such as leadership, domain knowledge, conflict management, etc., and in the end, consolidate reports so you can gain more insight on the person. I also find it helpful to practice "metacognition" and take notes of my reactions during the interview to isolate emotions from facts.

Quality over speed: "Time to fill" is a KPI frequently used to evaluate efficiency in hiring practices. It measures the time it takes to fill a vacancy since it originates and assesses the performance of the Human Resources Department. While it is important to reduce the hiring process duration to remain agile and competitive, maintaining the quality of the hiring process is equally significant. As a Human Resources professional, I always balance hiring quality with speed and try to meet or exceed internal customers' expectations. However, for key positions, I suggest evaluating the process on a case-by-case basis and maintaining open communication with stakeholders to ensure the process meets the necessary quality in a reasonable time frame. Rushing through the hiring process or taking shortcuts in positions that bring much value to the organization can lead to harmful consequences. Investing the appropriate time to find suitable candidates for critical positions and make informed hiring decisions avoids costly mistakes and builds a strong team.

Beware of sunk costs: Even if we invest a lot of time and effort in building an excellent recruitment process, it's not foolproof and sometimes fails. In the Human Resources industry, conventional wisdom states that new hires have failure rates of around 45% in the first 18 months. In my experience, the rate is closer to 30%, but depending on the position, it could be higher. However, the fact remains that we will lose a significant portion of talent regardless of our best efforts. Sometimes, the decision to let someone go is internally induced and may not be easy to accept due to the effort invested in the hiring process. When this happens, it's crucial not to fall into the sunk-cost mentality, where we continue to pursue a course of action due to a time and money investment, even if it doesn't make sense to maintain the person anymore. We might delay a firing decision because we have invested so much in bringing the person in that we "drag our feet," give fifth and sixth chances, and postpone the inevitable, but this is a mistake. False positives highlight flaws in our selection process, and it can be painful and shameful to admit that we failed. While giving feedback and supporting people's development is essential, it's also crucial to recognize that postponing a letting-go decision harms the organization and the person involved when the situation crosses the point of no return. Accepting the loss, making the tough call, and moving on is a better course of action.

Talent Portability

We customarily hold beliefs about talent being an ingrained quality of a person, an attribute that will be demonstrated in everything a person does and everywhere a person goes, and that cannot be taken away. However, there is evidence on the contrary; you probably have seen how talented individuals who have consistently delivered excellent results are moved to other areas or organizations and hit a dead end. The once outstanding employee is assigned to a different job or location with high hopes of replicating previous successes, fails, and falls from grace. I have witnessed it many times. How can this be possible? When this happens, a frequent response from talent management executives is that things occasionally don't work out as expected, even when the move is supported with first-hand knowledge of the person, evidence of good results, and thorough assessments. There is always a margin for error; it's just how it is, or so the thinking goes. This may be the case, but there may be more to it. We need to understand better the barriers and drivers of human performance in organizations.

Truth be told, we do not know enough about human behavior, and it is not easy to anticipate how humans will perform under different conditions: "We don't really know very much about what drives outstanding individual performance. Little clear-cut evidence supports or refutes prevailing beliefs about why some people excel". Boris Groysberg, professor of business administration in the Organizational Behavior unit at the Harvard Business School, wrote in his book "Chasing Stars."[21] We tend to focus on the person and assess performance and potential. Still, It is not intuitive to gauge the person as part of a system, which implies looking at individuals in combination with their surrounding context (the supporting network) and how the two conform to a binomial that explains performance. We are inclined to see talented individuals as if they were islands, just gifted all-terrain employees who will run with the ball no matter what. We venture to predict how employees will do in their next assignment based on prior performance, and we frequently oversee other factors that end up being critical to a positive outcome. The underlying belief is that talented people are "plug and play," but are they? This is not a new idea; more than a hundred years ago, in 1914, José Ortega y Gasset, Spanish philosopher, and essayist, wrote in "Meditations on Quixote": "I am me and my circumstances,"[22] which points out to the singularity of the combination person-environment. Consequently, when evaluating talent portability, it is very important to keep a systemic view and consider the work setting as part of the potential performance. The reality is that "talent is much less portable than what we think because performance isn't just one "P"; it stems from five —processes, platforms, products, people, and politics—and most of those you can't take with you," as Claudio Fernández Araoz writes in *"It's Not the How or the What But the Who."*[23]

When we address the context where the employee will perform as part of our talent mobility decisions, we add another layer of analysis into what aids or restricts performance. There is no way to guarantee a successful outcome every time, but adding the context as a data point will help us increase the probability of a better placing: "Exceptional performance is far less portable than is widely believed... exceptional performance appears to have been more firm-specific—more dependent on the firm's resources and capabilities—than is generally appreciated,"[24] says Boris Groysberg. By recognizing the importance of context in talent mobility decisions, organizations can improve their ability to place employees in roles and locations where they are likely to thrive, thereby maximizing their potential and contributing to overall organizational success.

Teams

When thinking about talent, we naturally focus on recruiting the best individuals. This is a logical and expected first step. However, when managing an organization, we must go beyond the person and consider how group collaboration boosts compounded talent. The team, not the individual, is the primary driver of results, and we must manage organizations based on this premise. In our business environment, teams are the basic unit of performance. Their dynamics are essential to sustain achievements over time: "It became obvious to me that almost everything great in the company happened in teams... start treating teams, not individuals, as the fundamental building block of the organization," as Adam Grant wrote in the preface of "Trillion Dollar Coach: The Leadership Playbook of Silicon Valley's Bill Campbell."[25]

This thinking is not intuitive. We are inclined to leverage the talent and skills of certain people to knock the ball out of the park, but in today's world, very rarely we will see heroic individuals doing all the heavy lifting to steer a company. "One of the most persistent and damaging myths in business today is the myth of the lone genius...very rarely do ideas spring from our brains perfectly formed...great ideas come from networks, not individuals."[26] Long gone are the days when a single person was at the epicenter of outstanding accomplishments or big transformations.

To further illustrate this point, I will, once again, use a sports analogy to provide color to our understanding of teams and team guidance, and I cannot think of a better example than Bill Walsh to show how one of the greatest coaches in history led teams to win championships. Bill Walsh was the head coach of the San Francisco 49ers. He won five Super Bowl championships in 14 years and is regarded as an innovator who changed how football is played. He described himself and his job in the following terms: "The ability to help people around me self-actualize their goals underlines the single aspect of my abilities and label that I value the most—teacher."[27] He saw himself as a helper of players and teams to become the best version of themselves, and to achieve this goal, he would share ideas and challenge everybody in his orbit all the time: "I would talk about different subjects with different players, with a squad, with the entire team, with position coaches, staff members, and others. I would discuss a topic from every angle, every approach....,"[28] he wrote in "The Score Takes Care of Itself: My Philosophy of Leadership." "Leaders sometimes wonder why they or their organizations fail to achieve success and never seem to reach their potential. It's often because they don't understand or can't instill the concept of what a team is all about at its best: connection and extension. This is a fundamental ingredient of ongoing organizational achievement."[29] There is a lot to unpack from this quote; Bill Walsh's management approach in football was transformational and generated outstanding accomplishments. He had a way of doing things that he described as the "standard of performance" that comprised his philosophy and leadership style, which is as current as ever and worth studying and which explains his success. But I would like to call your attention to the words "connection and extension" and go deeper into them because, in my opinion, they are fundamental to unlocking potential in teams.

How do you help teams connect (strengthen bonding) and extend (empower their reach)? To accomplish connection and extension, there must be a high level of trust from all team members, and for trust to happen, team participants must feel included, heard, encouraged to speak up, and free to defy the status quo. The now-famous "Project Aristotle" at Google, which occurred in 2012, illustrates how trust looks in teams in real life. The story goes that after analyzing all possible configurations in teams to find out the best design, researchers at Google concluded that the "who" part of the team did not seem to matter. What was more important was that everyone in the group had a chance to talk. If only a tiny part of the group talked, they found that collective intelligence declined. But if everyone felt safe and participated in expressing opinions, they saw that the collective intelligence of the group and its corresponding performance soared. Professor Amy Edmonson describes this phenomenon as "psychological safety." For a team to be connected and extended (everybody communicating and engaged as one), all members must actively participate in expressing opinions, especially dissenting views. The leader's guidance is essential, but what increases the team's performance is that everybody feels safe speaking up.

Following up on this idea, I would like to emphasize how talented teams can help in exploring and developing new solutions to pressing problems, and Pixar is a great resource to tap into; let's hear what Ed Catmull, co-founder of Pixar, has to say about it: "Getting the team right is the necessary precursor to getting the ideas right. It is easy to say you want talented people, and you do, but the way those people interact with each other is the real key... Getting the right people and the right chemistry is more important than getting the right idea."[30] Consider what Ed Catmull is saying and its implications for Regrowth in an organization: teams are more important than ideas, and having the right people and the right chemistry overrides everything else; if you have a talented and engaged team, good ideas will be forged. And Catmull offers another take to illustrate this point further: "If you give a good idea to a mediocre team, they will screw it up. If you give a mediocre idea to a brilliant team, they will either fix it or throw it away and come up with something better."[31]

Psychological safety is an essential ingredient for building a healthy team. The importance of preserving the team's health and the right chemistry among participants brings about a dilemma often faced by leaders: What to do with highly talented but toxic individuals who are indispensable to the company for their functional contributions but are harmful to the team's wellbeing. We all have experienced people who possess skills nobody else has in the company and are virtually irreplaceable but extremely difficult to work with. I love the take-no-prisoners approach offered by Reed Hastings, the co-founder of Netflix, who says, "You have to get rid of the jerks... it doesn't matter how brilliant your jerk is...The cost of jerkiness to effective teamwork is high. Jerks are likely to rip your organization apart from the inside."[32] The dilemma of the talented, toxic individual has only one possible outcome: sooner or later, you have to let go of this individual. Do not postpone the decision; it is best to do it as quickly as possible because the damage may be difficult to fix when the toxic employee finally leaves.

Teams play a crucial role in driving value for a company. They also serve as a representation of the company's environment for its employees. The team to which an employee belongs and the nearby teams with which they interact set the tone for how the company is perceived by its employees. When you are focused on your area of responsibility and solving problems in your day-to-day operation, it is challenging to sense the overall character of an organization; you simply can't cover more terrain than the one in front of you. Frontline employees often have a limited view of the company as a whole, and their perception will depend on their specific location within the organization. This condition reminds me of a well-known quote attributed to the late Margaret Thatcher, former Prime Minister of the United Kingdom: "There's no such thing as society. There are individual men and women, and there are families,". In the spirit of Thatcher's quote about society, we can assert that companies are entities that their people do not experience as a whole. People evaluate their companies using the reference of the team they belong to and the people they interact with—their "family," so to speak. They engage with the company through the team. A healthy team dynamic is vital for retaining and developing talent and positioning what the organization is all about with its constituents. Therefore, it is essential to understand the inner workings of the teams that comprise our company to ensure people's contributions and the overall company's success.

Talent Landscape

When an organization constantly incorporates high-caliber talent, it sets in motion a cumulative effect on the expected standard of performance for all employees, and the talent pool in the company puts pressure on the system to stay "at par" with the expected level. It is very organic how these individuals' collective abilities propel the entire organization toward excellence. "Hiring and keeping star players is about much more than just quality of work. It's a culture thing. When you retain only star players, you create a culture of competitive excellence,"[33] says Netflix's co-founder Marc Randolph.

When you work at a company and look at the roster of talented individuals holding positions, you can sense a consistent level of quality among them. This perceived quality sets a standard and creates a distinctive talent landscape that serves as a reference for your group. The higher the perceived standard, the more you feel you belong to an exceptional team. There is a French term that captures this feeling of pride, "esprit de corps," which alludes to the shared devotion of being part of something exceptional. As Hastings put it, "We found that being surrounded by the best catapulted already good work to a whole new level."[34]

Job Rotation and Talent Development

Your organization's talent base is a work in progress rather than a finished product. Once an employee meets the talent threshold set by the organization, it is essential to encourage and help their development. Talent is not a fixed characteristic but a dynamic feature requiring continuous improvement. Viewing talent as a fixed feature corresponds to adopting a machine-like view of the organization. Instead, the talent development journey should align with the ever-evolving customer needs and be renewed to remain relevant and competitive.

Companies typically offer training and development programs to their employees to enhance their skills in various areas such as manufacturing, negotiation, sales, leadership, decision-making, quality, digital, and more. According to The Business Research Company's report in January 2023, the global corporate training market size reached $380 billion by 2023. It can be challenging to determine the best learning programs for your company, and it's not my intention to recommend any specific training and development program. Instead, I'd like to emphasize the importance of having a coherent talent development plan as part of your talent strategy. Job rotation, which is widely used by companies today, is an effective practice to develop individuals and is often referred to as the Swiss army knife of managerial development. Companies emphasize job rotation and consider it the preferred tool to accelerate growth and development.

Job rotation is a practice that involves moving employees between different roles, functions, or locations within an organization. The conventional idea behind it is that this exposure will provide them with diverse experiences that will enrich their knowledge, round out their profile, and ultimately make them better at their work. In general, job rotations are productive for up-and-coming talent, especially in helping to improve their skill set and developing their business reach. It is essential to highlight that while highly specialized technical positions are exempt from this practice, most generalist jobs can benefit from job rotation.

My take on job rotation is that we must take it with a grain of salt (a large grain, indeed). This is not only for the reasons I exposed in the previous "Talent Portability" section but also because we should approach job rotation cautiously and not use it as a one-size-fits-all solution. Overall, job rotations can accelerate growth in learning new functional skills and foster adaptability, but we must not overestimate their impact. We should be wary of expecting significant returns when enhancing managerial skills with job rotations, as they can plateau over time.

Job rotation assumes that learning is directly proportional to the experience obtained with the accrual of assignments. The more the experience gained from different positions, the more the learning will be, or so the theory goes. However, the question remains: Will more experience always beget learning? As John Dewy, a prominent educational philosophy and pragmatism figure, has pointed out, learning is not a by-product of experience; reflection is. "We do not learn from experience... we learn from reflecting on experience," he said. However, job rotation will not produce the expected results if a dedicated, diligent reflection does not accompany the participant's experience, and this can only be achieved by incorporating short cycles of action and reflection as part of the process. Cycles of action and reflection are necessary to distill applicable insights, especially when there is limited knowledge to capitalize upon or when we are venturing into entirely new experiences. Reflection is critical to creating an array of practical solutions that can be used to deal with a wide range of day-to-day situations, and it is also helpful to develop a frame of reference that can guide our actions in the future.

Improving management proficiency also requires working on the person's ability to lead and leverage soft skills. It goes beyond functional capabilities and demands reflection and introspection that must be deliberately put into practice. It is essential to experiment and learn from mistakes. This type of learning comes from interaction with peers, observation of other leaders, seminars, executive education, mentoring, coaching, etc., to increase the quality of our reflection and action. Being authentic and vulnerable and feeling good in our own skin is not something that can be achieved with a few job assignments; it is a process that requires humility and personal commitment over time.

When using job rotation for talent development, it's important to consider that it has diminishing returns, especially in developing managerial or leadership skills. For instance, if someone moves from a finance treasury department manager to a logistics inventory manager, they will need to learn new skills such as demand planning, project management, and data analysis. This will enhance their overall understanding of the business. Now, suppose this person moves again from logistics inventory manager to operations product design manager. In that case, the individual will learn new skills such as supply chain management and product development. These job rotations help broaden the person's knowledge as new functional skills and disciplines are added, providing a broader view of how the company works.

However, job rotations do not necessarily increase managerial skills. Even if managerial skills could improve slightly with the rotations, they will eventually plateau. The reason is that job rotations are generally "lateral moves." With job rotations, individuals do not necessarily lead more people, add complexity to their tasks, or ascend in the hierarchy, which would be the case with a promotion, not a rotation. Job rotations help widen the knowledge of different areas of the organization. Still, job rotations are not the springboard that is commonly assumed when it comes to enhancing an individual's capacity to lead. To strengthen managerial skills, we must complement them with a shift in perspective, leveraging soft skills to improve performance.

The Flipside of Talent Management

So far, I have explored several topics related to talent management. I have emphasized the importance of improving our approach to talent by highlighting the need to use a structured method, rigor, and technology to enhance the probability of a positive outcome. I have always tried to leave out subjectivity in making people's decisions and focus on the specific talent attributes the position requires. I believe it is best to reduce noise and secure a good process.

However, I have learned that there is a critical flip side to this technical, hardcore approach; it entails addressing the overlooked, subjective attributes that we usually disregard when selecting or promoting talent. For instance, should being a decent, good-natured individual be considered a talent trait we must look for? Should kindness, thankfulness, and respect count?

I can attest that these criteria are usually considered secondary or not considered at all in most selection processes. Companies naturally favor the skills and other business-related traits required to compete and win in their industries. However, in the last decade, these character features have slowly gained recognition. I believe they will be considered fundamental in organizations in the near future as conscious capitalism spreads worldwide. I will give you three examples of renowned business leaders who have opened the door to these ideas.

Elon Musk is known as a shrewd, harsh, impulsive, and challenging person to work with. So it will probably surprise you to know that in a 2013 interview with Business Insider, Musk declared that he has put too much weight on talent and that it matters when somebody has a good heart: "I've made the mistake of thinking that it's sometimes just about the brain."

Another example comes from Sam Altman, the CEO of OpenAI, the American artificial intelligence research organization founded in December 2015. Altam was fired and immediately reinstated as CEO in November 2023. He was let go for a supposed lack of transparency with his communications with the board and hired back when most OpenAI employees threatened to quit and Microsoft support. He famously said, "You want to hire for values first, aptitude second, and skills third; most executive recruiters reverse that order." In the highly technical field of artificial intelligence, it is refreshing to see that values are considered essential.

Steve Jobs, who is one of the most accomplished business people of our time and was well known for his fiery behavior and short-fused temper, was once asked about his learnings when he left Apple and started Next Computers; he answered that he learned to take a long view on people. Even when he knew somebody was screwing up, he did not jump to correct them, "We are building a team here, and we are going to do great work here, not for the next year but for the next decade." He asked himself what he needed to do so the person who was screwing up would learn. This attitude sends a message to the organization to nurture others even if some skills are not yet fully developed.

How will these character traits impact the new talent management approach for the future? I do not know, but I believe they will become more critical and emphasize the importance of human markers. I am not proposing to downplay the significance of job-specific skills; I believe they are very relevant. However, in a world where artificial intelligence takes care of more tasks, it's essential to note that there will be opportunities for these personal attributes to become more significant in organizations.

The Elements of Performance

Talent density is a value driver embedded in a more extensive system, which constitutes the platform for unlocking organizational potential, along with culture and mindset. In the remainder of this chapter, I will address the specific determinants of talent associated with performance and lay the foundation for making it operational when pursuing an organizational transformation.

My thinking on talent density was enlightened when I read a groundbreaking document by Harry L. Davis and Robin M. Hogarth titled "Rethinking Management Education: A View from Chicago" (The University of Chicago, Booth School of Business,1992). The authors attempted to rethink the MBA education curriculum, which they believed was inadequate to "develop managerial talent capable of thriving in the new environment," as Davis & Hogarth put it in the paper. With this objective in mind, they developed the "Elements of Performance" framework, which consists of three critical determinants of action in business settings that explain how individuals can achieve exceptional performance. These determinants are conceptual knowledge, domain knowledge, and action skills. In addition to these determinants, they identified "insight skills" as the process by which we distill the learnings resulting from the corresponding actions.

The Elements of Performance model for Talent Density is the following:

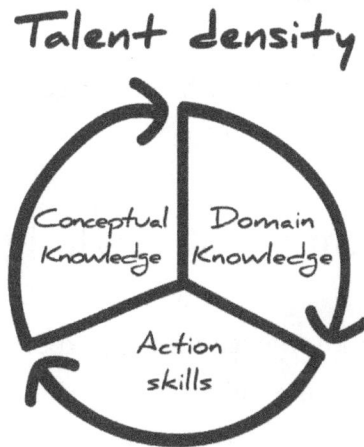

Adapted from Davis & Hogarth

Conceptual Knowledge

Conceptual knowledge refers to what is learned in schools and educational institutions. Almost all the content taught at schools or universities is included in this determinant. For college graduates, conceptual knowledge is the curricula related to manufacturing, accounting, finance, administration, economics, coding, marketing, Human Resources management, industrial safety, etc. "The value of conceptual knowledge is that it develops the ability to think broadly and rigorously in business settings,"[35] Davis & Hogarth explain. This determinant encompasses the concepts and ideas that will aid you in assessing and solving problems and undertaking opportunities at work. It also helps build the mental structure necessary to make sense of business-related activities. A significant portion of the training and development programs for employees sponsored or taught by companies is also included in this determinant, such as project management, inventory management, customer service, pricing, merchandising, sales, decision-making, critical thinking, time management, etc. People who excel in conceptual knowledge are commonly called "book smart."

Domain Knowledge

We acquire domain knowledge through experience in our field of action. "individuals acquire this knowledge by working at their jobs in particular firms and industries,"[36] wrote Davis & Hogarth. It is a by-product of "hands-on training and experience in particular job settings and is relevant to that domain,"[37] they also assert. When we work in a job position long enough, we will accumulate experience by virtue of continuous practice and experimentation that will lead to the acquisition of specific knowledge of our craft. This knowledge can be enriched by exchanging information with peers inside the company, customers, outside colleagues, experts, vendors, etc., which will help us sharpen our understanding of the job. For example, let's say you are a marketing manager in a consumer packaged goods company. With time, you will learn how your product is manufactured, warehoused, and distributed. You will also gather information from your customers that will allow you to know them deeply and understand their sensitivity to price, the products they buy simultaneously with yours, their seasonality, consumer trends, etc. You will also collect information directly from your store purchasers, such as what they value, how they place your product on the shelves, ideas for complementary lines, etc. Additionally, you may attend trade shows, talk with equipment manufacturers, visit packaging suppliers, experiment with digital communication, etc. You get the picture; it is knowledge acquired from years of experience at the job. The knowledge derived from the job experience is unique and challenging to obtain with means other than direct involvement: "Domain knowledge takes time to acquire and is not necessarily transferable to other areas,"[38] as Davis & Hogarth put it.

Another term that is used to describe this type of knowledge is "tacit knowledge," which "is the knowledge one may possess and apply successfully without being able to articulate it or even recognize its correct formulation,"[39] as Professor Emeritus of Philosophy and former Provost at Gettysburg College, Daniel R. DeNicola describes. As we accumulate domain knowledge, there will be much-codified information in our brain that we are unaware we have, which seems natural to us. "Out of the blue," we can retrieve it and apply it to our day-to-day tasks, which is instrumental in making good decisions and improving our performance.

Action Skills

Thanks to conceptual knowledge and domain knowledge, we can combine theory with experience; thus, our understanding of what to do to perform well is sound. We have the theory of how things work and the practical knowledge to support our performance in many circumstances. Yet, as valuable as they are, these two determinants are only necessary conditions for performance; they are not sufficient. We must still make what we intend to do happen; only effective action can get us there.

Throughout my professional career, I have often made the mistake of focusing too much on figuring out the problem to be solved without giving enough thought to implementing the solution. I used to believe that the most crucial aspect of problem-solving or seizing opportunities was determining what needed to be done. I thought that finding the best solution was 90% of the challenge and that presenting a logical and intelligent solution was enough to make everyone understand and buy into my proposal. I assumed people were rational individuals who would naturally support a well-reasoned plan. However, I learned the hard way that this was not the case. Although devising a plan is hard work, it is only half the battle. In addition to having a plan, you must also persuade others that your plan is sound and motivate them to work together toward its achievement. This is often more complicated than it seems.

Davis and Hogarth explain the tension between ideas and their implementation in the following terms: "Knowledge must be translated into action, and that requires action skills. These are the skills that enable individuals to set goals, sell others on the value of those goals, and work with and through others in their implementation. The value of action skills lies in the ability to achieve desired outcomes."[40] They make a powerful point: Knowing what needs to be done differs from making it happen. How often have people at your company had good ideas but hit a dead end because they did not get any traction with those who will carry them out? I have seen many consultants producing very well-crafted PowerPoint presentations, laying out everything that needs to be done in detail. However, they miss the "making it happen" part, and the results are disappointing. This goes beyond change management; it relates to inspiring action among colleagues. Today, I know that "making it happen" is so crucial for effective performance that it cannot be "something we will talk about later." It has to be "the key issue" to solve and deserves special attention.

Action skills are commonly referred to as "soft skills" (as opposed to the Conceptual and Domain Knowledge determinants that can be construed as "hard skills"), and they "require constant practice over many years in real-world situations,"[41] according to Davis & Hogarth. Sequencing action skills often follow a step-by-step process: setting a compelling goal, devising a plan to fulfill it, engaging the teams implementing it, and mobilizing all constituents to achieve buy-in. All of these phases require individuals with action skills to develop abilities in self-awareness, empathy, vulnerability, humbleness, negotiation, public speaking, storytelling, and teamwork, among others.

Designing for Talent Density

The determinants of talent density we have discussed can be used as a canvas for organizations to design their efforts to jumpstart talent development. By recognizing these different talent determinants, we can also create a talent planning agenda that involves evaluating key personnel's current levels of conceptual knowledge, domain knowledge, and action skills and identifying any gaps that need to be addressed. Moreover, these determinants can also help establish a benchmark for recruitment purposes.

The "elements of performance" model, comprised of the talent density determinants, encourages us to take a comprehensive approach to evaluating the various factors that influence our work results. As we carry out our job responsibilities, our conceptual knowledge, domain knowledge, and action skills seamlessly impact one another, enabling us to deal with everyday challenges. When all the factors are in sync and supporting each other, we achieve a virtuous cycle, increasing our performance level.

Let's consider how these factors play out in a real-world scenario. Let's say we must estimate the plant capacity to meet our client's expectations during the peak season. In this case, our knowledge of the subject matter will be vital in evaluating the technical variables that determine capacity. However, it's also essential to consider other factors affecting production, such as historic equipment yields, shrinkage, maintenance, and cleaning of the production lines. We must draw upon our experience and gather relevant information to do this.

Moreover, we must develop a plan of action and negotiate with our sales team, logistics, vendors, and clients to ensure a smooth process. All three factors - conceptual knowledge, domain knowledge, and action skills - must work together seamlessly to achieve the desired outcome as suggested by Davis & Hogarth.

When you look at the circle representing the three determinants in the model, you'll see a loop of arrows connecting conceptual knowledge, domain knowledge, and action skills. This shows that the model is an active and dynamic entity where each part affects and complements the others. The talent density dimension is the outcome of this dynamic system and, as we'll see later, influences a broader system, including the culture and mindset dimensions.

Regardless of your company's talent management strategy, this chapter underscores its crucial role in achieving business objectives. Along with organizational culture and mindset, Talent Density is one of the keys to unlocking the organization's potential.

CHAPTER 5

Culture

"Company culture doesn't exist apart from the company itself: no company has a culture; every company is a culture."
—Peter Thiel

"If you're really going to transform an enterprise, you've got to understand culture...It took me to age 55 to figure that out. Culture is everything."
—Lou Gerstner, former CEO of IBM

"Culture isn't something you can build up and then ignore. At Netflix, we are constantly debating our culture and expecting it will continue to evolve."
—Reed Hastings

I n the early days of my professional career, I was skeptical about how much organizational culture could influence business practices and behaviors. I read about it, but I thought culture's influence on business transformation was overrated. However, my thinking about culture significantly changed when I became the supermarket's channel manager in the northwest region of Mexico.

When I assumed the position, during my onboarding process, I had a long conversation with my predecessor to understand the challenges in the region. He mentioned that he had devoted significant effort to increasing our associates' engagement and commitment to their work, as many of our clients' stores had complained about our lack of involvement and poor performance. To tackle this issue, he prioritized fostering a customer-centric culture in our people's day-to-day activities. He worked with his supervisors and team leaders on specific programs and monitored improvement regularly.

While traveling across the region to meet with our clients and teams in the field, I witnessed two examples of the teams' progress in customer centricity that caught my attention. On one occasion, I visited a store and, as it was my custom, I headed toward the refrigerated section to look at our product's display to meet with the personnel working there and discuss their needs and how we could improve service to our clients. As I approached the area, I noticed one of our associates refilling the shelves, and something about her uniform caught my attention. She wore black pants, a white shirt with long sleeves, and a black vest, which was the standard uniform, but compared to the one we provided, it was evident that the fabric quality was better, the clothes' cut looked sharper, and the brand size was more prominent and a little bit brighter. Her uniform looked much nicer than the company's, and the brand's logo was more impactful. When I inquired about it, she told me she had her uniform custom-made by a tailor and decided she would no longer wear the standard company uniform:

Salesperson: The company's uniform is all right, but I needed to make a better impression on our customers. You know what they say: "You never get a second chance to make a first impression." So, I decided to wear a more professional-looking uniform, and I had it custom-made.

Me: Interesting. I understand your viewpoint. You think our uniforms don't help you make an impact, so you got yours made. If you don't mind my asking, did you pay for it yourself? Did the company reimburse you for the expense?

Salesperson: Yes, I paid for it myself, and I don't expect to be reimbursed by the company. I like wearing this uniform; it makes me feel more confident and professional. Besides, I think we should always strive to give our best to our customers, and wearing this uniform communicates that commitment.

I was caught off guard by what she said. My first reaction was against the idea; I was unhappy with her wearing a different version of our uniform because we had guidelines that all associates must comply with, and she violated the company's policy by not following the standards. On the other hand, I was impressed by her proactivity and appreciated her care about her image when dealing with our customers. She had gone out of her way to find a tailor, choose the fabric and the style, and pay for it herself! She intended to be at her best and care for her customers, ultimately benefiting the company. I found myself facing a dilemma: If I were to enforce the policy and ask her to stop wearing her tailor-made uniform, I could send a message to our people that I was limiting her initiatives and our customer-centric culture was not for real, and if I didn't, I could be opening a door for everybody to do whatever they want, and things could quickly get out of hand.

I left the store without saying anything about it. I decided to wait a couple of days before declaring my formal position so that I could have the opportunity to reflect more and come up with a sound judgment. While visiting another store during the trip, I had a similar experience with a salesperson at the deli counter that showed me that this was not an isolated event. This associate wore a standard white uniform with an apron and white tennis shoes. However, her tennis shoes were not plain white as our dress code dictated; they were embroidered with colorful sequins and glitter in the shape of the brand's logo of one of the products she was selling. I asked her why she had done that, and she replied that she was proud of our brand and wanted to add a colorful touch to her tennis shoes. She knew her customers would not see her shoes from the other side of the counter, but she felt lifted whenever she stared at the shining shoes, putting her in a better mood to take care of our customers.

Upon checking the sales records of the two associates, I found they delivered exceptional results, surpassing the average performance in the area. Moreover, they achieved high scores in almost all of their operational KPIs. I was thoroughly impressed by their efforts to go above and beyond their regular duties to provide excellent customer service. These associates were not following the dress code rules, but their actions spoke volumes about their dedication.

Some of my direct reports were concerned about the precedent these events could set with other team members who could start taking initiatives outside the established policies, and they prompted me to correct the situation. They wanted me to play by the book, even if it meant discouraging some of our people. However, it was clear to me that the benefits outweighed the costs, and I was concerned about the message such a decision could send.

So, I refrained from doing anything. I was now responsible for championing and spreading this customer-centric culture among all our associates and decided not to enforce the dress code guidelines in both instances. Given the circumstances of the cultural change we were promoting, my non-action was the best alternative to follow. Thanks to the customer-centric initiative, these two associates found new and creative ways to please our customers, even if it meant deviating from the corporate guidelines. This experience demonstrated that when the culture is adopted, people can incorporate and deliver the expected behaviors without needing specific company instructions. It may not play exactly the way we want, but it's the spirit of it that is worthwhile.

Sometimes, in business, doing nothing is a choice worth considering. So be it if I had to negotiate with corporate to make some rules more flexible, which I did as soon as I returned to headquarters. Our associates inspired me, and now, I had to support them.

The culture conundrum

Judging by what you can read on company websites, it would be fair to say that organizational culture is a well-rooted concept in the business world. In almost any company website, in the "about us" or "who we are" section, you can find plenty of statements upholding culture-related themes like purpose, mission and vision, values, guiding principles, aspirations, DEI (Diversity, Equity, and Inclusion) remarks, corporate social responsibility, etc, describing their fundamental pillars and their prescribed ways for interacting. Together with those statements, you may also find appealing pictures of happy, collaborative, productive employees, portraying their enthusiasm for belonging to those organizations, which makes you think that everyone working in these companies is a hundred percent on board with their principles, actively engaged, and the culture box is checked and going well. But appearances can be deceptive; we all know that.

I would like to ask you some thought-provoking questions. How much time do you dedicate to building your organizational culture compared to the time spent on finance, marketing, or operations? Is it less, more, or about the same? Do you consider culture a value driver for your company, or is it just another item on the Human Resources agenda that you are expected to handle? Are you a proponent of your organization's culture or simply an observer? These are not rhetorical questions; they intend to draw your attention to an often-overlooked driver that can make you succeed in the marketplace.

I suspect that you may not devote much time to developing your company's culture. If you are like most people, your day-to-day operations and budget constraints likely take up most of your attention (usually priority number one). As a result, other factors, such as culture, are placed on the back burner until the time is right, especially in times of crisis.

Building a solid culture should not be something we do when conditions allow it. Culture should be viewed as a powerful ally for implementing your business strategy; it is the vehicle to help your company navigate uncharted waters and spur organizational renewal. Satya Nadella, Microsoft's executive chairman and CEO, states, "At some point, the concept or idea that made you successful is going to run out of gas... The only thing that's going to enable you to keep building new capabilities... is culture."[1] A culture that adapts and builds the much-needed capacities to compete in the market must be the main focus of all CEOs or C-Suite teams. And this entails enabling your people to become the best they can be.

Organizational culture is crucial for companies, regardless of whether they are traditional or technological. In their book "Trillion Dollar Coach," Eric Schmidt, Jonathan Rosenberg, and Alan Eagle share the coaching philosophy and insights of Bill Campbell, a legendary executive coach who played a significant role in shaping the leadership styles and strategies of some of Silicon Valley's most successful companies. Campbell focused on people as the primary drivers of value in organizations: "People are the foundation of any company's success. The primary job of each manager is to help people be more effective in their job and grow and develop. We have great people who want to do well, are capable of doing great things, and come to work fired up to do them. Great people flourish in an environment that liberates and amplifies that energy."[2] Developing a system where people are supported and challenged will foster growth, innovation, and a strong sense of community, ultimately realizing individuals' potential and achieving collective goals.

Several successful organizations, such as Apple, Amazon, Google, Microsoft, Disney, and Netflix, have recognized the importance of culture and designed theirs as springboards to achieve superior performance. They are considered exemplary cases in this regard. However, despite the abundant evidence backing the benefits of organizational culture, many corporations still are not fully engaged with the idea, "executives often overlook a company's management culture when looking for ways to improve performance."[3] Why would that be?

I suggest two hypotheses about the barriers preventing the broader adoption of culture as a lever for value creation. First, we misjudge the magnitude of the required effort to build a culture. Second, establishing a link between culture and the financial metrics expressing economic value creation is difficult.

We underestimate the magnitude of the effort because we often fail to comprehend the relevance of the inherent challenges of bringing about a cultural transformation. Building a unique culture that enables top-notch performance is not a straightforward or predictable journey. It is the exact opposite. You will require a great deal of patience and perseverance to overcome the various obstacles that come your way, and it may take anywhere from three to five years or more to begin seeing results, with no guarantee of success. Along with defining what you want to achieve and how you will do it, which, as we will see, is a significant challenge in and of itself, you will need the complete commitment and active participation of the CEO and all leaders in the organization to implement it. They must become Chief Culture Officers and constantly preach the culture's message "ad nauseam."

CEOs who wish to transform their company's culture must lead by example and consistently display behaviors that align with the desired culture to show everyone that this is not another flavor of the month but a transformation that is here to stay. This personal involvement is a "must-have," not a "nice to have" if you want to succeed; otherwise, the attempt will inevitably fail. You will also need the commitment of all associates, who must be onboard and active; they will be required to take extra time and effort as they learn and exhibit the expected behaviors in addition to their regular responsibilities.

As you can tell, this is not a task for the "faint-hearted." Getting the buy-in and engagement of all stakeholders demands unrelenting dedication, hard work, and the investment of resources to design, implement, and monitor culture. The costs of the cultural journey are certain and immediate. The rewards are uncertain and take place in the future, and only a few companies are willing to endure the pain and sustain the effort long enough to obtain significant results.

The other hurdle that prevents culture's implementation has to do with assessing its financial impact. At its core, organizational culture is an endeavor that builds an intangible asset, and it isn't easy to establish its clear-cut, causal relationship with economic value creation. To explain this idea further, let us double-click into the definition of an intangible asset. From a purely financial perspective: "An intangible asset is a claim to future benefits that does not have a physical or financial embodiment...There are three major nexuses of intangibles, distinguished by their relation to the generator of assets: discovery, organizational practices and Human Resources."[4] These intangible investments are increasing in companies as we develop capabilities to differentiate from our competitors in the market: "The type of investment that has risen inexorably is intangible: investment in ideas, in knowledge, in aesthetic content, in software, in brands, in networks, in relationships."[5] However, the effect of this investment on people is still elusive.

Despite the many references in the business literature that associate people's intangible conditions with the creation of economic value in companies, like the ones that correlate diversity, employee engagement, or being a great workplace, among other factors, with distinctive value creation and positive stock price performance, there is still skepticism when it comes to financial benefits they generate. Rocio Lorenzo and Martin Reevs surveyed more than 1,700 companies across eight countries and wrote an HBR article to examine the relationship between managerial diversity, the presence of enabling conditions, and innovation. They found that "companies with above-average total diversity, measured as the average of six dimensions of diversity (migration, industry, career path, gender, education, age), had both 19% points higher innovation revenues and 9% points higher EBIT margins, on average."[6] Their findings are compelling, but even if there was no evidence of this sort, who can doubt that there is a positive correlation between diverse organizations or engaged employees and good company results? It is just common sense. However, it is overlooked since this association cannot be found in the financial statements when looking into the nitty-gritty of how a company creates value. There is no way to show the value of culture, or any intangible asset, in a balance sheet (unless the intangible asset was part of an acquired company and was accounted for in the purchase). The value of culture as an asset is baked into the numbers reported by the company and does not have a specific representation in the statement.

The Generally Accepted Accounting Principles (GAAP) state that the money invested in creating organizational practices and Human Resources must be classified as an expense. This means that it will be recorded in the profit and loss statement as an expense affecting the company's bottom line but not the balance sheet. The requirements set by the GAAP to capitalize on organizational practices or human resource expenses are challenging to meet. Therefore, they are rarely shown on the balance sheet as assets that enhance the company's value and are depreciated over time. Even when reported, isolating their impact and influence from other factors in creating economic value is often challenging and requires high subjectivity. As a result, investments in culture are usually viewed as costs, and it's tough to convince upper management to justify anything that detracts from the next quarter's bottom-line results.

According to Baruch Lev and Feng Gu, there are reasons to be optimistic despite the struggle of evaluating intangibles. In their book "The End of Accounting," they share how companies are gradually changing how they assess investment in intangible assets: "Corporate investment in intangible capital now surpasses investment in physical assets by a wide margin, and the gap keeps growing. The reason: During recent decades, intangible (intellectual) assets have increasingly bolstered corporate value and competitive edge, whereas tangible (physical) assets are essentially "commodities," equally available to all competitors, and therefore unable to create considerable value and confer competitive advantage... The increasing dominance of intangibles among corporate assets is widely recognized, with its consequences having become known as the "knowledge economy."[7]

The magnitude of the effort needed to build a culture and the difficulty of assessing its economic value creation are two barriers that reinforce each other and, in my opinion, deter the willingness to embark on this challenging journey. Once you know these barriers exist, I trust you will be better positioned to find ways to overcome them in your organization. It is not an easy task, but the good news is that if you can persevere and sort out these hurdles, you will be much better prepared to compete and win in the market.

One company that has overcome these barriers and stands out in leveraging culture as a driver for growth in a competitive industry is Southwest Airlines; its distinctive features of a fun and informal atmosphere, customer service focus, and community engagement, among others, together with their operational excellence, have contributed significantly to their enduring success. Claudio Fernández Áraoz, in his HBR article "Creating a Culture of Unconditional Love," summarizes the view of Herb Kelleher, co-founder and CEO of Southwest Airlines, on culture, as follows: "Just take a look at Southwest Airlines, the company which saw the greatest value expansion in the S&P 500 between 1971 and 2001. Herb Kelleher — its CEO for 35 years — once said: Given enough time and money, your competitors can duplicate almost everything you've got working for you. They can hire away some of your best people. They can reverse-engineer your processes. The only thing they can't duplicate is your culture."[8]

Culture Eats strategy for breakfast: The either/or fallacy

Ever since I have been involved in culture transformation activities and researched the topic, I have come across the quote "Culture Eats Strategy for Breakfast" in books, papers, presentations, and keynotes everywhere. It is a very popular quote and is attributed to Peter Drucker, the late management guru. However, according to the Drucker Institute at Claremont Graduate University, Peter Drucker never said that. They reviewed all his publications, speeches, and interviews, and this reference is nowhere to be found. The closest thing they could find with some resemblance to the spirit of the quote was: "Culture, no matter how defined, is singularly persistent."[9]

The phrase "Culture eats strategy for breakfast" is a catchy and memorable statement. It suggests that the success or failure of a company is more significantly influenced by its organizational culture than its strategies. This means that while strategies may change, a company's culture remains constant, providing the foundation for the company's performance and success. When I first read this quote, it made much sense to me. It emphasizes the importance of a human-centric approach in an organization, highlighting that how individuals interact is the core of the company's success. If a company gets the human environment right, everything else will fall into place, including the ability to adopt and implement the right strategy. I thought that this quote was like a golden nugget of wisdom. But, is it?

The more I reflected on this quote, the more I realized that the premise leads to an "either-or" fallacy, a false dilemma. It nudges you to choose one thing (culture) over another (strategy) when a much better position would be to say that culture and strategy complement each other. When a company sets them both at the table in harmony, it will eat the competition for breakfast. I agree with Ben Horowitz's take on the dilemma: "The truth is that culture and strategy do not compete. Neither eats the other. Indeed, for either to be effective, they must cohere... Pick the virtues that will help your company accomplish its mission."[10]

To better understand the relationship between culture and strategy, it is essential to delve into both. For that, let us bring to the fore what Roger L. Martin and A.G. Lafley present in their seminal book "Playing to Win" to shed light on how a company decides what strategy to pursue: "Strategy is an integrated set of choices that uniquely positions the firm in its industry so as to create sustainable advantage and superior value relative to the competition." At the core of strategy formulation is the decision of "Where to Play: "the set of choices that narrow the competitive field...in which markets, with which customers and consumers, in which channels" and How to Win: "How to win defines the choices for winning in that field. It is the recipe for success in the chosen segments, categories, channels, geographies, and so on."[11] In addition to the "Where to Play" and "How to Win," Martin and Lafley establish that strategy formulation requires defining a winning aspiration, the capabilities the company must have in place to support the strategic choices, and a management system to monitor performance.

As you can tell from these remarks by Martin and Lafley, the strategy's objective is to make choices that will integrate and produce an advantageous system for value creation in a particular market space. It determines the specific value your company must deliver to its customers to win against your competitors in the market. Culture supports the "means" to build the capabilities to provide the "end" of the value proposition to the customer. The strategy determines the "what" and the "how" the company will compete in the market, and culture lays out the scaffolding within the organization to be able to implement it. Culture, as valuable as it may be, is not a substitute for a bad set of strategic choices, and it cannot compensate customers for an inferior value proposition, "if your product isn't superior or the market doesn't want it, your company will fail no matter how good the culture is."[12] Culture may help you discover strategic choices and make decisions inside your organization to deploy them in the market. Still, it is not a substitute for selecting the right choices to compete and win in the market. That belongs to a different set of skills that the company must possess.

So let's not fall into the trap of thinking that culture and strategy are an "either-or" proposition because they are not; they are an "and" proposition. They work together, and the aim is to make it a virtuous cycle. Ideally, we are talking about developing an adaptive system that spurs reflection on actions taken, leaving room for proper adjustments as required. Culture empowers people to stay committed to the organization's core values while continuously seeking new ways to improve and succeed: "Successful cultures tap the motivation power of deeply held beliefs...But they also encourage change and innovation—the willingness to do whatever and go wherever."[13]

Culture is a verb, not a noun

"If you don't methodically set your culture, then two-thirds of it will end up being accidental, and the rest will be a mistake." Ben Horowitz.[14]

When figuring out a desired culture, it is customary for the CEO and the C-Suite team (typically responsible for leading this effort) to conduct lengthy sessions to select the values, ideals, principles, or behaviors that comprise all they want the company to become. The list of aspirations that result from those sessions is usually extensive, and additional work is often required to shorten it to a manageable few elements, generally around 5 to 7. One element that stands out as a constant in those exercises is that values are the preferred "weapon of choice" for companies to build a culture. Donald Sull, Stefano Turconi, and Charles Sull published an MIT Sloan Management Review article: "When it comes to culture, does your company Walk the Talk," on July 21, 2020, and among the many interesting findings of their research, they identified that companies prefer values when venturing in culture building: "Nearly all the organizations we studied rely on a set of core values as the guideposts for helping employees align their behavior with corporate culture. Of the companies in our sample, 72% referred to their company's culture as values or core values, and even employees at companies that use other labels — principles, philosophy, or ideals, for example — cited values as the foundation of their culture."[15] The authors studied websites and annual reports of nearly 700 companies, and they found that more than 80% of them published an official set of corporate values on their website: "The typical company lists a handful of values...Integrity was the most common, listed by 65% of all companies, followed by collaboration (53%), customer focus (48%), and respect (35%)."[16]

Sull, Turconi, and Sull also analyzed how the selected values actually drive employee behavior to build the desired culture: "We used data from the 2019 Culture 500, which ranks companies on nine of the most commonly cited values. Every Culture 500 company received a sentiment score that measured how positively employees talked about a specific value in the free text of their Glassdoor reviews."[17] Their findings were not encouraging: "The analysis reveals that there is no correlation between the cultural values a company emphasizes in its published statements and how well the company lives up to those values in the eyes of employees. All of the correlations between official and actual values were very weak, and four of the nine — collaboration, customer orientation, execution, and diversity — were negatively correlated."[18]

Many companies struggle to establish an effective culture. While some may believe that designing the culture is the hard part, the truth is that the real work comes after the initial planning. Once the culture has been defined, implementing it and getting employees to adopt it is the real challenge. Mark Randolph, Netflix co-founder, puts it in the following terms: "You can talk about your company's culture until you're blue in the face. You can put the most beautiful posters in your break room and carve your values in the corner-stone of your building. But none of that will make the slightest bit of difference if your words don't match your actions. Culture is observational. It's not what you say, it's what you do."[19] The truth is that no "bulletproof" playbook will guarantee success; you must make sure that the role models in your organization embrace the desired behaviors, practice them, and experiment to find the right choices to implement your culture transformation.

You don't find out who's been swimming naked until the tide goes out

In the 1994 Berkshire Hathaway Inc. shareholders meeting, Warren Buffet discussed how companies can make "dumb" decisions in reinsurance that don't become apparent until years later, often only coming to light during tough times. He famously stated, "You don't find out who's been swimming naked until the tide goes out." Buffet's quote applies to many business situations, but I find it particularly relevant for companies that are attempting to build a strong culture.

When everything is going well in a company, and the results are positive, it's easy for everyone to present themselves in the best possible way and become champions of the desired culture. Leading by example is uncomplicated when things are running smoothly; remember what Publilius Syrus (85–43 BC) once said, "Anyone can hold the helm when the sea is calm." However, culture is a contact sport, and the real test occurs during stressful times when results are not favorable, emotions run high, and everyone is under pressure. In such situations, people's true colors are revealed, and you find out who has been swimming naked. Command and control practices tend to take over during challenging times, and trust becomes scarce. Principles such as "it's okay to make mistakes" and "respect others" crumble under the pressure of the situation. Leaders who usually excel can struggle to conduct business and maintain the desired culture simultaneously. Their behavior under stress harms the organization's credibility and becomes a liability to the cultural transformation.

Everyone needs to be aware of their positive and negative actions to curtail problems down the road. Culture is a fragile, cumulative process that takes time to become a habit. Therefore, all leaders must be aware of themselves and pay special attention to those who could derail the cultural effort due to their temperament and volatility. Identifying and working with these individuals makes it possible to ensure that everyone is on the same page and moving in the same direction towards building the desired culture.

Bill Walsh, former head coach of the San Francisco 49ers, used to say: "The culture precedes positive results. It doesn't get tacked on as an afterthought on your way to the victory stand. Champions behave like champions before they're champions; they have a winning standard of performance before they are winners."[20] We must commit to consistent effort and maintain these standards, even during difficult business situations. It's essential to ensure that all team members meet the established standards, especially the weakest links, to sustain success in the long run.

Bridging the culture's knowing-doing gap with dressing-room leaders

I will share several sports-related examples in this book that can be applied to business scenarios; most of these examples are well-known stories reported in the media. However, I had a unique opportunity to learn first-hand how a sports team leverages its culture to ensure consistent success. I visited the headquarters of the Real Madrid soccer team, which is one of the most respected Clubs in the world and has won the most Champions League trophies. and had a conversation with their Sports Director at the time, Emilio Butragueño. He is a retired Spanish professional footballer nicknamed "El Buitre" and is a soccer legend in his own right.

I was interested to know how Real Madrid maintains its identity despite players constantly leaving and new ones joining. Moreover, I wanted to learn about the secret behind their winning spirit, which is renowned for their ability to make spectacular comebacks and win games that seemed to be lost. Many interesting topics were covered during our conversation, but one stood out in how they were able to uphold their culture, and that I believe is essential to scaling culture in organizations: "the dressing room leader."

According to Butragueño, in Real Madrid, the Head Coach can decide on the team's playing style, training methods, and physical programs. The practices that are designed to deploy its playing style are his decisions. However, the team's identity is non-negotiable. It is a backbone that does not change with the Head Coach. Real Madrid's identity has made the institution great and allowed it to become one of the most popular soccer teams in the world. It is a steady pillar that holds the organization together and must be preserved, no matter who runs the team at any given time. While coaches may come and go, the team's identity and culture must remain intact.

Real Madrid recognizes that even with the best coaches, there is always a gap between them and the players, which can create a void in the team's spirit and performance. So, to maintain Real Madrid's identity and address the coach-players gap, they developed the concept named "dressing room leader." This is a distinguished player within the team who takes on the responsibility of steering the team's identity within the group and dealing with fluctuation in performance and ego clashes, which are inevitable in groups of highly talented players. The "dressing room leader" must be a respected player and be considered an icon of Real Madrid's mentality. He usually has a long tenure with the team, does not mind providing reality checks to players who don't have their feet on the ground, regardless of their fame, and is capable of instilling their philosophy of resilience, 100% winning attitude, and humility in all the players. It is a peer with the gravitas to transmit the institution's philosophy that coordinates with the Head Coach, facilitating these principles and invigorating their mentality to face their next adversary.

The Head Coach must also demonstrate these values and lead by example, symbolizing the team's ethos on every occasion. The "dressing room leader" does not substitute for that but complements the coach's message in the intimacy of day-to-day peer exchanges. This concept can be applied to scaling culture in organizations. It is a form of distributive leadership that is a valuable tool to help embed the identity and desired behaviors within teams and work closely with their colleagues to ensure everyone is on the same page—some Food for thought.

Reaching cultural transformation tipping point

One of the challenges of scaling culture in any organization is that you must cross a certain threshold to gain momentum and leverage its power. It is tempting to believe you can reach this inflection point using only marketing or communication efforts, such as an internal campaign with gimmicky, catchy messages that immerse all employees in how culture should be lived. I hate to burst your bubble if you think this way, but it will not work. No matter how good your internal communication campaign might be, it will inevitably come short because for the system to change, you need personal, life-living, aha moments that transmit the behavior, not catchy phrases or images with ideal portrayals. Culture can only be established by a direct, intimate experience, with leaders performing by the stipulated behaviors and individuals assimilating the insights gained in the interactions and making sense of them. Culture is adopted by osmosis. Roger L. Martin, former Dean of the Rotman School of Management at the University of Toronto from 1998 to 2013 and an author of several business books, describes this very compellingly: "For me, any culture change is a retail, not wholesale exercise. Wholesale is when organizations make sweeping grand proclamations about doing things differently. Retail is when they pay particular attention to each and every interaction and use those individual interactions as a catalyst to do things differently".

The proximal condition of culture adds another layer of complexity to an already demanding subject. Since a communication campaign will not do the job by itself, you need to leverage the interactions in the organization and try to use them as culture-enhancing moments. Leading by example is the only way; you must walk the talk and encourage other leaders to do the same. Discuss it, bring the topic to your town halls, hear what the employees think, adjust where needed, and repeat.

When attempting to scale culture, it is essential to remember that you must not compromise the standards set with cultural behaviors. They must be executed as they were laid out consistently. For instance, if you establish "create a safe space to make mistakes" as a behavior, you must comply with it 100%, day in and day out. If you only support this behavior occasionally, halfway, or apply it depending on the circumstances, it will not take hold as a cultural behavior. Even worse, it will create confusion. It's a binary situation; you do it the way it's supposed to be done, or you don't. When there are incongruences in the standards, you reach a mediocre version of your intended objective. Danny Meyer, the Founder & Executive Chairman of the Union Square Hospitality Group, offers an interesting view on the impact of a culture where unwanted behaviors coexist with the desired ones: "The culture you have in your organization is the sum of all the wanted behaviors that you celebrate minus all the unwanted behaviors that you tolerate."[21]

One important thing to remember when scaling culture is the windy road you will encounter. The process will never resemble an ascending, straight, 45-degree angle line. Our logical thinking mind may suggest that this is the pattern to follow, but it is not a realistic way to depict a human-centric journey. In my experience, scaling culture feels like attempting to untie a big bundle of tight knots, like the ones found in the pile of accumulated rope that you often see on a pier or in an old marine vessel. As you try to untie the superficial knots, you discover more loops and twists inside the pile that are not visible in the first place. It is frustrating at times, but you must persevere until fewer knots come your way, and eventually, you will have a smooth rope, loose and free. The process will make you want to drop everything at times because of the thinking that the desired cultural behaviors will evolve and strengthen as time goes by; it's only natural to expect that you will see more and more of them. You do at times, but as you untie one knot, frequently another one appears; it is a test of your fortitude. Cultural progression stops and goes, and sometimes it gets stuck.

Scaling culture in an organization entails working with a dynamic, live system. You will face some forces that push you forward, while others will push you back. The driving forces occur when you declare and demonstrate the behaviors you want to achieve, the teaching moments with leaders and associates during workshops, all-hands-in-deck meetings, and other initiatives promoting the desired change. On the other hand, the restraining forces come from organizational inertia, perceived lack of commitment from leadership, and other factors that might slow down cultural development, such as outdated policies, time constraints, conflicting incentives, or competing priorities. The system might freeze at some point, with facilitating and restraining forces opposing, balancing each other out, and leaving you stuck. To keep progressing, you must find ways to solve the tension between these driving and restraining forces. How do we do it?

After learning from falling many times on this path, I will tell you what has worked for me; it was a counterintuitive finding since my natural tendency was to put considerable effort into facilitating the driving forces through spreading the culture Gospel. Still, I learned that you will get the best bang for the buck if you prioritize weakening or eliminating the restarting forces rather than pushing with the facilitating forces. Of course, you still need to teach the desired culture and showcase the importance of its adoption, but make a solid effort to eliminate outdated policies, conflicting guidelines, etc. In layman's terms, expose the "it is the way we have always done it" thinking and bring to the fore the "stuck switches" held in the organization because, once you get rid of them, the desired behaviors will have an easier path to adoption. The late Daniel Kahneman, known for his work in behavioral economics, for which he was awarded the 2002 Nobel Memorial Prize in Economic Sciences, represented change as a spring that is compressed, "when we want to move people from A to B, we push them... (the spring will gradually compress) and when you compress the string it will push back harder."[22] The turning point is when you weaken the pushback force of the string; even if the push is not so strong, resistance will be eliminated, and people will have an easier way of moving from point A to point B.

You will know you've reached the tipping point of cultural transformation when the force of the barriers becomes weaker than the force of the drivers. Once you reach this moment, your work will ensure that this gap, where barriers are weaker than the drivers, widens and continues in this direction. I understand it's easier said than done, but keep this thought in mind, and I can assure you that your journey will be on the right track.

Not everything that can be counted counts and not everything that counts can be counted

William Bruce Cameron's quote is spot on to head this section because one of the topics I find more controversial is evaluating progress when attempting to scale culture. I have mixed feelings about the practical value of measuring culture since the process is, at best, a proxy that doesn't represent the actual state of affairs. To measure culture, we typically use scales for the desired behaviors that establish a value based on intervals, with the difference between any two consecutive points being the same throughout the scale. Unlike objective measurements like temperature, distance, and weight, our culture measurement is based on the judgments and opinions of those surveyed. They assign a value to the observable behaviors in the company using the scale; then, we consolidate the results, and we hope the "wisdom of the crowds" will cancel out extreme scores and errors and give us a fair number. The reasoning behind the practice is that if the sample size is representative, averaging different people's judgments will give us an accurate picture of reality. However, the question remains: does it?

I've extensively discussed the most effective method for measuring company culture with CEOs and C-suite members. While I understand the need to determine where you are in the journey and adjust where necessary, I am convinced that, more often than not, we end up mistaking the map for the territory. This becomes even more problematic when performance bonuses are part of the process because there is much noise from everyone involved, making the evaluation process questionable.

It would be better if you considered it a directional, uneven, and rollercoaster-like movement of adoption. It is organic and never stands still; therefore, we must accept that using interval scales to measure its progress can be misleading. Assessing change by quantifying a score's incremental progress is hardly the best approach to show the actual adoption of beliefs and corresponding organizational behaviors over time. We lock in assessing what numbers tell you, using two or even three decimals to describe the shift's depth and complexity. We declare progress, for instance, because this year, we got a 4.46 value in the "it is okay to make mistakes" principle compared to last year's score of 4.21. Are we making progress because the numbers show we are 6% better? Does the scoring of 4.46 versus 4.21 reflect something relevant to begin with?

I believe it's important to incorporate a variety of perspectives and tools into our culture's assessment process. By keeping an eye on the direction of cultural change and reaching out to different groups and outliers (like newcomers and long-time members) using both qualitative and quantitative methods, we can gather more insightful information than we would from a traditional single survey. Integrating this evaluation approach can provide a more representative measure of our transformation journey. This holistic approach ensures we capture diverse experiences and viewpoints, helping us better understand the organization's path. While companies may prefer the "certainty" of numbers to measure progress, I'm convinced this approach leads to an incomplete representation of what is happening in the organization. A quality-based approach would yield better results.

In the remainder of this chapter, I will introduce a cultural model that has proven helpful to me and is part of the Aspen Root Framework for unlocking organizational potential. It will highlight the areas you must work on when building an organizational culture. It is simple and actionable, unlike other approaches I have explored, which were very complex to manage and implement.

Determinants of Culture

Let's begin this conversation by briefly discussing the concept of culture. Organizational culture has gotten the attention of scholars since 1950, and there are several approaches and definitions that strive to understand the phenomenon and capture its workings. Many prominent authors like Edgar Schein, Charles O'Reilly, and Geert Hofstede, among others, have devoted much of their lives to providing valuable reflections on the subject. These authors mention shared assumptions, norms, values, attitudes, rituals, attributes that distinguish one group from another, etc., as the essential items that shape a particular organizational culture.

In this book, I will not attempt to propose yet another definition of culture; there are several dozen already, and in the end, "corporate culture means different things to different people."[23] Therefore, I don't think it would be a good use of our time to go deeper into defining something that is currently "over-defined." Instead, I will provide a framework to help operationalize the actions whose outcome is to deliver a desired culture.

In the day-to-day, culture is an intangible whole, an entity that employees acknowledge without understanding its inner structure; they just make sense of it. Culture is communicated in how things are done in the company, what is expected from you, and the emotions, stories, memories, and experiences people share and live regularly. That is the overall cultural vibe, but at times, the mood can be particular and, for instance, shape the way meetings are conducted, the proper reactions when your boss asks you to work on the weekend, or if it's appropriate to ask for a raise to your boss or request vacations.

As with the Talent dimension of the Aspen Root framework introduced in Chapter 4, I will advocate the three determinants that build on each other and represent the inner workings of an active, living cultural system. I will examine them separately to shed light on each one, but it's essential to point out that they work as a feedback loop, reinforcing each other to generate the culture. For those designing the desired culture, these determinants start as independent categories but often blend and overlap.

The three determinants that give shape to organizational culture are "The Creed," "Contextual Affect," and "Stewardship."

Culture

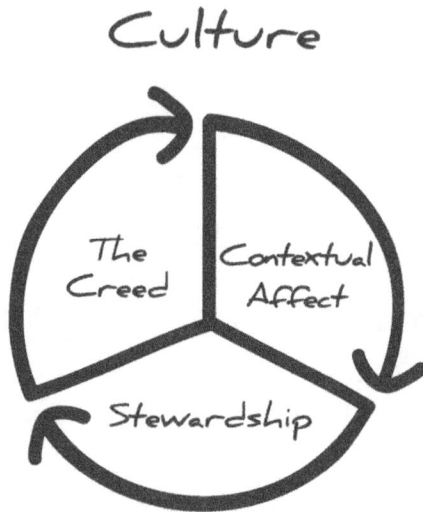

The Creed

"The Creed" is a declaration made by an organization about what it wants to become. Once the company sets the desired aspiration, employees can internalize this idea, generate the mental models that support it, and adopt associated behaviors. When all associates assimilate the stated mental models and corresponding behaviors, the "Creed" becomes a collective state in the organization encompassing a shared way of being and doing. It specifies what the organization stands for, its North Star and values, its reason for existence beyond profits, what is allowed and not, and what you can expect when you join in. The "Creed" encapsulates the company's identity and aspirations, and everyone is called to embrace these ideals.

Organizations use various descriptive elements, such as core values, principles, behaviors, ways of thinking, and ways of interacting, to develop "The Creed." values are the preferred way to communicate to employees what the company is all about and what is expected of them. I previously referred to a 2020 MIT Sloan Management Review study, which surveyed nearly 700 large companies. An interesting finding in this study is that around 50% or more of the companies that were analyzed coincided in upholding three values: Integrity (65%), Collaboration (53%), and Customer (48%).[24] The consensus on these three values suggests that many companies want to ensure that their people are ethical and honest, can interact well, and take the customer's perspective in their work performance. While we all can agree that these three values are essential for an organization to function, the fact that so many organizations share them raises the question of how to make them a distinctive trait in how they do business so they can be differentiated and gain an edge.

Simply stating the desired values and outlining the expected behaviors people must adopt is a first step, but it will not be enough to sink them in. Values need to be anchored through unique company practices that give them substance; otherwise, we risk navigating a sea of sameness compared to other organizations. We can achieve this goal by instilling routines embodying these values so that the practice begets our desired behaviors. To illustrate this idea, let's look at how Pixar has achieved a distinctive trait in the much sought-after value of collaboration. When making movies, Pixar periodically evaluates if their productions are liked and if they are delivering the impact they want. To do this, they instituted a " Braintrust " session where everyone involved in the movie can express their opinions: "The Braintrust, which meets every few months or so to assess each movie we're making, is our primary delivery system for straight talk. Its premise is simple: Put smart, passionate people in a room together and charge them with identifying and solving problems, and encourage them to be candid with one another... The Braintrust is one of the most important traditions at Pixar...The Braintrust sets the tone for everything we do."[25] Actions speak louder than words; Pixar walks the talk of collaboration with the Braintrust session and creates an experience that conveys this value to its people more than any poster on the wall or communication campaign could do.

Despite the fact that core values are widely used, organizations are not limited to relying on them to design their "Creed" and can incorporate other types of descriptors to reach their goal. AB InBev, for instance, chose not to create its Creed with values. Instead, they leverage ten principles divided into three sections that communicate it: Dream, People, and Culture. Among the principles you can find: "*We dream Big*" (we are building a profitable, growth company). "*We recruit, develop, and retain people who can be better than ourselves*" (we are measured by the quality and diversity of our teams). "*We are a company of owners*" (owners take results personally and lead by example), or "*We manage our costs tightly to free up resources that will support profitable top-line growth.*"

Amazon is another example of a company that has chosen "Leadership Principles" over core values to leverage its "Creed."

They have sixteen to describe "how Amazon does business, how leaders lead, and how we keep the customer at the center of our decisions."[26] Some examples are *"Customer Obsession"* (leaders start with the customer and work backwards). They work vigorously to earn and keep customer trust. Although leaders pay attention to competitors, they obsess over customers); *"Invent and Simplify"* (leaders expect and require innovation and invention from their teams and always find ways to simplify. They are externally aware, look for new ideas from everywhere, and are not limited by "not invented here." As we do new things, we accept that we may be misunderstood for long periods of time); *"Bias for action"* (Speed matters in business. Many decisions and actions are reversible and do not need extensive study. We value calculated risk-taking); *"Learn and Be Curious"* (leaders are never done learning and always seek to improve themselves. They are curious about new possibilities and act to explore them).

When creating your company's organizational creed, it's important to approach it like an artist crafting a sculpture or painting a picture. As a leader, you aim to create a world and emphasize the qualities that matter most to the company, which everyone must hold and demonstrate at work. You can build your identity with values, principles, or a mix of both; it's fine as long as the "Creed" platform is congruent with your company's aspirations. Remember that every design element of the desired identity should work together to convey a coherent message. Having a clear rationale behind the choices of values or principles is essential to avoid sending mixed signals or creating confusion within the organization. If, for any reason, some of the ideas included in the "Creed" collide, it's crucial to explain their reasoning and how they can work together in a way that is easy for everyone to understand. I have seen how enforcing principles related to experimentation or agility, where mistakes are part of the process, can conflict with the mandate of delivering results, where there is no space to fail. Ensure that the whole and the parts of the "Creed" integrate and make sense.

In my experience developing "Creeds," I have learned a few lessons that I believe can be helpful:

Be Distinctive. Your "Creed" will become your way of being. It will permeate your customers, associates, vendors, and community. Your Creed sets your organization apart from others, and making an impact on your people and the market is crucial. Even if others have already stated the same principles or values as you, it's important to frame them in a way that highlights your company's unique perspective. You can show how your values are lived differently by using stories, anecdotes, practices, or compelling phrases specific to your organization's history or way of doing business. Even if you use widely accepted values like innovation or integrity, you can still frame them in a way that makes them your own and communicates a proprietary signature.

Avoid unnecessary complexity. When creating a "Creed," leaders often try to include as many attributes as possible to cover a broad range of goals. This is a natural tendency because generating multiple ideas is easier than distilling and simplifying deep insights. However, it's better to focus on a few key attributes that can significantly impact rather than trying to include everything imaginable. Start with the few that make the most sense; you can refine and adjust your "Creed" over time. It's commonly believed that humans can remember 5 to 9 digits with an average of 7, so remember that keeping it short and sweet is better. When crafting a "Creed," choose a few fundamental principles to make a difference and build on this foundation.

Conformity in the aim, not in the means. When creating a 'Creed,' we aim to set a shared behavioral objective and emphasize its importance in achieving our goals. This helps to create a critical mass and advance the organization as a whole towards that goal. However, while the outcome may be clear, and the intent is to move the organization in this direction, we must avoid the standardization of means; everybody should be entitled to contribute from their diverse perspective. As long as the principles and values are maintained, we must respect how each person upholds the goal in their own way. We aim to move forward together, enriching the concept with diversity and avoiding micromanagement or robotization of people and processes.

Balance your pain points with ideals of what could be. When communicating the values or principles in "The Creed," we should be mindful of how we frame our message. We can either focus on pain points or harmful conditions we want to move away from or state our message as an aspiration we can strive towards. Moving away from pain can be a powerful motivator, but I suggest using it sparingly to avoid overindulging and diluting its force. Using positive aspirations as goals is a powerful way to frame your message. For example, if you want to instill the principle that everyone should give their best in your "Creed," you can say, "In this company, we don't procrastinate; we don't sack it off," or "In this company, we jump to action and give it our very best until the task is done." If you pick a negative view to illustrate a principle, you should balance it with a positive perspective in another principle to maintain a balanced tone in the overall identity. When verbalizing values or principles, it is essential to provide an ample spectrum to leverage the positives and negatives so you do not get stuck in one mode and amplify their impact.

Beware of overdoing a good thing. One of the paradoxes that you must consider when setting values and principles is that virtues and defects go hand in hand. Something good can become destructive when taken to an extreme. For example, being focused, persistent, and unwavering in achieving your goals is good. Still, if you go beyond a certain point, those virtues can turn into stubbornness, closed-mindedness, and rigidity. Similarly, emphasizing that people should take full ownership of projects can unintentionally lead to disregarding others, creating isolated teams, and hindering collaboration. Remember that the dose makes the poison, so be cautious about how virtuous values and principles are applied in your organization and strive to find a healthy balance.

The litmus test of reality vs illusion

To achieve "The Creed," organizations must manage two distinct "realities" that do not entirely align. The first reality is the intended or desired outcome, which is what the stated values and principles dictate as the aspiration. In contrast, the second reality is the day-to-day reality experienced by individuals, which is how they behave and what they do in reality. It is crucial to recognize the gap between these two realities and continuously work to achieve the stated identity. Behavioral deviations from the set values and principles are expected to occur in the organization, and we must acknowledge that those ideals will be challenging to achieve fully. However, we must continuously work to close the gap on any possible deviations because failure to do so can lead to the perception that our narrative is hollow, deceptive, and even hypocritical, seriously hindering our transformation journey. In the end, it is our actions rather than our words that determine success. What is seen and felt in the organization trumps what is wished for. We must be prepared for the demanding journey ahead, as achieving the ideal state will require bursts of effort and sustained commitment over the long term.

Many companies that stall, face challenges, or experience a changing environment must review or adjust their "Creed" at some point. Even if things are going well, it is essential to periodically evaluate whether the "Creed" platform still makes sense and whether the company's chosen identity is valid to deal with situations in the foreseeable future. I strongly recommend conducting a self-audit of your "Creed" at least every five years to ensure that you are on the right path or if any changes are required.

Out of all the elements necessary to building an organization's identity, much attention has been given to the purpose component of the "Creed," and rightly so. It is considered the guiding force that unites the organization, inspires it to remain relevant, and sheds light on the transformation journey. Let's take a closer look at this component.

Purpose

One essential component of "The Creed" is having a well-crafted, captivating purpose that communicates why your company exists beyond making money. Over the past decade, we have seen a growing emphasis on the importance of organizational purpose in the business world and with reason. As conscious capitalism is becoming a driving force globally, purposeful companies are better positioned to make a positive impact by delivering value to humanity.

Undoubtedly, generating profits is very important for any company. Stockholders must get an adequate return for their investment; otherwise, the company will cease to exist, leading to losses for all stakeholders. However, it would be shortsighted to understand companies only as cash-generator entities. We must recognize that for-profit enterprises significantly impact the community in many ways. They provide benefits for their employees, suppliers, customers, and society at large. The contribution of these companies goes beyond the mere transactional exchange with customers; they enrich the lives of all those involved with the organization. Hubert Jolly, the former chairman and CEO of Best Buy and author of the book "The Heart of Business," underscores purpose's impact in organizations in the following terms: "I believe that business is fundamentally about purpose, people, and human relationships—not profit, at least not primarily. Companies are not soulless entities. They are human organizations made of individuals who work together toward a common purpose."[27]

The company's purpose encompasses all the benefits an organization provides to its internal and external stakeholders. It defines the reason for the organization's existence and why it would be missed if it didn't exist. From the perspective of people working at a company, purpose is crucial because it helps establish a personal connection with the organization beyond the contractual relationship, unleashing the energy necessary to achieve individual and organizational goals. As the race to attract top talent becomes increasingly fierce, a clear sense of purpose becomes essential for drawing in and retaining the best individuals.

One of the things that I often see when companies craft their purpose statement is a tendency to ladder up excessively and position it in a territory where it is difficult to differentiate. Many organizational purposes begin to look the same at a very high level; they express that they want to help people achieve their dreams, have a better life, live fully, be healthy, be happy, thrive, etc. From a high-level perspective, this is fine, but the organization risks entering into a sameness territory that leads nowhere. It's crucial to balance being aspirational to inspire your audience and being relatable, closer to the ground, to connect with them. This equilibrium is what creates an engaging purpose that can engage all stakeholders, internal and external.

The French emperor and military leader, Napoleon Bonaparte, understood how to strike this balance well and used it to rally his troops to conquer vast territories. Napoleon's rule was a transformative period that reshaped Europe in numerous ways; he profoundly impacted France, Europe, and the world. He once said that soldiers do not risk their lives and die for the salary they get, but they do so willingly if it is to accomplish a greater ideal. When mobilizing his troops, Napoleon's message was moving and, at the same time, concrete, centered on nationalism, glory, and the vision of a victorious nation. The soldiers embraced this ideal and fought for it, even if that meant losing their own lives.

When a company's Purpose profoundly resonates with its people, it becomes the compass that guides and motivates work and the benefits it provides to others. We all work to make a living and want the companies we work for to do well, but our engagement goes beyond financial conditions. Jules Goddard and Tony Eccles, authors of the book "Uncommon Sense, Common Nonsense," underscore how critical Purpose is to mobilize the organization towards achieving noble goals: "Most of us don't work to enrich shareholders even though we recognize the virtues and merits of capitalism. We work to express our talents, earn a living, socialize with colleagues, participate in exciting projects, and perhaps make a difference in the world. Effective organizations play to these motives".[28]

Embarking on any transformation journey requires enormous energy to overcome the inevitable challenges that will come. An inspiring Purpose can recharge individuals in the organization with energy and become the sought-after source of motivation when things get complicated, or energy levels run low. "Getting invested in what the company stands for because it resonates with what makes you get out of bed in the morning is one of the essential ingredients of engagement. Clearly articulating and feeding that connection between personal and company Purpose for every team member is, therefore, one of the most crucial roles of any leader."[29]

Contextual Affect

The second determinant of culture in the framework is "Contextual Affect," which refers to the impact of the organizational context on people's behavior while they perform their duties. I chose the noun "affect" to describe the implications for context because it pertains to emotions, moods, influence, or the expression of emotions carried by the environment, which significantly impacts how we perform in the organization.

When we think of context in the organization, our mind takes us to the physical setting, including its architecture, layout, decoration, and furnishings. These aspects and their corresponding messaging influence how we work and sometimes explain our productivity or lack thereof. However, context is a broader concept and encompasses intangible elements such as operating procedures, protocols, policies, and implicit or explicit rules that determine how we conduct our jobs. The main point here is that the surrounding conditions of the organization either facilitate or hinder people's performance. I previously mentioned W. Edward Deming, a revered figure in Japan's Industrial Revolution, in this book. He famously stated the influence of context with a potent citation: "A bad system will beat a good person every time."

Context as a pain point

Among the many references on the impact of context on business performance, there is one that I find particularly enlightening, which is Sumantra Ghoshal's "The Smell of the Place"[30] speech. He delivered it during the World Economic Forum at Davos back in 1995, and his insights are still as fresh and relevant today as they were 30 years ago. Ghoshal was a professor at INSEAD and London Business School, and his research focused on how contextual factors influence organizational performance. He offered an exciting approach to improving performance in this regard. Unfortunately, Professor Ghosal passed away in 2004.

Ghoshal used an evocative metaphor comparing the Calcutta and Fontainebleau forests to describe how context can be a pain point and a restriction to performance. Professor Ghoshal was born in India, in the city of Calcutta, and he worked as a professor at INSEAD, located right next to the Fontainebleau forest. He relates how he visited Calcutta every summer when his children were on vacation to relax and spend time with family. Still, he found it difficult to find solace at 102 or 103 degrees with 99% humidity. The temperature made him tired, and he didn't want to go out; he only wanted to remain indoors where it was fresh. He couldn't help but compare his mood in Calcutta with how he felt in spring when he walked in the Fontainebleau forest: "You, go to the forest of Fontainebleau in spring, oh the firm desire to have a leisurely walk, and you can't; the moment you enter the forest, there is something about the crispness of the air, there is something about the smell of the trees in spring you want to jump, you want to jog, you want to catch a branch, to run to do something, and that I believe is the essence of the problem. Most companies, particularly large companies, have created downtown Calcutta in the summer inside themselves. Then they complain; they say you are lazy, and you don't take the initiative, and you don't cooperate; you are not changing the company. But it is not about changing me; I have a lot of energy in spring in Fontainebleau, and I am a bit tired in summer in Calcutta ... at the end, the issue is how do we change the context, how do we create the Fontainebleau forest inside companies."

In his speech at the World Economic Forum in Davos, Professor Ghoshal discussed how companies create an environment based on the four C's - Constraints, Compliance, Control, and Contract, which he calls the "Smell of the Place." This environment is what people have to deal with while doing their jobs. The rules, protocols, and procedures organizations establish to enhance performance and achieve growth can create conditions that hinder them from reaching it. They can suffocate and disempower their employees and limit their ability to produce results. The professionalization of management needed for growth can be a double-edged sword - a blessing that could quickly become a curse. Ghoshal's metaphor of Calcutta and Fontainebleau forests serves as a reminder that detached managers, bureaucracy, and old-school systems run counter to organizational creativity and hinder overall performance.

We need to regularly assess whether our company's procedures and policies are helping us reach our goals or getting in the way. Are they still serving our objectives, or are they hindering our progress? The systems in place are often stagnant and have not been reviewed in a long time. They have been operating for many years without proper analysis.

Factors Shaping Contextual Affect

The organizational context of a company is shaped by various factors that come together to form a system. To describe the factors that influence a company's internal context, we can categorize them into four groups: I) work structure, II) performance appraisal, III) physical environment, and IV) regulations, symbols, and traditions. It's important to note that this is not an exhaustive and comprehensive classification but rather a method for recognizing fundamental elements that define a company's culture from a contextual standpoint. Now, let's delve into each of these categories.

I) Work wiring (policies, protocols, and processes)

This category showcases the written and unwritten guidelines for managing various aspects of a business, such as assets, procurement, manufacturing, distribution, information technology, finance, R&D, marketing, sales, and others. These guidelines are functional and help the company operate efficiently. They align the organization to deliver products and services to customers. The objective is to standardize the operation, making it stable and predictable, and operate in a way that significantly reduces risk, thereby increasing the likelihood of success. This predictability and risk mitigation should instill a sense of security and confidence in our operations. In this section, you can find the work-related policies such as remote work, code of conduct, conflict of interest, travel expenses, vacations, recruiting, onboarding, parental leave, DEI (Diverse, Equitable, and Inclusive), and ESG (Environmental, Social, and Governance) initiatives.

As organizations evolve, these systems must be reviewed and updated, as the processes designed to help the organization can hinder its performance if they are not updated to reflect current conditions. A deliberate approach to validating their merits should be taken to ensure they are still helpful. Otherwise, they can become a straitjacket that limits people's capacity to attain the company's goals.

II) Performance evaluation and incentives

Companies typically follow a yearly budgeting process to set ambitious goals for total revenue and profitability. The finance department usually leads this process and aims for a healthy return on investment. The goal is then broken down into geographical regions, product families, product-client combinations, etc. These objectives are assigned to various departments, including marketing, manufacturing, distribution, and sales. Throughout the year, the organization closely monitors progress to identify potential shortfalls and adjusts to meet the goals. Individuals working in areas where progress is lagging will be expected to work harder to achieve the objectives if they appear out of reach, as variable compensation (bonuses) is calculated based on fulfilling these objectives. The annual operating plan results evaluate performance, provide feedback, and determine potential salary increases and promotions. Sales quotas and efficiency measures are implemented to incentivize sales, production, and distribution personnel. These measures follow a similar logic and compensate for performance.

Incentives for performance are a common practice that involves sharing profits when certain milestones are reached. They are designed to link performance with investors' success. However, it's crucial to ensure that these incentives do not create silos, pit individuals against each other, or hinder collaboration across different areas. If the overall performance system is not well-aligned, various departments may compete against each other to achieve their goals, which could lead to friction and unnecessary rework. This approach can be dysfunctional because different areas might prioritize their interests over the company's best interests.

It's clear that a balanced approach to performance evaluations is crucial. While quantitative evaluations provide a necessary structure, they can also stifle teams' willingness to take risks and explore new opportunities. This is where quality evaluations come in, allowing for some discretion and encouraging the company's advancement.

Interestingly, some organizations have stopped linking compensation to objectives setting and are revamping their performance evaluation process with alternative criteria. This is an intelligent decision. Performance Evaluation will continue progressing in a way that aligns the organization and inspires its people to achieve their best rather than hinder performance.

III) Physical setting

How an organization's workspace is arranged and its overall appearance sends a powerful message about its values and identity to its stakeholders. Every aspect of the layout and furnishings sets the tone for human interactions and reflects the company's essence. Even if companies haven't intentionally designed their environment to communicate a message, they should know that it impacts their people. Furthermore, companies must ensure that their physical identity aligns with their strategy and the qualities they want to foster among their people. For instance, if a company operates in the low-cost industry, having luxurious offices with high-end furnishings and expensive decor would be inconsistent and send a contradictory message. Similarly, if a company promotes innovation and creativity, it would be counterproductive to have a closed and restrictive workspace that inhibits the flow of ideas. While it may seem common sense that the desired identity should match the setting, it's surprising how often they do not align.

There is one example of the consistency of context as a determinant of culture that has brought much value to the organization and comes from none other than Steve Jobs. During the 1990s, Pixar had to construct a new headquarters to accommodate its growth and better suit its requirements. At that time, Steve Jobs was the majority shareholder and actively participated in the project by designing the building himself. He aimed to ensure that the workspace's layout promoted collaboration, which is a fundamental element of their creative process and is deeply ingrained in Pixar's culture and way of working: "Steve was a big believer in the power of accidental mingling ... (he) presided every detail of the new building's construction, from the arched steel bridges that straddle the central atrium to the type of chairs in our screening rooms. He didn't want perceived barriers, so the stairs were open and inviting. He wanted a single entrance to the building so we could see each other as we entered. We had meeting rooms, restrooms, a mail room, three theaters, a game area, and an eating area, all at the center of our atrium (where to this day, everyone gathers to eat, play ping pon, or be briefed by Pixar's leaders on the company's goings-on) This all resulted in cross-traffic—people encountered each other all day long, inadvertently, which meant a better flow of communication and increased the possibility of chance encounters"[31] This example illustrates that when the work environment fosters the desired organizational traits, employees are more likely to embrace its principles and adopt its values with less resistance.

Due to the pandemic, the traditional work environment has changed significantly in recent years and is no longer the principal place of work. The pandemic has dramatically impacted our work, and many people are still working in a hybrid model or home office. It's still uncertain what the future office will look like, and we don't know what will work best. However, it seems clear that the office remains the preferred option for innovation, creativity, and sharing ideas, as interpersonal relationships are crucial for organizational culture. Therefore, I suggest paying close attention to the physical setting, as it is critical to shaping the overall atmosphere and has a significant impact on advancing the organizational identity.

IV) Rules, symbols, and rituals

"It was the summer of 1995, back when Jeff Bezos could count his Amazon employees on one hand, and those few employees needed desks. Bezos' friend and employee number five, Nico Lovejoy, says Bezos himself found a scrappy, cost-effective solution right outside their doors. "We happened to be across the street from a Home Depot," said Lovejoy. "He looked at desks for sale and looked at doors for sale, and the doors were a lot cheaper, so he decided to buy a door and put some legs on it." With that, the Amazon "door desk" was born. What neither of them knew at the time was that the scrappy, do-it-yourself desk would turn into one of Amazon's most distinctive bits of culture. More than 20 years later, thousands of Amazon employees worldwide still work each day on modern versions of those original door desks."[32]

Rules, symbols, and rituals are powerful cultural drivers; they bundle emotions, feelings, and experiences and represent values much better than words can. They can generate social cohesion around a desired identity. The above citation of "The Door Desk" captures a moment in Amazon's history that reflects its values of frugality and resourcefulness, which have been central to its cultural standards and business ethos. Jeff Bezos wasn't necessarily looking to set a symbol when adapting doors as desks. Still, the anecdote got traction and became a representation of what being an "Amazonian" is.

Furthermore, together with other attributes, it became a recognition token at the company: "The Door Desk Award goes to a person who exemplifies Frugality and Invention. The Just Do It

Award is an abnormally large, well-worn Nike sneaker given to employees who exhibit bias for action. It usually goes to a person who has come up with a clever idea outside the scope of their job."[33] Symbols crystalize history and aspirations. When you look at the history of humanity, there are examples of symbols that represent ideals or philosophies that have withstood the passing of time and connect with vast audiences, such as the Statue of Liberty, the Peace symbol, or the Red Cross, to name a few. These are examples of historical symbols that tell a compelling story and communicate a powerful message.

One of the most effective rituals I have found when supporting a human-centered approach in organizations and guiding productive conversations in meetings is a practice associated with the Systems Thinking perspective, which has been used for decades. This ritual is precious when an organization puts its people at the center of an organizational transformation. Experts like Peter Senge and Fred Kofman have detailed this practice, which involves having check-ins at the beginning of meetings and check-outs at the end.

Participants typically arrive at the start of meetings with emotions, worries, and expectations that often go unacknowledged. This can negatively impact their effectiveness and engagement during the meeting. By asking for check-ins at the beginning of the meeting, the participants can emotionally connect, learn about their current personal state, set expectations, and align everyone on the meeting's objective. This simple practice can yield significant returns. It is worth its weight in gold: "The check-in process opens up that space for understanding and fuller communication by allowing us to bring concerns into the group. Once we acknowledge that something is on our mind, it is much easier to focus on the meeting."[34] Likewise, in the check-out, we can end meetings productively by bringing forward a reflection of its value and setting out the following steps, "The check-out process allows each person to say what they want and be appreciated and celebrated by the group. They might ponder the process, consider the content, ask questions, or even make requests for further conversations,"[35] says Fred Kofman.

In a recent experience working with a sales team, I encountered a person who, during our interactions, kept checking her phone and appeared disinterested in relevant business topics. We organized a meeting to discuss a new product launch, and I requested a check-in; when it was her turn to speak, she opened up about her child having a health issue and how it had made her feel anxious and overwhelmed and affected her sleep. What at the beginning seemed to me like a lack of commitment on her part turned into a "how can I help you" situation. The team responded with compassion and support and adjusted her workload for the launch accordingly. This simple yet effective practice of checking in with each other helped the team stay focused on the task and prevented issues that could have arisen. The team united and supported each other in a time of need, strengthening their trust and increasing the overall effectiveness.

There are other examples of rituals at organizations that strengthen culture. Many companies have a tradition of recognizing their people's hard work and dedication. Some of the most common ones include celebrating years of service, acknowledging achievements, and rewarding those who embody the company's values. For instance, organizations that strive to foster innovation often have an annual event where failed products or ideas are showcased, emphasizing the importance of experimentation and taking risks. This approach reinforces the notion that failure is not necessarily bad as long as it leads to insights or learnings that can be used to improve future endeavors.

Rules, symbols, and rituals help set a context that shapes a company's culture, creating a sense of connection and belonging among its people. When these elements are aligned with the company's "Creed," they become powerful tools for transformation and unlocking people's potential.

Stewardship

Stewardship is the third determinant of organizational culture in the model. It is vital in shaping the organization's culture and plays a significant role in conveying its identity and operating system in daily work settings. Essentially, it is how the organization embodies its values when teams encounter everyday challenges, making it a critical component of the overall culture.

I chose the term "Stewardship" to name this determinant over the widely popular term "Leadership" because I wanted to convey how anybody could put it into practice without the need to be a so-called "Leader." There has been much discussion about the difference between "Leaders" and "Managers," where the latter are portrayed as short-sighted, control-oriented, and transactional. And the former are visionary, inspirational, and game changers. I wanted to avoid any positive or negative characterization of whoever has a guiding role in teams since, in my opinion, it has important implications for how culture is enacted. It should be accessible to everyone working in teams. The "Stewardship" naming bypasses the trap of defining a "persona" and highlights the action of steering the organization, which seems agnostic enough and fitting for any individual and chosen culture. Moreover, "Stewardship" is a more neutral and action-oriented manner to describe this crucial role. Notwithstanding the value that leaders' vision and inspiration bring to an organization, I believe we have underrated the importance of steering teams and conduction the organization to fulfill its objectives.

The "Stewardship" of teams is crucial to any organization's success. It defines how to work and interact with others and should not be isolated from the organization's values and principles. Instead, it should be intricately connected with them, reflecting what the organization stands for. The approach to interacting with teams must be rooted in the organization's ethos and mutually support each other. This underlines the values and principles the organization aspires to uphold while performing its functions and serving its customers. To be sustainable, the "Stewardship" model must be consistent with "The Creed" and "Contextual Affect." This is how the organization's culture is demonstrated in actions, not just words.

Stewardship: person-specific or company-specific?

In my experience working in complex organizations, I have seen how companies include "Leadership" models to complement their talent development initiatives. Leadership is customarily seen as an extension of individual abilities that must be enforced to achieve the organization's goals. I prefer to view it as a component of the desired culture because it signals a way of being and interacting to help teams and the organization attain the best outcome. Following this logic, if you design your Stewardship model as part of your culture, you can better integrate the three determinants, Identity, Contextual Affect, and Stewardship, as a virtuous circle that feeds and reinforces itself.

Deciding to place Stewardship as a talent development topic or a cultural company trait may seem a secondary consideration; in the end, what difference does it make where you put it if it delivers the result? I will advocate that it does make a difference and that managing initiatives in the appropriate categories, in this case, culture, is essential to make the best decisions and maximize their impact.

Stewardship is a contact sport

For teams to achieve their goals, members must actively engage in healthy discussions and confront each other's ideas. There is no easy path to progress; facing challenges and working through difficulties is necessary for individuals and organizationss to Regrow. Therefore, a good Stewardship model should not aim to avoid conflicts or force artificial harmony but rather create an environment where different ideas can be respectfully discussed to determine what's best.

Stewardship should promote collaboration and trust. Each team member's unique contribution is essential to the team's success. Even in difficult circumstances, the Steward should utilize everyone's contribution for the team's benefit. Open and honest communication is always encouraged so all ideas are explored and critically examined rather than dismissed.

To illustrate how Stewardship is a contact sport, I would like to refer to a story shared by Steve Jobs, where he learned the benefit of the healthy confrontation of ideas. Jobs relates his experience as a kid with an 80-year-old neighbor who showed him how a rock tumbler could turn ugly rocks into beautiful polished ones: "he pulled out this dusty old rock Tumbler. It was a motor and a coffee can and a little, you know, band between them, and he said, come with me, and we went out to the back, and we got some rocks, some regular, old, ugly rocks, and we put them in the can with a little bit of liquid and a little bit of grit powder, and we close the can up, and he turns this motor on, and he said to come back tomorrow, and this can was making, you know, racket as the stones were in. And I came back the next day and we opened the can, and we took out these amazingly beautiful, polished rocks. The same common stones that had gone in, through rubbing against each other, with a little bit of friction, a little bit of noise, came out as these beautiful, polished rocks. And that's always been in my mind my metaphor for a team working really hard on something they're passionate about. It is through the team, through that group of incredibly talented people, bumping up against each other, having arguments, having fights sometimes, making some noise, and working together, that they polish each other, that they polish the ideas, and what comes out of these are really beautiful stones."[36]

The story of Steve Jobs teaches us a valuable lesson about the power of collaboration and constructive conflict. By working together, a team can refine and enhance each other's ideas, resulting in much better outcomes. Managing a team is not about avoiding conflict altogether but embracing it as a necessary part of the process. Productive friction is essential for unlocking a team's full potential, driving innovation, and achieving organizational objectives. Ultimately, the way we navigate this "bumpy" road speaks volumes about our company's culture and values. The way we steward teams represents the culture in action.

Can one size fit all?

The concept of Stewardship is crucial for translating a company's desired identity and purpose into the dynamics of its teams. Stewardship operates within the organization's specific context, depending on its structure and rules, which can either facilitate or hinder the teams' progress. For Stewardship to be sustainable, the model and its components must embody the essential traits of the company's declared spirit and be capable of challenging the status quo it aims to overcome. Therefore, the model must be custom-designed according to its goals. However, regardless of these conditions, I believe that good stewardship models share several essential elements that can help any organization unleash untapped potential.

I advocate a Stewardship model consisting of four fundamental components that serve as a backbone for any organization seeking innovation and Regrowth. These are necessary but not sufficient conditions and must be enriched with other drivers ad hoc to the organization's needs. These elements are the starting point and aim to foster collaboration, promote a free exchange of ideas, and ensure accountability—all crucial and indispensable for companies to compete in fast-paced market change environments. The components are:

- Ownership
- Supporting others' growth
- Truth versus Ego
- Psychological Safety

I will provide a comprehensive overview to help you better understand each component. It's important to note that each topic is extensive and could quickly fill an entire book independently. Nevertheless, I will delve into each, enabling you to evaluate its importance and value. Exploring each component in depth will clarify its role and significance within the overall model.

Ownership

As mentioned, I worked for a consumer packaged goods company in Mexico and was the General Manager of supermarket sales nationwide. I experienced an event that showcased the impact of taking ownership firsthand. We encountered a significant issue: the sales of drinkable yogurts had dropped by nearly 20% over two weeks in the southern region. Being a responsible manager, I quickly convened a meeting with my entire sales team to identify the root cause of the problem and take immediate action to address it. This decline coincided with the onset of the winter season, a notable change in this area. While people in the North might have seen it as warm weather, switching from wearing a T-shirt to a sweater for the locals was a big deal. We promptly analyzed the issue during the meeting, and I encouraged my sales team to contribute their insights and propose potential solutions. The head sales supervisor for the area said:

"This has been a very atypical season for the Cancun area; it has been colder than usual. Nobody craves cold drinks in this weather, and yogurt drinkables are indeed cold drinks. The general temperature has been so chilling that when customers walk inside the supermarkets, they stay away from the open coolers; people want to avoid contact with fresh air at all costs. Unfortunately, we cannot control the weather, and we have to wait for the cold spell to pass before we can expect sales of drinkable yogurt to pick up again. Let's remain patient and optimistic for when the weather warms up, and then we can see an increase in unit sales."

That statement got me thinking. For sure, cold weather is something we can't control, but there must be something we can do about to promote sales; we cannot lower our guard and wait it off without trying something. The sales team included many experienced salespeople who knew their jobs well and had a close relationship with store managers, so I began to ask questions, probing for fresh ideas. What follows is an exchange with the most veteran salesperson on the team:

Me: Have you talked to the store managers? What are they telling you about sales in general?

Salesperson: They say our yogurt drinkables category has been hit the hardest. However, other categories are doing fine, and in fact, some are showing nice sales increases.

Me: That's interesting; which categories are increasing?

Salesperson: Produce and dry goods are doing very well; it seems people are staying at home and cooking for the family.

Me: Is there a way we could capitalize on the trend of these two categories? Any ideas?

Salesperson: We could negotiate a temporary display in the produce section of high-volume stores and the headers of some dry goods aisles. We can place small coolers with doors and promotion displays. Fresh fruits go very well with drinkable yogurt to make a healthy dessert, and protein bars are a good match, too.

In the group discussion, someone exclaimed: That is good thinking! I can negotiate temporary spaces in the cashier lines to drive impulse purchases; if people still drink cold soda in this weather, they might as well like to try something healthy, like drinkable yogurt.

The energy in the room changed as everyone got excited and started sharing ideas on how to solve the problem. Instead of feeling helpless, the group took ownership of the problem and felt empowered to find solutions. What started as a drama about the cold weather became a collaborative brainstorming session, with salespeople sharing their ideas to tackle the challenge. Seeing how empowered they felt once they took responsibility for the problem and started developing creative solutions was inspiring.

Blaming external factors for our failures removes our power to change the situation. Instead, taking responsibility and focusing on what we can do to solve the problem will energize us to devise ideas to deal with it. Instead of being passive recipients of our circumstances, we become proactive problem-solvers, working towards finding a solution and driving positive change. This way, we take control of the situation and work towards finding a solution.

Why is ownership a crucial component of Stewardship in any organization? We don't know when the next crisis will come and can't control what will happen. The only thing we can control is our response to the challenge. When individuals take ownership of their problems, they are more likely to actively seek solutions instead of being bystanders who only watch and refuse to commit. Viktor Frankl, in his book "Man's Search for Meaning," beautifully summarizes the concept of ownership: "Everything can be taken from a man but one thing: the last of the human freedoms—to choose one's attitude in any given set of circumstances, to choose one's own way."[37] An organization that leverages its people's ownership will be empowered and better prepared to use its inventiveness to deal with any problems that come its way.

Supporting others' growth

To talk about this component, I will refer to sports once again. In teams, it is not uncommon to see teammates driven by a fierce competitive spirit, encouraging one another to improve their skills and perform to the best of their abilities; sometimes, they get very vocal. They are united in their goal to win, with the coach playing a crucial role in their training and game plan to achieve this objective. During the game, players work together to execute the team strategy and push themselves to execute well; they support each other to achieve their goals, always keeping the team's best interests in mind. By collaborating and urging each other to be their best, they can accomplish great things on the field and secure victory.

I want to share one example that illustrates the "Supporting Others' Growth" dynamic from Michael Jordan's Chicago Bulls of the 1990s. As we all know, Michael Jordan is one of the greatest basketball players in history. His accomplishments are still recognized worldwide by players and basketball fans alike. However, even with his exceptional talent, the Chicago Bulls could not win championships before 1991. From 1986 to 1989, the head coach, Doug Collins, implemented a game system where the team would pass the ball to Michael Jordan and trust that he would score and eventually bring the win. Unfortunately for them, although the team would advance and reach the finals, they could not beat their nemesis, the Detroit Pistons, to win the NBA championship.

On July 10, 1989, Phil Jackson became the new head coach of the Chicago Bulls, replacing Doug Collins. Jerry Krause, then Bulls' General Manager, hired Jackson hoping he could bring about a transformative change in the franchise that would lead to winning championships. Jackson's innovative playing system involved a "triangles" formation, which ensured that most players touched the ball. In the sports television documentary "The Last Dance," produced by ESPN Films and Netflix, several players, including Michael Jordan, talk about how the team benefited from the system and how it helped them grow individually and as a unit. Here are some quotes from Chicago Bulls players back when the new system was introduced:[38]

When players were introduced to the new system...

"**Scott Pippen**: He (Phil Jackson) brought a different approach to the game. Doug's approach was more catered to Michael, and Phil's approach was more catered to the team.

Michael Jordan: I wasn't a Jackson fan, you know, when he first came in, you know, because he was coming in take the ball out of my hands, Doug put the ball in my hands.

Phil Jackson (to Micheal Jordan): I don't anticipate you're going to be the scoring champion in the league. The spotlight is on the ball, and if you're always the guy that's going to have the ball, teams can generate a defense against that, which is what happened with the Pistons the last couple of years,

Michael Jordan: He (Phil Jackson) said I'm not worried about you, but we got to find a way to make everybody else better; we got to create other threats.

Phil Jackson: That special thing that has happened when the largest icon the NBA's ever had understands, "I don't have to have the ball in my hands all the time."

What happened when they help each other improve...

Michael Jordan: My energy started to gear toward my teammates and pushing them to excel.

Horace Grant: Michael forced the hand of a lot of the players to really dedicate themselves to off-season training like OK, we're going to spend the summer dedicated to this proposition, and we're not going to be runners up, we're going to be champions.

Horace Grant (referring to Michael Jordan): I see that screaming devil. You make a mistake; he's going to scream at you. It's going to belittle you. He demands almost perfection, and when you see your leader working extremely hard in practice, I feel like if I don't give it my all, I shouldn't be here.

Scott Pippen: He taught me how to stay in the gym, and he's got a lot of time and starting to build the confidence that I needed.

BJ Armstrong: More than any other player, Scotty benefited from playing with Michael Jordan because Scotty had this raw athletic ability, but what we didn't have was what Michael brought every day, which was to drive to be the very best every single day, the mental focus of the game.

BJ Armstrong: Being around Michael every day like that just brought it out of us; Scotty evolved, Horace evolved, and I evolved.

Scott Pippen: It was a great feeling. We matured in many ways, physically and mentally. It was time for us to become the top team in the game."

Before Phil Jackson's "triangle system," the team depended on what Michael Jordan could do himself to win games. However, after introducing the system, the players began playing as a cohesive unit, helping each other, and everybody grew their skills thanks to their effort and Michal Jordan's. Between the years of 1991 and 1998, the Chicago Bulls won a total of six NBA championships, cementing their place as a dynasty and one of the most legendary teams in the history of the sport.

From my experience with large organizations, I've noticed that the teamwork and collaboration seen in sports teams isn't always present. Personal agendas often take over, with people focusing solely on their own interests. The idea of helping others improve and the team spirit that goes along with it can be hard to find in established companies that have reached a plateau. As demonstrated by the Chicago Bulls, it's teams, not individual players, that win championships. Therefore, organizations need to make a concerted effort to promote and foster collaboration, high standards, and ambitious goals, while ensuring that everyone is genuinely dedicated to supporting others and offering help.

Why is it essential to support the growth of others in an organization? Even if a company has achieved success and gained customer loyalty, it risks becoming irrelevant if it doesn't continually improve. For a company to evolve, every team member must take responsibility for their own development and commit to helping others be their best. In organizations, teams are the key to developing a sustainable business model that consistently wins and stays ahead of customer needs, avoiding the trap of complacency.

Truth over Ego

As humans, we frequently assume that our decisions are guided by logic and a quest for truth. However, our emotions, usually subtle and unnoticed, significantly shape our thoughts and opinions and guide our decision-making. More frequently than we care to admit, we rationalize our feelings and use them as a foundation for our so-called logical reasoning. If we were to examine how we select a given path among the many alternatives we can choose from, we would discover that emotions and feelings have a more substantial influence than we recognize.

Even if our decision-making process turns out to be hazy and needs to be reviewed due to our emotions' interference and will never be entirely objective, it ends up being less harmful than what a false validation of our identity can produce. If upholding our identity gets in the way of our reasoning, our decision-making process will be based on what the sense of our worth is or should be. This can lead to distorted logic and a need to accommodate the pretended superiority that comes with hierarchy, accumulated experience, presumed foresight, or the need for respect.

Self-identity plays a significant role in our decision-making at work. Our desire to be seen as valuable and competent individuals can sometimes hinder our ability to make the best choices. Factors such as our position in the chain of command, academic background, or past achievements can lead to an inner struggle that prompts us to prioritize our ego over making the best decisions.

Although the ego is a natural part of human nature and is necessary to a certain degree to function well, it often doesn't align with the organization's best interests. Our tendency to protect our self-image can overshadow the pursuit of optimal solutions or opportunities. This tension between seeking truth and preserving our egos can ultimately harm the organization's performance. To address this, organizations should prioritize truth-seeking by selecting the best ideas regardless of their source and working to reduce the influence of egos, especially among those in leadership positions.

To better explain the concept of ego or its absence in business, let's consider a conversation mentioned by Kim Scott in her book "Radical Candor: Be a Kick-Ass Boss Without Losing Your Humanity." In the book, Scott recounts a discussion with Andy

Grove, the renowned CEO of Intel, about whether she should join Apple. This conversation illustrates how Steve Jobs handled the balance between truth and ego.

"**Andy Grove:** F*ing Steve always gets it right.

Kim Scott: I laughed, thinking he was making a joke.

Andy Grove: No, you didn't understand me. Steve always gets it right. I mean it precisely, like an engineer. I am not joking, and I am not exaggerating.

Kim Scott: Nobody is always right.

Andy Grove: I didn't say Steve is always right. I said he always gets it right. Like anyone, he is wrong sometimes, but he insists, and not gently either, that people tell him when he's wrong, so he always gets it right in the end."[39]

Grove explains in the conversation how Steve Jobs's ability to shift focus from "being right" to "getting it right" allowed him to make the best decisions to win in the market. This mind hack directs our attention towards finding the best solution, enhancing our sense of worth based on our ability to devise what solves a problem, even if the idea is not ours, rather than always needing to be correct and emerge as the hero. Under this concept, we will choose the most effective alternative by prioritizing getting it right over being right, regardless of who takes credit for the idea. This means adopting a different mindset driven by the goal of getting it right rather than seeking recognition and praise. Shifting from ego-driven validation to the fulfillment of achieving the best solution to the problem is what produces inner satisfaction.

Another take on the same idea comes from Ray Dalio, the founder of Bridgewater Associates, a billionaire investor and hedge fund manager. Dalio shares the following on resolving the Truth over Ego tension: "To be effective, you must not let your need to be right be more important than your need to find out what's true." and "I just want to be right—I don't care if the right answer comes from me. So I learned to be radically open-minded to allow others to point out what I might be missing."[40]

Why should truth be prioritized over ego in an organization? For an organization to operate effectively and meet the needs of its customers, it must be willing to pursue ideas that have the greatest chance of success. If leaders prioritize fulfilling their egos over implementing the best ideas, the organization will squander valuable resources, lose employee engagement, and risk losing talent. Therefore, it is vital to keep egos in check when navigating the challenges of the job and confronting uncertainty. Choosing truth over ego at all times is crucial and requires deliberate effort and continuous self-examination; it is an ongoing process that cannot be abandoned.

Psychological Safety

Before we begin this section, please take a moment to think about your experiences in meetings. Have you ever been in a meeting where you felt unsafe expressing your ideas? Or a meeting where you didn't feel included and felt like a piece of furniture in the room, with nobody noticing your presence? Or a meeting where you feared challenging the traditional way of doing things because you might be reprimanded for cutting against the grain? I bet you have. It's a common experience for many of us; it is unpleasant and de-energizes anyone involved. I am also going to bet that, besides being awkward, it was an unproductive team meeting because several good ideas were prevented from seeing the light of day. The open exchange of viewpoints was limited, and as a result, there were fewer ideas to consider. It was wasted potential.

Teams are the life and blood of companies; they drive results, and their dynamics are essential for competing and winning in today's business environment. Psychological safety refers to the necessary conditions that enable teams to work well by encouraging the free exchange of ideas to advance the organization's goals. Timothy R. Clark, author of the book "The 4 Stages of Psychological Safety," underlines the importance of psychological safety in the following terms: "Organizations that lack psychological safety and compete in highly dynamic markets are galloping their way to extinction."[41]

In chapter four of this book, when we explored the Talent dimension, I briefly explained psychological safety as a condition to help individuals "connect and extend". Now is time to highlight its importance in stewarding groups of people to achieve their best and build the foundation upon which all stewardship must be conducted.

Fostering psychological safety within an organization goes beyond explaining and understanding the concept. It requires a deliberate effort to integrate it into the everyday interactions and practices of the workplace. We can harness its potential benefits by making psychological safety the platform of the organizational culture. This means encouraging open communication and valuing diverse perspectives so that individuals exchange ideas freely. When psychological safety becomes ingrained in the fabric of our operations, everyone can feel empowered to contribute their best, ultimately leading to improved teamwork, innovation, and overall organizational success.

How does this look in practice? In meetings, if you are the team's steward, you must ask for the opinion of someone outside your direct line or report whenever you have a chance. You must prompt individuals who stay quiet to participate. Ask follow-up questions like 'Tell me more' or 'How do you see this impacting our team's goals?' Be the last to offer an opinion, and do so after the team has had the opportunity to express their views. This fosters inclusivity and diverse perspectives, encourages deeper discussion, and ensures everyone's voice is heard, contributing to more well-rounded decision-making. Amy C. Edmondson, a Professor of Leadership at Harvard Business School and author of the book "The Fearless Organization" put it in the following terms: "It's not sufficient for organizations to merely hire talented individuals. If leaders want to unleash individual and collective talent, they must cultivate a psychologically safe environment where employees feel comfortable contributing ideas, sharing information, and reporting mistakes."[42]

The significance of psychological Safety in organizations cannot be emphasized enough. It's not just a good business practice; it's a necessity. However, I've noticed that traditional, old-school settings often overlook this crucial aspect. The hierarchical nature of bosses or individuals who believe they know everything in the organization must give way to this new way of interacting. If they do so, the benefits for the organization will not just be significant; they will be game-changing.

CHAPTER 6

Mindset

*"The view you adopt for yourself profoundly
affects the way you lead your life."*
—CAROL DWECK

*"You can't start a fire / You can't
start a fire without a spark."*
—BRUCE SPRINGSTEEN

*"I would say consistent discipline has been one of those
Prodigy-like strengths that I had... I did have something
inside of me that no one could see from the outside, this
level of discipline that I could accomplish something that
was really important and really special."*
—TOM BRADY

W hile working at the CPG company I mentioned, I
had the opportunity to serve as a senior manager for
several years, overseeing the northwest region of my

company's supermarket channel, where a major supermarket chain was headquartered. My duties included managing my company's sales relationship and implementing growth initiatives with this client. At the time, the supermarket chain had approximately 120 stores, most of which were large formats, and they were a very important retail operation in the region, accounting for 40% of the region's revenue and with good profitability levels. To boost sales, I teamed up with the chain's purchasing manager to create an ambitious promotion to sell my company's products, offering cashback to the chain if they achieved a specific sales target. After a few weeks, the promotion ended, but the sales target was not met; it fell short by about 20%. I was summoned for a meeting with the supermarket's purchasing manager to review the promotion results. She was known for being tough and having a fiery personality, but she was also fair, and we had a good working relationship. This is what happened in the meeting.

Me: We evaluated the promotion at the company, and it went reasonably well. Unfortunately, we did not reach the agreed sales target, so we will not award you a cashback.

Purchasing Manager: We did our part, and it was your fault if the sales were not reached. I want my cashback, no excuses.

Me: I don't know what you are talking about. Why do you think it is our fault? Your stores operate the sales floor, not us, and you had enough products to sell at competitive prices. The fact is that there wasn't enough customer traffic and the displays in the stores communicating the promotion were badly placed, that is why we did not reach the sales target.

Purchasing Manager: That is not true. Your company ran attractive promotions with my competitors simultaneously, leading to low store traffic. You created this mess; I want my cashback now! (raising her voice)

Me: But your competitors had different products, the promotion in your stores was custom-made to fit your customers' needs. You were very happy and approved the assortment we suggested. Sorry, but it does not make sense to award a cashback if you did not comply with your end of the deal.

Purchasing Manager: Say whatever you want. I want my money, and I don't accept any excuses! (She smashed the table with her fist.) We will delist your products from our supermarkets if you don't! I want my money!

The conversation became heated and intense, quickly reaching a dead end. I was on the verge of losing my temper, and it crossed my mind to yell at her and tell her I didn't care if she delisted my company's products. She had not honored our agreement, and she was extremely rude. If a major conflict was inevitable, I felt that I could explain the situation to my bosses, and they would understand if I decided to end the relationship with the client. However, something about her behavior seemed off. I sensed she was not telling me something, and her demeanor was unlike anything I had seen before. While I was very upset, I felt I needed more information before walking away from the table. Ending the relationship with a client is a critical decision, and I wanted to be fully prepared if that was the necessary course of action.

To gain some time, I pretended to receive a phone call and asked her for a few minutes to take it. I left the office, took a deep breath, and tried to collect my thoughts. I was convinced I was correct; there was no valid justification for her falling short of the goal and expecting to receive the cashback. If I were to accept her demand, it would set a terrible precedent for our relationship. However, I also felt something was hidden that I wasn't considering. At this point, my focus was not solely on winning the argument but on solving the problem and maintaining the relationship. Upon returning to the room, I asked her:

Me: Do you agree that trust is an indispensable part of any relationship and vital to our collaboration to grow sales and create value?

Purchasing Manager: Yes, I do, and you broke our trust by not supporting us in the promotion.

Me: It appears that we have strongly opposing views on this issue and have reached an impasse. While we both agree that maintaining trust is crucial for our collaboration, there seems to be no solution to this dilemma that wouldn't result in one party losing trust. We need to find the most fair way to resolve this deadlock.

Purchasing Manager: And how can this happen?

Me: Let the higher powers decide for us. We will accept whatever they choose, even if it does not serve our particular interests.

Purchasing Manager: Higher powers? What are you talking about? Are you crazy?

Me: Let's do a coin toss, and luck will decide for us. If the coin lands on heads, you win, and I'll pay the cashback. If it lands on tails, I will not pay. We don't need to agree on who is right or wrong; the higher power will choose. But you must accept that this is the only time we will call the higher powers to break a tie between us. What do you say? Are you on?

At this moment, the Purchasing manager got visibly nervous. She stood up from her chair, stumbled, started rubbing her hands, and rapidly closed the curtains of her office.

Purchasing Manager: Okay, let's do it. But we need a trial toss first; it's just for practice and does not count. Okay?

She nervously opened her purse, took out the largest coin she could find, and kissed it. She asked me if I was ready, and I nodded. She crossed herself with the coin, blew air, and flipped it. It was tails!

Purchasing Manager: Wait, wait. Remember, this flip was a trial. I am just warming up. The next one is for real. She kissed the coin again, crossed herself with it, and flipped it again. It was heads. She won!

She jumped all over the place, held her arms high, and screamed, "I won! I won!" She couldn't be happier, and she even hugged me at some point. She immediately produced a note with the cashback amount for me to sign, and I signed it. I congratulated her and told her that while she won the coin toss, I needed help to figure out how to increase our business because now I had a problem. She responded that we could plan something and agreed to a later call to talk about it. She dismissed me, and I left the office. Although I lost the coin toss, I felt that the game was not over and that I would have more opportunities.

A few days after the coin toss, a colleague from the company, who knew people who work at purchasing in the supermarket chain, shared some interesting information with me. A week before our meeting to review the promotion results, the supermarket's purchasing department underwent an organizational change. The Purchasing Manager now reported to a new boss, who was determined to make a strong impression. The new boss was angry with her for not meeting the sales targets to qualify for cashback. Despite her explanations, he threatened to fire her on the spot. He made it clear that if she didn't secure the cashback from me, she would lose her job. She was in a desperate situation as she was the sole provider for her family and couldn't afford to lose her job.

Unbeknownst to me, by proposing the coin toss to break the tie, I allowed her to save her job. She now had an opportunity to get the cashback, and she was lucky to get it. She never told me, but I heard she was very grateful because I devised an unusual solution that helped us both save face and continue our working relationship.

When I exited the room for a few minutes, pretending I received a phone call, I regrouped mentally and cleared my thinking instead of breathing my fumes and figuring out how to retaliate. I took perspective and tried to look beyond the obvious to see the whole picture and find out what was missing, even though I didn't know the entire story about her boss then. I believed I was justified in sticking to my position and not granting the cashback because we had an agreement and she didn't fulfill her end of the deal. However, I was open to finding a better way to handle a complex situation. The coin toss gave me a 50% chance of winning without having to give in, which seemed like a reasonable option given the circumstances. It was also an opportunity for her to get away with a win without meeting her part in the agreement. When I asked the question about trust and what needed to happen for us to succeed, I hoped to take us both out of the narrow focus of the exchange and wished she would reveal something that could help me expand the playing field and look for a solution. Fortunately, she engaged, and by letting the "higher powers" break the tie, we found a path to work together, albeit it was unusual.

We built a profitable business relationship that lasted many years, and a few months later, I recuperated the cashback with other promotions. Questioning my beliefs, dealing with high-stakes emotions, and making sense of the big picture were instrumental to my finding a way out of the deadlock. I enhanced my mindset and came out winning in the long run.

Decoding the mind's blueprint

The concept of mindset originated in psychology and describes individuals' various mental settings and ways of thinking. Over the past few decades, the idea of mindset has gained popularity in the business world due to its usefulness in describing intangible mental stances that, when expressed as behaviors, have the potential to create value in organizations.

Let's double-click on the meaning of the term, What is a Mindset? Mindset is a mental frame, a lens through which we see and make sense of the world. Such a mental frame is constituted by beliefs, codified experiences, values, biases, etc., arranged in a certain way to help us deal with reality. We need a mindset to help us simplify a complex environment because we cannot process all the information we receive at once through our senses. Hence, we need a frame to filter data and use the proper information to help us make decisions. For instance, to conclude that it is likely to rain, we don't need to mentally compute the environment's barometric pressure, humidity, wind speed, etc., at every moment. If we see thunderstorms and dark clouds coming our way, we can confidently say it will likely rain. This is based on previous experiences that helped us build a mental representation that asserts thunderstorms + dark clouds = rain. We use these mental equivalences in our daily interactions to make sense of what is happening around us and react accordingly. By definition, a mindset is personal, although some elements can be shared with many individuals and thus become common traits.

A particular mindset configuration will nudge a series of behaviors congruent with that view of the world. For example, if we hold a scarcity mindset, we will demonstrate frugal, prudent behaviors that reflect this mentality and, consequently, avoid spending beyond our means. A scarcity mindset will block us from even considering behaviors others may find normal, like purchasing full-price clothes or splurging on a nice dinner on a special occasion. The logic behind designing and implementing specific mindsets in organizations is that such a mental frame will translate into shared behaviors that can advance achieving the desired results.

In Chapter Three, I emphasized that we are in the mindset business and that the organization's mindset is our playing field. Therefore, the success of our efforts to regrow through transformation will depend on how effectively we position the ideas and beliefs that support the organization's goals in our people's minds and encourage behaviors that will make these goals a reality. We should not underestimate the importance of mindset development; it is a complex endeavor that will help individuals at companies make sounder decisions. We should give as much attention to designing the desired shared mindset in an organization as we typically do with talent density and culture initiatives. Most importantly, we must ensure that the entire talent density, culture, and mindset framework is articulated as a coherent system that creates a self-reinforcing loop. Unleashing the organization's potential at scale requires setting a flywheel in motion that influences the ways of thinking and acting of our constituents and achieves a compounded effect by aligning everyone in the same direction.

As much as we may want to shape mindsets across the board, permeating the whole organization, it is critical to recognize that the decision to embrace an idea and implement it is always a personal choice. While the collective mindset happens at a larger scale, it still depends on the individual's commitment to follow through. Adopting new beliefs and ideas at the individual level is not straightforward; it's a complex process influenced by personal experiences, biases, social interactions, and the organization's specific context. This complexity makes the mindset business messy and tricky, requiring a long-term commitment to make it a reality.

What you think, you become

The heading of this section is a quote attributed to Buddha, and the whole citation is the following: "The mind is everything; what you think, you become." I like this quote because it reflects how mindsets not only scaffold our thinking but are an intangible source that informs our actions and eventually shapes our identity. Our thinking is the force that makes sense of the world and sets boundaries to what we can achieve; therefore, it is a valve that unlocks or limits our potential. How we signify previous experiences and beliefs is critical to future success for any given task; it will provide us with a go or no-go signal and calibrate our efforts. Suppose we deem the goal we want to pursue too ambitious, and we will come short in its achievement. In that case, we may relinquish it or lower the bar, or maybe we can go the other way, decide it is worth pursuing, and challenge ourselves to go for it even if it looks like a long shot. Our thinking assesses and decides using our self developed mental frames. As Henry Ford said, "Whether you think you can or you think you can't, you are right." The takeaway is that upholding an appropriate mindset is the first step to becoming all you can be. It is a necessary condition for any organization or individual to rise to its potential.

It is worth noting that mindsets do not just happen to us; we are both the authors and the actors playing a role based on a set of learned beliefs. Those beliefs become our internal compass and roadmap to solve problems, undertake opportunities, and evaluate our performance. The best analogy I can find to illustrate this condition is that of software. At the mindset level, we are simultaneously the coders of the program and the operating system that executes the instructions, and we are also responsible for debugging it when it does not work well.

Ideally, we should deliberately evaluate our mindset to determine if it is delivering the expected value for us, and if it is not, we must change it and improve it. To access our mindset, we must look "under the hood" and examine the structure of our thinking to evaluate the beliefs, biases, values, etc., that support it. When the software gets stuck, that is when our beliefs compromise our desired performance; we must roll out our sleeves and debug the program or rewrite it. We must let go of beliefs that do not benefit us because they cannot simply be tweaked; they must be replaced with new ones that can serve us better. Debugging our mindset is difficult because we are accustomed to a particular way of thinking and have a vested interest in maintaining it. It's like performing surgery on ourselves; it's tough to rearrange or remove what doesn't work in our minds, but who will if we don't do it? Improving our mindset requires serious self-assessment, clarity, rigor, and discipline. You are responsible for your thought processes and must be prepared and willing to decide when to change.

The situation becomes interesting when an organization wants people to adopt specific mindsets and beliefs to encourage certain behaviors. As we discussed earlier, the process of adopting or letting go of beliefs is personal, so it is always challenging to implement this at a large scale. To accomplish the goal, we require, first and foremost, the willingness of our people to incorporate or substitute beliefs and adopt a mindset. The process follows a similar pattern to the one we reviewed in culture in Chapter Five; leaders must be role models to advance the adoption. However, we must pull an additional lever to facilitate the task; it is a significant factor for success and entails replenishing the source that will feed the process to its completion.

Energy x direction

"In physics, we learned that energy is finite. It's not true in human dynamics. Energy is something you create out of nothing."—Hubert Jolly

When you try to get the organization to embrace new beliefs or mindsets, you can rest assured that you will inevitably face internal barriers and pushback from many of your constituents. The resistance level will be directly proportional to the scale of the change: the more significant the change, the more effort it will take for people to adapt, and consequently, the more resistance you'll face. You know what I mean if you have been part of a change initiative in an organization. It can be frustrating because getting everything to go as planned is tough, especially when trying to get people on board with something new. You have to understand that the adoption process will involve ups and downs and will often hit frustrating roadblocks that may make it feel like no progress is being made. It can be painful and tiring, but that's how it is.

The diversity of perspectives among participants and the inherent complexity of groups are important factors that contribute to this problem. People are unique and not all the same. However, another reason for the stall, perhaps even more critical than the diversity of perspectives, explains the difficulty in adopting beliefs and mindsets on a large scale. The heart of the problem lies in energy availability. The change process requires significant mental and physical energy from members of the organization, and the sourcing and replenishment of that energy is a critical factor for success.

When I talk about having the necessary energy for change to happen, I am not only referring to the mechanical energy needed to go about fulfilling daily duties (which is the energy required to perform) but also the mental energy that pushes the "will of a group" forward to overcome the natural friction and obstacles entailed in a transformation process. When designing the plan for the organization to transform and perform in a new way, we must contemplate the stream of fuel required to feed the process; that is, we need to consider the initial mental fueling to get started and the many subsequent mental refuelings necessary to recharge the people's inward sources of energy and catalyze them towards the attainment of the objectives. The organization's intentional, voluntary energy renewal is crucial for embracing the desired beliefs and mindsets. Based on my experience, when cultivating energy within the organization, it is always better to exceed the required amount than risk falling short. The more energy you can generate within the system to drive the transformation forward, the greater the likelihood of success.

Let's pause to double-click on the energy sourcing challenge. I just asserted that, in a transformation process, organizations consume lots of energy and must plan for its availability until the end. You do not want to run out of gas before the work is done. But what kind of energy do you need? Where does the energy required to transform come from? How can we generate it sustainably?

The reason behind the planned transformation is the driving force that will fuel the change process. If we want to encourage the adoption of new beliefs and mindsets, we must ensure that our people fully embrace the "why" and make it their own. Doing this will generate the resilience needed to persist and ensure that everyone is wholly aligned and committed while navigating the challenging path of transformation. Unbeknownst to us, there is a boundless reserve of energy within the organization waiting to be harnessed, and it is up to us to unleash it and convert it into action. This energy reserve stems from the ideas and mental images of individuals and the organization's aspirations, which we can unlock with the "why" of change. When the "why" of change resonates with people, it becomes the source that empowers its members to excel in pursuit of a meaningful vision.

The big "why" of the organization is articulated by its purpose, which, as discussed in the culture chapter of this book, states the reason for its existence beyond making money and signals a path to follow in the pursuit of greatness and the service of others. The purpose is the compass that aligns everybody in the organization to accomplish a worthy goal. But I will suggest that no matter how powerful the purpose of the organization might be, it is not enough to source all the energy we will eventually need in a transformation; we must complement it with additional levers to scaffold its pull and accelerate the thrust required for the adoption of beliefs and mindsets. Let's take a closer look at this idea.

The "purpose" of an organization is composed of a "noble" aspiration and a positive vision of success that its people can use as a reference to strive for the end goal. To illustrate its workings, let's take, for example, Microsoft's purpose: *"To empower every person and organization on this planet to achieve more."* This purpose establishes a hopeful goal to inspire and guide the organization to help others become more productive and reach their goals. It is a worthy vision; the motivation for Microsoft's people lies in the satisfaction and pride of assisting others to improve, gain an edge, and perform better to fulfill their life's objectives. While Microsoft's purpose statement helps align its people, we must ask ourselves if it alone generates enough energy to motivate them to advance through thick and thin and overcome the challenges they will inevitably face. I advocate that we must explore further what else we can do to enhance the energy emanating from the purpose statement that will fire up the organization.

Science provides a solid foundation to help us in the quest to amplify organizational energy resources and prompt action. Research demonstrates that people tend to be more influenced by messages highlighting potential losses than those focusing on potential gains. The fear of losing is a powerful force and substantially impacts behavior more than the promise of gaining something. Jimmy Connors, the number one tennis player of his time, is attributed to have said: "I hate losing more than I love winning," which is a colloquial way to express the concept of loss aversion. Daniel Kahneman and Amos Tversky explored the ramifications of loss aversion in their "Prospect Theory" and won a Nobel Prize in Economics in 2002 for their contributions to behavioral economics. They discovered that losses loom larger than gains in making decisions and undertaking corresponding actions. In any given situation, we are more likely to be motivated by avoiding a loss than by a potential benefit to be gained. There is even an estimate of how much more powerful loss avoidance is compared to gain seeking in human behavior: "We are roughly 2.5 times more sensitive to losses than we are to gains of similar size. A message framed as a potential loss might, therefore, be more persuasive."[1]

Using the lens of energy creation to mobilize an organization, and based on the "Prospect Theory" logic, I suggest that we complement the purpose statement with messages around loss avoidance that can produce higher energy in the organization than those pursuing a positive, gain-oriented objective. The idea is to use targeted loss avoidance affirmations consistent with the core idea contained in the purpose, to scaffold it, create tension and contrast, leverage the discomfort they cause, and ultimately motivate our people to change.

Loss aversion messages can evoke emotions and even distress that we can use to our advantage, but we must be careful not to provoke anger or rage. If we can harness these emotions effectively, we will have significant energy to drive our transformation efforts. However, if we take it too far, we risk opening a genie's bottle and unleashing uncontrollable forces. The aim is to use these loss aversion messages sparingly to cultivate a sense of justified or virtuous anger to strengthen the company's purpose.

To show how we can use loss aversion to scaffold the purpose and boost energy levels in the organization, let us revisit Microsoft's purpose: *"To empower every person and organization on this planet to achieve more."* In the journey to achieve this aspiration, Microsoft will have to deal with many barriers that can compromise its accomplishment, among them intense competition from prominent established players, unlawful copycat products, unfair regulatory conditions in some countries, restrictions in trade due to its high market share, inequitable business practices, cybersecurity threats, etc. Although Microsoft's purpose statement motivates its people to overcome these barriers, we could strengthen the proposition with complementary messaging and use targeted "loss aversion rallying calls" to increase energy and prime the organization to deal with these barriers more intensely.

Here are some "loss aversion rallying calls" that deal with the identified barriers in Microsft's example and that the company could use to build up the energy level:

For intense competition: "We must engage vigorously in the competitive business landscape to safeguard our company's prosperity and the welfare of our people, ensuring we consistently earn and maintain our customers' loyalty."

For unlawful copycat products: "Safeguarding the integrity of our innovation is critical. Failure to do so jeopardizes our ability to deliver the high-quality, safe products that our consumers rightfully expect and deserve."

For cybersecurity threats: "We are currently under siege from internet intruders who are attempting to hold our company hostage, posing a significant threat to our survival. It is imperative that we take immediate action to thwart these attacks and safeguard our operations."

Well-directed anger can be a powerful energy source; we are "righting a wrong" to serve the company's higher purpose, and these emotions play a role. By channeling our anger toward addressing injustices and serving our company's higher purpose, we can use it as a driving force for action. These feelings are also present when we are facing a crisis. Winston Churchill is often quoted as saying, "Never let a good crisis go to waste." We all know that critical moments are opportunities to bring out our best. Righteous anger is a valuable tool for generating energy and direction and unlocking organizational potential. Still, we must be careful when using it as a catalyst because anger is an emotion that can lead to hostility or bring out the worst in us. Do not unleash anger; instead, channel it constructively with a positive tone in service of a worthy goal to take advantage of its benefits.

The evidence of things not seen

When asked about the secret to his success, Jim Carrey, the Canadian-American actor, and comedian who has made several blockbuster movies that have gained recognition worldwide, commonly replies that it is due to his faith in himself to create the reality he wants. He famously said, "Faith is better than hope," underscoring the nature of relentless faith as a driver to accomplish your goals over having the wish for things to happen the way you want.

Carrey's thoughts about having faith in ourselves have resonated profoundly with me. I believe it will with you, too, because they convey that faith in oneself is a prerequisite for initiating positive change and progress in our lives, setting a system in motion to be focused, take action, and turn things around to reach our full potential. Faith in oneself encourages us to trust our capabilities and persevere in pursuing our goals.

When we have faith in ourselves, we are better suited to adopt empowering beliefs, build the confidence needed to overcome challenges, and maintain the determination to keep moving forward, even when there is no evidence that we can achieve our goals. Faith nurtures a positive attitude to life, and while it can be said that it is not grounded in facts and, therefore, may be wishful thinking, I will argue that it is an essential component to any transformation, whether at the organizational or the individual level. Faith paves the way for becoming all we can be, and we must use it as a lever to guide our path to growth.

When you examine what has driven the most remarkable accomplishments in human history, you will find that faith has always been present. Take the late United Kingdom's Prime Minister Winston Churchill, one of the best examples of someone who had unwavering faith in himself and his ability to succeed against the most incredible odds. What he accomplished by leading the United Kingdom through victory during World War II is unbelievable. He not only leveraged his faith to stay put during the difficult times but was able to transmit his faith to the United Kingdom's population at large, which explained why they could withstand the many hardships that preceded their final victory over the Germans.

The late Steve Jobs was also a firm believer in the power of faith and trusting oneself. At Stanford's commencement speech in 2005, he said, "Sometimes life hits you in the head with a brick. Don't lose faith" or "Have the courage to follow your heart and intuition. They somehow already know what you truly want to become. Everything else is secondary." Understanding and harnessing faith can be a complex matter. It may seem counterintuitive initially, as we often encounter irrational expectations leading to unproductive outcomes. However, we can also find many examples where seemingly unattainable goals were achieved due to unwavering self-belief.

Two stories of outstanding individuals who have leveraged faith have deeply inspired me. I would like to share them to further probe into the concept of faith. One belongs to the sports world, with Tom Brady, and the other to the business arena, with Ben Horowitz.

In the book "The Dynasty," Jeff Benedict relates the story of the Patriots' football organization and how it became one of the most lauded teams in the sport's history. Benedict shares a sneak peek of Tom Brady's mindset and the beliefs that have made him a legendary quarterback. I think we can all agree that Brady has always shown an unwavering faith in himself and believes in achieving his goals through a relentless work ethic. In the book, Tom Brady elaborates on his approach to football in the following statement: "In the end, my life is focused around football. It always has been. It always will be, as long as I'm playing. I've given my body —everything, every bit of energy—for eighteen years to it. So if you're going to compete against me, you better be ready to give up your life. Because I am giving up mine."[2]

If we look inside Tom Brady's mindset and examine the structure of the network of beliefs that support it, we can see how his identity is intertwined with football. For him, football is not just a job; it's a way of life. Brady's mindset would show that discipline and his unwavering attitude to give his best are essential elements to becoming the best player he could be. He strongly believes in continuous improvement and is committed to his craft, upholding unconditional accountability, making no excuses, and fully dedicating himself to achieving his best version. Most importantly, we will see how Tom Brady's faith in himself constitutes the backbone that builds the foundation for his mindset and belief system; it is the key to becoming an extraordinarily competitive player.

Brady's exceptional performance drove him to achieve impressive results, indirectly influencing the team. His unwavering faith was contagious to his teammates, inspiring them to believe in themselves and adopt similar mindsets and beliefs. This cumulative impact of shared faith and mindsets, accompanied by their skills, propelled the Patriots to eleven Super Bowl appearances and six wins. I am convinced that Tom Brady could not have accomplished unprecedented success in professional football without faith in himself.

The other case of faith driving exceptional performance that I want to share belongs to the business world. It showcases Ben Horowitz, the cofounder and general partner of Andreessen Horowitz, a venture capital firm founded in 2009 with assets of 42 billion dollars as of May 2024. In his book "The hard thing about hard things." Ben shares his personal experiences on founding and scaling startups and elaborates on the specific trait that has served him well during challenging times: "People always ask me, `What's the secret to being a successful CEO?` Sadly, there is no secret, but there is one skill that stands out, it's the ability to focus and make the best move when there are no good moves. It's the moments where you feel most like hiding or dying that can make the highest difference as a CEO."[3]

Ben Horowitz's mindset as a founder is firmly rooted in the faith that he can overcome adversity. He believes there is always a way out of a crisis, no matter how severe it may appear. Even when everything seems lost and there's nothing more you can do, he believes you can find an alternative approach to help move the company forward. Ben Horowitz is known for facing the brutal facts head-on, never sugarcoating reality. He obsessively prepares for the direst circumstances and believes that insecurity is the path to security.

Keeping an alert mind and expecting the worst will prepare you to deal with an unforeseen crisis. If you think your company is vulnerable and can fail at any moment, you will be on the lookout to face your most pressing problems and fix them to survive. You must have faith in your capacity to face and overcome difficulties. In the startup industry, 95% of new businesses will fail, and only 5% will succeed. When managing a startup, the odds are against you, even if you make sound decisions. A mindset for overcoming adversity is essential to survive in this line of business. The faith Horowitz holds in himself helps him solve problems, permeates the rest of the startup organization, and generates the conviction to strive to live one day at a time when everything appears bleak.

Faith binds your mind

Faith plays an essential role in shaping your mindset. It generates a cohesive system that binds your mind, which helps you process what happens to you and your response. Faith anchors and strengthens your belief system and feeds the energy required for you to move forward and face your challenges.

Faith, or the lack thereof, is crucial in facing life's "make it or break it" situations. It forms the foundation for building our character and achieving our potential. However, scaling faith in an organization presents a significant challenge. You cannot improvise faith; you cannot spread faith without a genuine, honest proposition. Even then, it will not stand if it doesn't manifest daily by its constituents, which implies that those in authority must demonstrate faith and express it when leading others. Despite appearing fuzzy and difficult to bring about, faith is a necessary platform for people to become all they can be and accomplish the seemingly impossible. Faith is a driving force that propels individuals to strive for greatness.

Determinants of Mindset

I must begin this section with a disclaimer because if there is a section in this book where I will oversimplify a very complex topic, this is the one. I want to come out clean from the get-go because I will use broad, general ideas and be superficial in describing a very profound subject. The mind is a deep and complex matter; I do not intend to produce new concepts or revolutionary insights into its inner workings. Instead, I will use available information from subject matter experts, together with my experience with mindset development in organizations, to present the case for the actionable things you can do to leverage the potential of your people, help them become whatever they want to be, and help the company reach its goals. I aim to explore each mindset determinant and deepen the understanding of its essential components to jumpstart ourselves and our people into a self-enhancement path.

Mindset is the last dimension of the Aspen Root Framework and consists of three determinants: Identity, perspective-taking, and agency. As with Talent Density and Culture, these three mindset determinants feed into each other, strengthening the system and producing a reinforcing loop that helps convert thinking into action and action into thinking. I recognize that these determinants are an arbitrary categorization since the mind is a whole that cannot be compartmentalized; I intend to treat these determinants as different windows looking into the same house so we can focus our efforts on the actionable levers that heighten potential at scale in the organization.

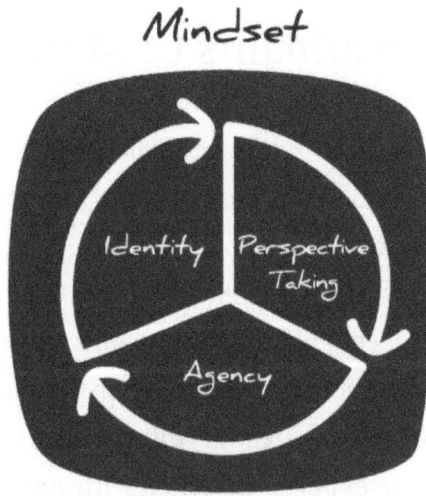

Identity

Think of identity as the determinant that encapsulates the sense of who we are, our personal view of the world, and how we fit in it. Our identity is essential because it articulates the information about ourselves that resides in our minds and comprises the settings that assess how we see ourselves, what we believe we can achieve, and what we think we are capable of doing. The limitations of what we can achieve are based mainly on the stories we tell ourselves rather than being rooted in hard facts or undeniable evidence; they represent learned convictions or ideas we have acquired throughout our lives. The limits to our potential are not set in stone and can, therefore, be changed.

Our identity is a complex interplay of experiences, both big and small, that shape our thoughts, beliefs, and behaviors. From major life events to everyday interactions, each experience imprints on our conscious and unconscious minds, influencing how we perceive the world and make decisions.

This resulting mindset serves as the lens through which we interpret new experiences and navigate our interactions. Our thoughts and beliefs inform our actions, and at the same time, our actions shape and reinforce our mindset. It's not a one-time process but a continuous feedback loop in which our internal state affects our external behavior, and our external experiences influence our internal state.

In describing the personality of individuals, there is a widely used model you are probably familiar with called the iceberg model. The visible portion of the iceberg is what you can see above the surface, but it is only a tiny part of the whole. The image of the iceberg shows us that what you can observe in the behavior of a person in day-to-day activities is only a fraction of his whole, which is what is referred to as the "tip of the iceberg," the portion above the surface. Still, the majority of the weight of the iceberg lies below the surface, which constitutes the mass that must be moved for the iceberg to advance. In that large body of ice, you find the person's mind structure, which encompasses the values, beliefs, and mental models that give shape to the person's identity and actions; the deeper you go into that mass, alas, the mind, the broader and heavier it gets. In this section, I will attempt to make visible portions of the iceberg that are vital for the mobilization of the organization and the liberation of its potential.

I) Mental Models

The majority of the territory comprised in the area of what "lies below the surface" in our minds and that gives shape to our identity, is unknown or undisputed by us. Our mind is virtually uncharted territory, and given its influence in determining our behaviors, we should better understand its nature. In our minds, we can find the self-imposed restrictions that explain the outcomes of our daily lives and work.

The range of possibilities that set the boundaries of our performance is closely tied to the mental models we employ to interpret and understand the world. As discussed earlier in this chapter, mental models shape our perceptions and guide our decision-making process. Mental models are the "cognitive shortcuts" that we commonly employ to establish a view and perspective of how reality works. We utilize them all the time, and they rarely are questioned or updated to integrate new information. "Mental models can be simple generalizations such as "people are untrustworthy," or they can be complex theories, such as my assumptions about why members of my family interact as they do."[4]

In his book "The Fifth Discipline," Peter Senge introduced the concept of mental models in the 1990s to create awareness of these representations and to improve the quality of conversations in organizations. Mental models are very useful in dealing with assumptions and limiting beliefs held in individuals and teams; being aware of them nurtures a healthy reflection on the ideas we hold as being true and helps us examine their validity as conditions change. Peter Senge's work continues to be relevant to this day and, in my opinion, is essential to leverage people's potential at scale in organizations: "The problems with mental models arise when they become implicit—when they exist below the level of our awareness."[5]

Understanding the concept of mental models helps us analyze the structure of our thoughts. It enables us to consider different viewpoints to solve problems or take advantage of opportunities. This introspection can be a game-changer, providing new insights and driving innovation in a business environment. A prime example of challenging mental models and the associated limiting beliefs can be found in Elon Musk's SpaceX Company. Elon Musk aims to make the human species multi-planetary and establish a colony on Mars. To achieve this vision, he founded SpaceX to make space travel viable and affordable. Recognizing that high costs impeded the industry's growth due to single-use spacecraft, Musk focused on reusing space launch vehicles and ensuring their safe return to Earth's atmosphere.

The prevailing assumption when Musk evaluated the problem was that rockets could not be reused because their sustained damage was not repairable. Above all, the industry's mental model was that of risk mitigation and safety. However, Elon Musk did not have it; he believed there was a way to maintain the highest safety level and simultaneously reduce operation costs, and he challenged the mental model of space transportation of his time: "Like many old science fiction stories, Musk imagined a rocket turning around and slowing down by firing its engine, softly landing. No violent reentry furnace, charring the outside of the vehicle. The process could be automated—no necessary human to fly it."[6]

We are now used to watching SpaceX rockets gently reenter the earth's atmosphere and safely land on platforms in the middle of the sea. But this was unimaginable just a few years ago; Musk refused to be limited by the accepted safety mental model and was able to significantly reduce the costs of space travel: "By 2018, the Falcon 9's cost per pound into low-Earth orbit was twenty-three times cheaper than the old space shuttle."[7]

The takeaway from SpaceX's story is that organizations and their people must relentlessly challenge their mental models, questioning the customary way of doing things all the time. SpaceX shattered long-standing industry norms by reimagining space travel, pioneering reusable rockets, and revolutionizing how we envision space exploration. This demonstrates the profound potential of challenging preconceived notions and daring to rewrite the rules. It is the only way to solve gnarly problems and pursue Regrowth, especially in difficult-to-differentiate markets.

In defying our mental models, we assume an identity that refuses to accept restrictions and is rooted in the fundamental belief that things don't have to be as they always have been. We must adopt an unrestrained persona to rise to our potential. This shift in mindset allows us to become the architects of our destiny, driving us to seek unconventional solutions and carve out new paths to success. Let me unpack this idea further.

II) Growth mindset

"A simple belief about yourself—a belief we discovered in our research—guides a large part of your life. In fact, it permeates every part of your life. Much of what you think of as your personality actually grows out of this "mindset". Much of what may be preventing you from fulfilling your potential grows out of it". —Carol Dweck.[8]

As a young researcher in the 1970s, Carol Dweck was obsessed with understanding how people cope with failure, and to probe into this, she turned to studying how students grapple with hard problems. She noticed some students thrived with challenges, while others perceived them as threats to their worth and tried to avoid them. Her research findings established that students can hold two opposing positions while facing a challenge: believing that their human qualities are carved in stone, their "factory settings" are all they've got to solve problems, and there's nothing they can do about it. Or that their human qualities can be cultivated, that with effort, new strategies, and help from others, they can develop abilities and skills they do not currently possess or improve over what they already have, and that they can deal with whatever life presents to them. She named the first end of the spectrum "Fixed Mindset" and the other end "Growth Mindset": "Individuals who believe their talents can be developed (through hard work, good strategies, and input from others) have a growth mindset. They tend to achieve more than those with a more fixed mindset (those who believe their talents are innate gifts)."[9]

Those with a growth mindset view failure as an opportunity, a temporary situation they can overcome. They believe that even if things may be difficult and appear insurmountable, if they put in enough effort and resourcefulness and look for the help of others when required, they can learn how to turn things around. The message in the growth mindset is simple but unequivocal: we are always a work in progress, and we can further our talents if we are willing to do whatever it takes.

A growth mindset is a potent belief that opens the door to deep transformations. It can shape our identity and empower us to overcome our perceived limitations. Of course, there will be problems that are beyond our capacities and that a growth mindset will not be able to resolve, but the point here is that we can push the boundaries of what we think is possible and come closer to reaching our goals and become what we aspire to be: "Do people with this mindset believe anyone can be anything, that anyone with proper motivation or education can become Einstein or Beethoven? No, but they believe that a person's true potential is unknown (and unknowable); that is impossible to foresee what can be accomplished with years of passion, toil, and training,"[10] says Carol Dweck.

The ramifications of adopting a growth mindset as a critical component of your identity are far-reaching; it is a belief that can make a difference in all kinds of people, disciplines, and organizations. The fact that it is a belief that we decide to embrace or not is what makes it truly incredible. It is up to us to choose to remain restricted by a fixed mindset or adopt a growth mindset and begin the journey to attain what we can become. Nothing is blocking us from making this decision; we are free to do it, and still, we seem to have problems holding up a growth mindset consistently; it is tempting to fall back into the fixed mindset gravitational pull. Adopting a growth mindset is not easy; it requires breaking away from our habits and putting in dedicated effort and hard work. However, despite the challenges, it's more than worthwhile, as it can propel us closer to achieving our goals. It's about acknowledging that we can shape our own paths and continually enhance ourselves.

To unlock the full potential of its people, an organization must assume a growth mindset. This means creating an environment where challenges are seen as opportunities to learn, effort is recognized as the path to mastery, and constructive feedback is valued for improvement. When an organization prioritizes cultivating a growth mindset, it fosters innovation, encourages risk-taking, and supports the continuous development of people's skills, ultimately driving overall growth and success.

Perspective Taking

In our daily lives, we are busy operating, trying to accomplish our goals, and fulfilling our commitments. We usually function inside a self-made bubble, where it is easy to get absorbed into the tasks at hand and lose sight of the bigger picture. We focus on what is right in front of us and cannot detach to see the whole system and how our decisions create consequences that might impact us down the road. If we base our thinking only on what is immediate, it will be challenging to make effective decisions since we can't see further ahead in the cause-and-effect dynamic. This activity is known as "the inside view," which brings to the fore only the things we have in front of us and understand clearly.

However, in order to be more effective in our thinking and decision-making process, we must complement the "inside view" with an "outside view," where we can step outside ourselves to gain a better perspective of the problems we are facing. The "outside view" allows us to look at the whole system and better judge the different possibilities of our actions. We take perspective to try to understand the whole. We should strive to balance our natural inclination to rely solely on the "inside view" and include the "outside view" to increase our effectiveness. This can help us understand the situation better and make more well-rounded decisions by considering a more comprehensive range of factors and potential outcomes.

The challenge lies in being able to detach from the "inside view" because "stepping outside ourselves and really getting a different view is a struggle."[11] We must be more fluid in going from the micro to the macro to improve our impact: "It's natural to be drawn to the inside view. It's usually concrete and filled with engaging detail we can use to craft a story about what's going on. The outside view is typically abstract, bare, and doesn't lend itself readily to storytelling. So even smart, accomplished people routinely fail to consider the outside view."[12]

How many times have we addressed the wrong problem or failed to anticipate the repercussions of our actions because we couldn't foresee the larger issue ahead? Gaining perspective is crucial, as it prepares us to face the more significant problems that we cannot see with a narrow view, shaping our mindset for greater effectiveness and reaching our full potential. Warren Berger, the author of the book "A More Beautiful Question," explains it in the following terms: "When we do step back, what do we see? We're seeing essentially the same realities and situations. But with more distance, a bigger picture comes into view. We may now be able to see the overall context; we might notice the patterns and relationships between things we'd previously thought of as separate."[13]

Taking perspective requires being open, curious, and humble; it is not as intuitive as it may seem, especially when we feel strongly about something. We must adopt what, in the Zen tradition, is known as the "beginner's mind." By adopting this perspective, individuals can foster creativity, improve their problem-solving skills, and enhance their overall learning and growth.

Perspective-taking is a determinant of Mindset because an undetached view helps us deal with our natural biases, enhance our understanding of a phenomenon, and, most importantly, inform our thinking and actions. Taking perspective can be very consequential in our personal and professional lives, equipping us with the tools to make sound and well-informed decisions. In the words of Peter M. Senge, C. Otto Scharmer, Joseph Jaworski, and Betty Sue Flowers, authors of the book "Presence": "If we can simply observe without forming conclusions as to what our observations mean and allow ourselves to sit with all the seemingly unrelated bits and pieces of information we see, fresh ways to understand a situation can eventually emerge."[14]

There is a critical thing to remember about attempting to take an "outside view" to devise the whole picture. Despite the benefits of opening our minds to the system's first-, second-, or third-order consequences, there will always be a limit to how much we can predict the moving parts of a changing system. We must balance the broader view with the actions we can take now to avoid getting lost in the woods.

Agency

It may seem odd to discuss agency, an activity-based component, as a determinant of mindset, which is a way of thinking component. At first, identifying agency as a mindset determinant appears counterintuitive since thinking and doing belong to different realms. But as I have delved into the subject, I have realized the profound interconnectedness between action and thought: acting is vital in shaping our thinking since our actions strongly influence our thoughts and beliefs. It also works the other way around; our thinking informs our actions. The mind has the potential to impact our behaviors, and our behaviors can also shape our thoughts in new directions.

Action generates information, and we must capitalize on it to devise the best solutions and increase our performance. When we reflect on our actions, we shape our beliefs and mental models. The pre-Socratic Greek philosopher Anaxagoras highlighted how action influences our thinking with the following statement: "It's by having hands that man is the most intelligent of animals."

The conviction to act and get insights that inform our beliefs is crucial in developing a mindset that unlocks individual and organizational potential. I have always believed in the power of action, especially when we lack enough information to make sound decisions. Many times, the best approach is to start doing something to address our problems and adjust our course as we progress. However, I want to emphasize that I am not endorsing blind or random action. I believe in investing some time in devising well-informed, "smart actions" because I am convinced that this way, we can increase our probability of success. But make sure it is not overdone. Despite our natural inclination to plan extensively and be as prepared as possible before launching a project or taking action, there comes a point where planning must cease, and intuitive action must take over.

In our daily lives, there are many examples where we benefit from acting to inform our thinking. One classic example is learning to ride a bike. Before attempting to ride, we may have theoretical knowledge about balancing and pedaling. Still, it's only through getting on the bike and trying to ride that we truly understand the dynamics of balancing and steering. Swimming is another example of an activity that requires action. No amount of thinking about swimming techniques or watching tutorials can prepare you for the experience of being in the water. You have to physically get into the pool, lake, or ocean and start moving your body to understand the dynamics of swimming.

Having discussed the importance of agency in shaping our mindset and thinking, it's time to examine the drivers of agency that propel us in our chosen direction. I suggest that two key components form the foundation of agency: self-efficacy and persistence.

I) Self-efficacy

"Beliefs of personal efficacy constitute the key factor of human agency. If people believe they have no power to produce results, they will not attempt to make things happen."[15]

I have always admired Albert Bandura's work; he is one of the greatest psychologists in history and an authority in the field of human will. He introduced the concept of self-efficacy, and his ideas are essential for understanding how individuals and organizations push their boundaries beyond what they think is possible. The concept of self-efficacy is simple yet very powerful: When you face a difficult challenge you don't know how to tackle, you can turn your mind to a situation in your past where you faced another significant obstacle and overcame it by applying your skills. The central belief is that if, in the past, you were able to leverage your abilities to figure out a solution to a seemingly impossible problem and succeed, you can do it again. Your recollection of the success story under dire circumstances is a testimony that you can trust your abilities; it gives a reason to believe in your capacity to employ agency to face adversity and come out with a favorable outcome: "Perceived self-efficacy is not a measure of the skills one has but a belief about what one can do under different sets of conditions with whatever skills one possesses."[16]

We all have personal or professional stories of achievement in which we encountered a problem we didn't know how to handle but managed to solve. Even regular activities such as golf, cooking, gardening, playing a musical instrument, school projects, business deals, etc., can provide us with examples of how we successfully dealt with challenges in the past and overcame them. These stories offer evidence that we can draw confidence from and use them to bolster our belief in our ability to tackle current and future problems effectively.

I have leaned on self-efficacy many times in my life. This belief has enhanced my agency, boosted my performance, and allowed me to overcome dire challenges. I want to share a personal story about self-efficacy that helped me solve one of the most significant problems I have faced in my life. It is related to the marriage of one of my daughters, and it has become a self-efficacy anecdote for me that I refer to frequently, confirming that it is a compelling belief to hold.

My daughter had her wedding at a vineyard in Valle de Guadalupe, Baja California, Mexico, which is 1,500 miles away from Monterrey, where we live. Planning a remote wedding was quite different from what we were used to, but we believed it would be worth it due to the beautiful experience it promised. On the wedding day, after the religious ceremony, I drove my daughter and our family to the location for the photo session. It was a beautiful landscape within the vineyard where the bride, groom, and families would take pictures to capture the memorable day. Time was tight as it was around 4:00 pm, and we only had a couple hours of good light for the photo shoot.

While driving to the location for a photo shoot, I encountered several closed avenues. It turned out a bicycle race was taking place in Valle de Guadalupe, and the police had blocked off the circuit. Unfortunately, one of the closed avenues led to the location of the photo shoot. I learned through the radio that the bicycle race was scheduled to finish at 6:00 pm, meaning the photo session would have to be called off since the sun was set to go down then, and without natural light, the photos could not be taken. It was a disappointing situation, as the venue was chosen specifically for its beautiful landscape, and without sufficient light, the backdrop would be useless. My daughter was very upset and started to panic while my wife asked me if there was anything I could do to resolve the issue.

I parked by the blocked avenue and got out of the car. I walked up to a police officer in a patrol car that was blocking the avenue and asked for help. However, he refused to talk to me and insisted that I needed to move quickly, saying I was obstructing traffic flow. He didn't listen to anything I said; he just turned his back on me to continue directing traffic. Feeling discouraged, I decided to return to the vehicle. As I started walking back to inform my family that it was impossible to pass through, I saw the distress on my daughter's face from a distance. I stopped, paused for a moment, took a deep breath, and reassured myself, "You can solve this problem; you have negotiated deals with tough people before with good results; you can do this." Some images of past intense negotiations crossed my mind. I walked back to the police car, trying to figure out what to do and devising a strategy on the go.

Me: Officer, there is an emergency, and I need to talk to your supervisor.

Policeman: What??

Me: There is a serious situation that requires immediate attention, and I need to speak to your supervisor.

Policeman: (looking incredulous) All right; he grabbed his radio and called his supervisor, who showed up a few minutes later.

Police Supervisor: What is the emergency?

Me: There is a big problem. I will explain it to you in a moment, but first, I need to ask you if you are a father.

Police Supervisor: What? Yes, I am a father.

Me: Do you have a daughter?

Supervisor: Yes, I do, but I need to know what the emergency is.

Me: Do you mind telling me her age?

Police Supervisor: Sixteen years old. I need to know what is the emergency now, or I am out of here.

Me: I bet that if she had a serious problem, you would do anything in your power to help her. As fathers, we don't want our daughters to suffer.

Police Supervisor: What does my daughter have to do with the emergency? I had enough; I am leaving.

Me: Officer (pointing to my car), my daughter is in that car and faces an emergency. Today is her wedding day, and if you look closely, you will see that she is wearing her bridesmaid gown. It is the most important day of her life, and to conclude the ceremony, we must cross the blockage and get to where the wedding will take place. I am sure you can relate to this since you have a daughter, and as a father, you want the best for her. You have the power to solve her problem, so please, please, help my daughter realize her dream.

Police Supervisor: (remaining silent for a moment). Okay, I understand. I will help her and let you through, but I do not want you to jeopardize racers; I will escort you. You must follow my car at low speed and obey my instructions.

Me: Of course! I will drive slowly and look at your signals. Thank you very much for your help. You have made my daughter's day, and she will never forget it!

As I made my way back to the car, I couldn't help but notice the anxiety in my daughter's eyes. She was eager to hear the news. I reassured her that everything was fine and we could continue with the photo shoot as planned; she was very happy. The police supervisor guided us, and we reached the venue promptly.

This self-efficacy story reached a critical juncture when it became clear that calling off the photo session was not an option, and I had to do something about it. At that moment, I reassured myself that I could succeed because I had conducted tough negotiations before and had been successful. Then, I took action to devise a solution to the problem. Fortunately, it worked. You can imagine how important the outcome was for me as a father; it's something that I will never forget.

Since then, I have held this story as an example of how self-efficacy is a belief that can increase your performance and get you the results you want; it fuels your agency and can make a difference in your life. Cultivating self-efficacy is a game-changer for any organization that can incorporate it into its collective mindset and leverage its power. I cannot recommend it more as a belief to nurture the collective mindset and unlock potential.

II) Perseverance

The importance of perseverance and its benefits for improving performance has been widely documented in many fields. There is abundant evidence showing how people enhance their skills and achieve mastery in their respective areas of interest by consistently dedicating time and effort to their pursuits, embracing failures as learning opportunities, and maintaining a steadfast commitment to their goals despite challenges and setbacks: "It is safe to conclude from many studies on a wide variety of disciplines that nobody develops extraordinary abilities without putting in tremendous amounts of practice...No matter which area you study –music, dance, sports, competitive games, or anything else with objective measures of performance– you find that the top performers have devoted a tremendous amount of time developing their abilities."[17]

Perseverance is essential for success. It empowers individuals to overcome challenges and progress toward their goals, enabling them to achieve anything they set their minds to. It is a critical factor for unlocking potential and should be a focal point for any organization seeking to keep up with the fast pace of change. Perseverance is challenging to develop at the organizational level because it stems from individual motivation. Conventional wisdom dictates that a company can only do so much to keep its people's intrinsic motivation high so that they can withstand inevitable headwinds and achieve success. It is generally assumed that some individuals will be motivated and work hard to improve while others will not. This is seen as a natural aspect of human behavior, suggesting limits to what a company can do. But is this truly the case?

I firmly believe that companies can help develop persistence in their people significantly. Here are four things they can do:

a) Foster mental representations

The late Anders Ericsson, a leading authority on human performance, found that, when it comes to applying sustained effort to improve performance, people are in charge, "I have found it is surprisingly rare to get clear evidence in any field that a person has reached some immutable limit on performance. Instead, I've found that people just give up and stop trying to improve."[18] Additionally, Ericsson found that a critical element that individuals leverage for improving performance is developing mental representations that guide their efforts; these mental representations serve as parameters to assess progress and inspire individuals to continue when they feel like quitting. This is where organizations can help individuals embrace the process by encouraging them to have a compelling objective to follow.

Mental representations can be mental models, beliefs, aspirations, purposes, or the image of a role model that individuals aspire to emulate. They create a goal that establishes the gap from where they are now to where they want to be. The more specific the mental representation, the better results people will have in attaining their objectives: "What sets expert performers apart from everyone else is the quality and quantity of their mental representations."[19]

Organizations can significantly support the development of mental representations among their people by setting aspirational goals and clearly defining what success looks like within the organization. For instance, they can share success stories of individuals who have excelled in their roles or achieved significant milestones, inspire others, and provide a clear image of the type of professional and leader they can emulate in their career development. This practice can generate energy and direction for all.

b) Encourage gradual improvement

Motivation and capability go hand in hand when it comes to the persistence required to develop a skill. The better you get, the more motivated you are, and the more motivated you are, the better you get. This self-reinforcing cycle is crucial for developing any skill, whether learning a new language, mastering a musical instrument, or excelling in a particular sport. Achieving a compounding effect requires a commitment to stay put: "Studies of expert performers tell us that once you have practiced for a while and can see the results, the skill itself can become part of your motivation."[20]

Organizations play a crucial role in fostering persistence among their people by encouraging continuous improvement. This can be achieved by stimulating individuals to take small, manageable steps toward their goals and helping them to evaluate their progress regularly. By doing so, organizations can support the development of a positive cycle of persistence, which can contribute to substantial personal and professional development for their people.

c) Encourage self-awareness to decrease barriers

Persistence is a habit that benefits from our ability to observe what is helping or hindering us in achieving our goals. To do this, we must be self-aware and understand our emotions, thoughts, and behaviors. Once we know these aspects, we can assess our situation holistically and make the necessary changes to overcome our barriers.

Organizations can help individuals become more self-aware by encouraging reflective practices and offering initiatives supporting emotional intelligence. Helping your people examine their own system dynamics and develop the right environment for persistence will nudge the driving forces and diminish restraining processes critical to improving performance.

James Clear, the bestselling author of Atomic Habits, encourages us to take a systemic view of habit formation that is helpful in developing persistence: "If you have trouble changing your habits, the problem isn't you. The problem is your system. Bad habits repeat themselves again and again, not because you don't want to change, but because you have the wrong system for change."[21]

d) Recognize progress whenever possible

By recognizing those in the organization who are advancing in their persistence abilities, the organization demonstrates that it values its people's efforts to improve themselves, thus motivating them to keep progressing. Acknowledging people's accomplishments helps them gain confidence in their abilities, leading to a cycle of improvement and increased resilience in facing challenges.

Recognizing and assessing persistence skills can be challenging because evaluating the internal processes in people's minds that lead to persistence is complex and subjective. We often rely on assessing observable performance and may not always fully consider the internal factors enabling improvement. Still, it is essential to make an effort to incentivize persistence, recognize progress whenever possible, and preferably do it immediately, right in the moment it happens. Provide timely feedback when people are making progress, as immediate recognition boosts their motivation: "What is immediately rewarded is repeated."[22]

A Recap of the Mindset Determinants:

In my experience working with organizations, I've seen how frequently mindset becomes a topic of discussion in the context of Regrowth and transformation. Everyone recognizes the importance of cultivating a desired mindset and attempts to take practical steps to attain it, but the reality is that it's a complex topic to embark upon. Figuring out how to influence the collective mindset in the desired direction will continue to be challenging in an organizational setting.

I explored three determinants of mindset to show how we can manage this critical dimension and further integrate it with our efforts with the talent and culture dimensions within the Aspen Root Framework. The goal is to develop a coherent system to unlock the organization's potential to regrow when confronting a stall.

In a nutshell, the mindset component entails activating the following determinants:

Identity: by working with mental models and beliefs and encouraging a collective growth mindset approach. This way, we can go beyond the self-imposed limits of our thinking and venture into new territories.

Perspective-taking: to complement our task-oriented, inside view with an outside view that looks at the overall context of our problems and opportunities and helps us adjust our course when needed.

Agency: to underscore that our actions inform our thinking. When performing, we must leverage self-efficacy and persistence to keep advancing when we inevitably face the challenging situations that an ever-changing world brings to us.

Enhancing mindsets involves managing identity, perspective-taking, and agency at the organizational level. This collective effort will help us achieve the company goals and lead our people to reach their full potential.

CHAPTER 7

The Regrowth Journey

"You do not drive a plant to grow...Nor, we would argue,
do leaders "drive" their organization. The organization is
a human community. It is a living system...There is no one
driving it. But there are many tending the garden."
—Peter Senge

In the preceding chapters, we explored concepts and ideas that describe the individual components of a Regrowth journey for organizations, visiting each element separately to gain a thorough understanding of each one of them. Now, it is time to see how they integrate and operate together and, most importantly, how to devise a path to design and implement a transformation journey. I will revisit and summarize the main ideas we have covered and attempt to illustrate how the system works.

This book is rooted in the idea that stalled organizations can reclaim their growth momentum by unlocking people's potential. Organizational inertia has to give way to new ways of thinking and doing; for that, we need a mindset shift. To attain this goal,

I suggest organizations take the following steps to shift their collective mindset:

- Recognize that growth is mostly an inside job; it is organization-driven.
- Identify the transformation's "where to play" territories.
- Determine the winning path according to the selected territory.
- Launch the transformation, reach critical mass, and maintain a change momentum to compound the impact.

The Regrowth journey demands commitment and a steady hand from everyone in the organization, especially those in leadership positions. Be prepared to face ambiguity and maintain high spirits; it is a bumpy road.

I) Double down on your people's humanity

In the introduction, I talked about how typical companies grow slowly, at about 2.8 percent, according to McKinsey, and only one in eight reach a double-digit growth pace. The data shows that, for all practical purposes, most companies attain meager growth or stall. I also discussed how growth is driven by customers' buying of our products, which, by definition, is an activity that takes place in the market, that is, outside the company. Yet, the reasons for stalling are linked to the actions we undertake or fail to undertake inside the company to deal with what is happening outside in the customer's world. This is why I suggest that growth is primarily an "inside job;" it is the result of the dynamics of the organization in the quest to gain the customer's preference. Despite the inside-outside dynamic, many managers still blame external factors for their poor growth performance and point out the competitive landscape, government regulations, changes in consumer trends, industry shifts, etc., as the reasons for their inadequate results, but this is a flawed diagnostic for the root cause of the problem. The truth is that poor growth performance in organizations is not something that happens to us, like a disease; a company's stalling is a self-inflicted wound.

Conventional wisdom suggests that to grow, we need to excel at organizational initiatives that operate at the capability level or the product level. Consistent with this line of thought, we customarily implement practices like innovation, agility, marketing, product development, data analytics, or business intelligence, to name a few, to jumpstart the company into a growth trajectory, and more often than not, we disregard the development of practices that help the organization incorporate the beliefs and mental models necessary to adapt and transform. Functional skills are indispensable to growth; this is a fact and is not subject to discussion, but not at the expense of pursuing the mindset enhancement of our people, which must be embarked upon with the same level of intensity as the one entailed furthering functional skills, to strengthen the foundation that unlocks potential and drives valuable growth in the organization. Upholding the human spirit in the organization creates a shared platform to help make sense of what we intend to accomplish and simultaneously generates the impulse to make things happen. As markets and the business environment get less and less predictable, it's only logical to concentrate on developing the organization's resourcefulness fabric that will aid us in adapting to the new reality and effectively managing whatever the world brings our way.

The central idea I want to highlight here is that we must promote an organization's human-centered stance to spearhead growth. This is not a check-the-box activity; we must do it with a profound conviction. It is imperative to deal with an ever-changing world where the only way to compete and win is by unlocking our people's capacity to contribute.

Lately, I have been asked how the human environment will look inside organizations once technology substitutes many of the functions that are performed by people today. There is concern about how worthwhile it is to help our people develop their mindset when, sooner or later, they will end up being replaced by an algorithm. The expectation is that Artificial Intelligence will provoke massive layoffs and software will take over humans in organizations. My response to this gloomy vision is that although technology will undoubtedly expand its reach, humans will remain of the utmost importance in organizations, with a repurposed aim. Technology's wider reach will make us bring to the fore what is uniquely human and uplift it. The spirit of collaboration, connection, inspiration, creativity, and the potential to become what we are meant to be as individuals and organizations will be heightened. For sure, many routine activities like data analysis, inventory management, maintenance programs, and low-value-added repetitive tasks within the organization will be taken over by artificial intelligence, which will increase efficiency and effectiveness in the execution of processes and end up benefiting society. Artificial Intelligence will inevitably displace some people, requiring us to strengthen those activities where humans can make distinctive contributions.

Organizations must recognize that their people have dreams and aspirations; they want to be developed and seek opportunities to put their talents to work. In an ideal scenario, their purpose will align with the organization's purpose, making their job a fulfilling, meaningful experience. However, even if they were not aligned, they could still have the opportunity to be a part of something great, engage with their work, and feel they were making a difference. To make this happen, organizations need to declare and single-handedly pursue their people's mindset enhancement and do it with the same intensity with which they go after other functional practices; it is critical for sustainable growth. This conviction has to be demonstrated by the CEO and the C-Suite team and should be a priority on the organization's agenda. We usually see stalling as a problem, but in reality, it is a symptom of an organizational flaw, and to alleviate it, we must unlock our people's ingenuity and potential. We must actively energize our people's journey to becoming the best version of themselves; in doing so, we will help them push the boundaries of what they think is possible, and, as a consequence, the organization will accelerate its growth path, it is a win for all parties involved.

II) Map the knowledge journey

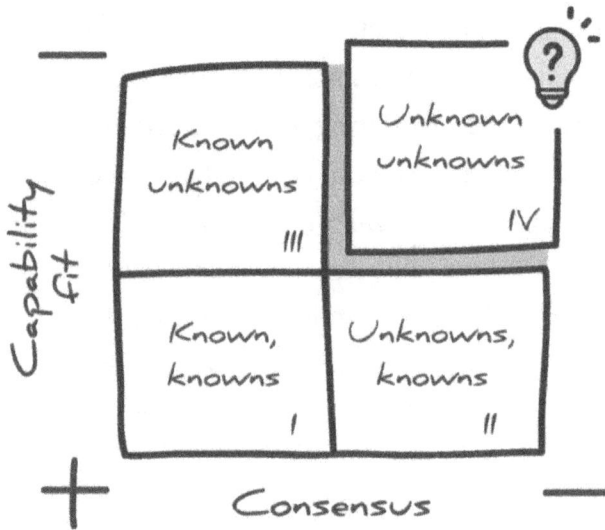

In the quest for growth, established companies must improve what they are already doing on behalf of their customers and venture into doing new things to continue gaining their preference. As we discussed previously, this is a dynamic system; the pace of change in industries and markets is accelerating, putting pressure on organizations to develop differentiated products and services to keep up with their customer's increasing expectations.

To solve this problem, companies must constantly develop knowledge, hopefully, proprietary knowledge, to get an advantage and provide better solutions to their customers' needs so they can compete and win in the market. The pressure to create knowledge is always on; companies must find ways to stay relevant with their customers, whether with their current or new offerings. Otherwise, they will hit a wall and stall.

In Chapter Two, I suggested a knowledge advantage framework to map your efforts. The axes in the matrix represent two critical areas where companies must make consequential decisions. On the horizontal axis, we find the degree of consensuality of the ideas the company attempts to pursue. On one end, we have consensual ideas, which are typically safer bets. If we were to look at consensual ideas using a Gauss curve bell, they would be placed near the average; most people would agree that these ideas could work.

Notwithstanding their general approval, they would also be "more predictable" and probably are being attempted by other companies in the market, so the expected growth and returns would not be as significant. On the opposite end of the horizontal axis, we find the less consensual ideas, which are outliers and "improbable" by nature and, therefore, more disruptive (they lie in the tails of the Gauss curve bell mentioned above; not too many people would agree they can work). Given their uniqueness, they have the potential to produce more significant growth and returns. Still, they are riskier and have a lower probability of success. In the vertical axis, we find the degree to which the company's capabilities are a good fit to support the ideas it wants to take on. The ideas to pursue will require suitable capabilities to make them happen, so we must determine if we can leverage our current capabilities or develop new ones. Knowledge creation applies to capabilities and ideas; they go hand in hand when delivering value to our customers. It wouldn't make any sense to develop the best telephone, tire, or shampoo for our customers if we cannot provide it as expected and on time; it would defeat our purpose, and we would lose sales to our competitors.

The thing about today's business environment is that even in the space where we have consensus in ideas and fitting capabilities to execute them, there is high pressure to evolve. It seems to be a comfort zone, but it is not. To stay alive as a company, we must develop and apply knowledge constantly to renew our current operations, and much more so if we want to venture into unknown territory, attempting something that we have not done before, where there is no certainty and the risk is higher. It is several orders of magnitude more challenging to explore the unknown, generating much tension within the organization, even if we are on the right track. This is precisely the point I want to underline in this section. When attempting to explore spaces that lie beyond our core, we must assess the implications for our people in both the knowledge-creation process and its operationalization because there will be hardships and problems that the organization must be capable of withstanding and resolving. We customarily think about the challenge of developing new ideas or capabilities as just having the functional skills to do it, but it goes beyond that; ultimately, it is a make-it-or-break-it situation for the organization that will depend on how our people handle the process.

Think of the organization as a vessel, the vehicle that will take us where we want to go. As such, it is designed to take you to the places where you are currently doing business; however, when you decide to look for growth opportunities, inevitably, your organization will have to wander and explore new territories, you will stretch your systems, and experiment with new ways of doing things. The further away you venture from your core, the more you will challenge the vessel to go to new places and do new things, and the more stress and adaptation it will have to endure. If your organization is hardwired to perform only in today's business, it will suffer when you want to take it to new places with different operating conditions. This argument reinforces the logic for developing an adaptable organization and thinking of it as an intrinsic part of your growth path. Cultivating an adaptable system with the bandwidth necessary for renewal should be the priority for those organizations that want to compete and win in today's and in the future business.

I have often heard how organizations want to be disruptive and create game-changer products and services in their industries. It is the mantra that drives innovation and growth functions and is a mandate from the CEO and the Board. Everybody wants to become the next Amazon, Airbnb, or Tesla. This is very good, but I want to know to what extent they are also committed to developing the organization that will take them there. The dynamics in quadrant IV, "Unknown unknowns," are challenging for established companies to sustain, given the contrarian nature and the managing style of the renegades that create that kind of product. It looks like the most important thing is having a disruptive team and the functional skills to do the job. Still, from the perspective of an existing organization, it has more to do with the systemic human interactions that make the process possible than anything else. If you have a vehicle that can only be driven on paved roads, it will struggle when you take it cross-country. Good luck if you want to use a Ferrari on a mountain bike road; be prepared to grapple with adversity and frustration.

III) Embrace a new perspective of the organization

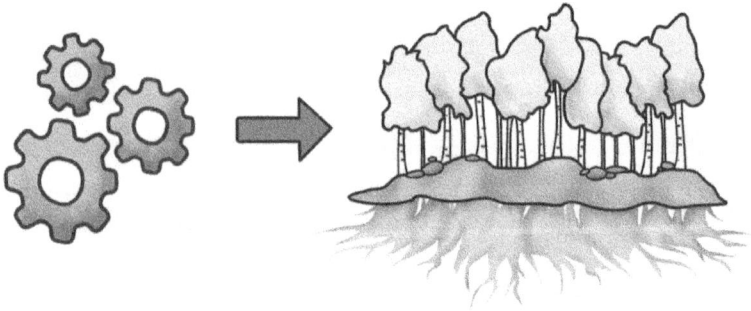

The perspective leaders hold to make sense of the organization's undertakings constitutes a mental model that will impact their decisions and actions and ultimately determine their roadmap for growth and performance. In Chapter Three, I introduced two metaphors that describe an organization, the machine and the biology metaphor; they constitute two opposing ways to explain their inner workings and the corresponding beliefs that drive them. Let us briefly review them again.

When addressing the machine metaphor, it is vital to refer to the work of Frederick Winslow Taylor, the American engineer who wrote the Principles of Scientific Management (1911) and made significant contributions with his time and motion analysis, where he attempted to determine the optimal sequence and coordination of tasks in production. Taylor aimed to make organizations as efficient as possible and approach human contributions like another gear in the production process. Later, other thinkers like W. Edwards Deming built on this idea and embarked on the quest for perfection and optimal performance as the guiding principle in business. The central idea in the machine metaphor is that organizations are machines made out of parts, and they must attain optimal efficiency; by optimizing the parts, we will optimize the machine as a whole. The manager's job is to evaluate the efficiency of each part, that is, departments or functions, and eliminate the inefficient use of resources, non-value-added activities, and waste to increase productivity and streamline the company's performance.

On the other extreme, we have the biology metaphor. This perspective portrays the organization as a living being, a biological entity, evolving constantly to respond to the challenges presented by its surroundings. If we observe how nature works, we find that living organisms evolve in response to the changing conditions of their environment. These organisms "improve" or "get better" by adapting and adjusting to deal with whatever may jeopardize their existence, which does not necessarily correspond with our standard definition of efficiency. In nature, there is no pre-conceived or overarching goal for improvement; evolution is context-specific and triggers a natural selection process to be able to survive. For example, think of how strains of bacteria have developed traits to become resistant to drugs as a result of the overuse of antibiotics by the population; it has been an evolution process where organisms use complexity and diversity to evolve specialized structures as a way to adapt and enhance their probability for survival. The specific biology metaphor I discussed in Chapter Three is that of the Aspen Grove, a collection of tens, hundreds, or even thousands of trees that spring from "one single root."

The mental model of the organization we select, whether the machine or the biology metaphor, will be very consequential for our decisions in a Regrowth journey. Let us run a thought experiment to surface what happens when we use one mental model or the other.

As I mentioned, the machine perspective drives us to break the company into departments and assess the efficiency of each one. For this task, indicators to measure performance are selected, and people are expected to work relentlessly on their improvement; the goal for each department is to optimize them as much as possible. On the production floor, for instance, the team would use indicators such as scrap rate, downtime, units produced per hour, cost per unit produced, machine utilization, or factory capacity, to name a few. In sales, the indicators would be revenue per employee, customer acquisition cost, conversion cost, customer lifetime value, etc. In logistics, fill rate, transporting cost per unit, warehouse utilization, damaged goods percentage, etc. This same logic will apply to all functions, and areas like HR, Marketing, Finance, R&D, IT, etc., will have indicators to achieve the optimal state. Each department will benchmark its performance with other internal or external peers, past historical data, industry standards, etc. The idea is that all departments in the company will attempt to beat the selected benchmarks and become as efficient as possible. When your job is focused on optimizing, you adopt an optimization mentality, and this will be the lens through which you see the world; you will be looking at every opportunity to be more efficient.

In the machine mental model, the optimization mantra will steer your behavior; you will define your job as achieving maximum efficiency. This may bring good results for a while, but what happens when business conditions change? What happens if you hardwire your activities to perform optimally on a specific business model and the environment shifts? Or what if you drive optimization in your department at the expense of other departments and create a dysfunctionality? How flexible would you be to adapt once you have "cut to the bone" and thus leaving no room to move? Well, then you will have a problem. We all agree that a threshold of efficiency is always desirable, but remember that "the dose makes the poison," and with the machine metaphor, you are all in.

The representation of the company as a machine is a well-engrained concept in business, and people are incentivized to attain ever-ambitious goals. The pursuit of efficiency is very alluring; it suggests that your department and the company are arranged as clockwork, which is desirable. The biology metaphor challenges you to use another mental model, which demands extra effort from the engineering minds. Let me be clear: I do not advocate discarding efficiency indicators. Of course, you need high levels of efficiency to achieve a viable operation, but this should not be the overriding factor; you must balance it with your capacity to adapt and respond effectively to unexpected events.

In the biology metaphor, as we have stated, we depict the organization as a living system. The unit of analysis is not a single department but the whole organization as it delivers the product or services its customers expect. We start with the end in mind, which is what the customer needs, and reverse-engineer the interrelations and processes involved in delivering it. This approach enables us to establish the necessary operation standards for efficiency and productivity while identifying areas where flexibility and adaptability are needed. The priority is to nurture the source and ensure its flexibility to adjust. To better understand this systemic approach, consider the analogy of tending a garden. When you watch a garden, you ensure the proper soil for plants to grow, nourish it with fertilizers and provide the water needed, remove the weeds, prune the plants, and eliminate any pests. You provide support for unique plants and will pay attention to the specific needs of your garden, given the climate in the area or the light it gets, and work on the conditions that foster its growth. Tending a garden is an excellent example to demonstrate that you must strike a balance, caring for the whole system while efficiently performing specific tasks.

Now, let us unpack what "tending the garden" looks like in an organization. The first thing we must understand under this imaginary scenario is that systems adapt according to their capacity to coordinate and learn; both activities reinforce each other. As for the coordination, we will tend the garden by ensuring the free flow of feedback within the organization at all levels, which entails removing internal barriers and fostering the exchange of relevant information and ideas. We must also secure the flow of information from the outside, which captures the customers' view, allowing the organization to be continually mindful of their needs and expectations. A vigorous internal and external feedback loop will help align all the teams and regulate the system. As for learning, tending the garden in the organization implies understanding transversal processes, how departments collaborate, their willingness to experiment, and how teams reflect on their on-the-job experiences and distill insights that can be applied on the job.

Most importantly, it involves how people adjust their behaviors due to their reflections. The biology metaphor's systemic approach requires leaders to take a long-term view of people. Bosses must play the role of coaches; they are not supposed to provide all the answers to the problems their teams are facing; instead, they must guide and facilitate the learning process and let their people figure out the solutions themselves. The picture of success is people contributing and learning; it will demand patience from the leaders and being able to juggle the urgent needs of the business and the people's learning process, but it is the only way to develop an adaptable organization that meets its goals and simultaneously, helps its people grow.

The machine and biology metaphors are supported by beliefs that strengthen each mental model and anchor people's behavior. These beliefs underscore the tension between the two metaphors and highlight how they drive the company to two completely different outcomes: perfection or learning.

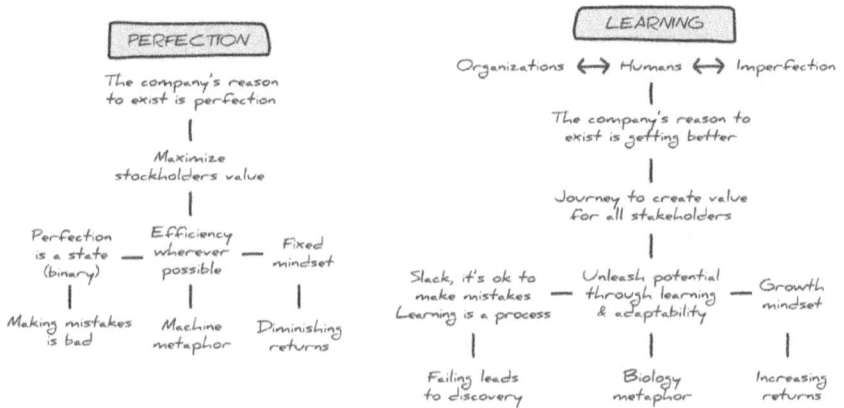

The machine metaphor's logic is rooted in the idea that the company can achieve a perfect state, and we must seek it. But I suggest this thinking leads to a trap and should be avoided. Let me explain:

Many managers think perfection is bliss, the "nirvana" of efficiency. Customarily, managers chase perfection by setting high-performance indicators in their departments so their teams can focus and work relentlessly until they achieve them. Once the teams attain their objectives, the work is done, and the problem is solved. Since the goal has been reached, the team stops pushing, and there is no need to continue. Now, they belong to the elite group, so why bother to do more? If managers attempt to set bolder indicators, the team will do its best to hold its ground and sandbag because team members will be exposed if they don't make the new numbers; it is a fixed mindset behavior. Perfection has a twin brother, which is the fear of failure; you do not want to dare to accomplish more and compromise the status you have reached; there is nothing but downside ahead. If you fail, there could be repercussions for your professional standing with your boss and the security of your employment. Paradoxically, perfection thinking hinders the very objective it is intended to accomplish and leads to complacency; it ends up being a trap. Seeking perfection is a curse; do not fall prey to the charms of this false state of grace.

Aspiring to become a perfect organization implies having perfect people, and this idea leads to several organizational dysfunctions. For one, so-called perfect people don't think they need to improve and, in my experience, are prone to have big egos. They see themselves as an outstanding finished product, so they always succeed and do not have to improve further. In discussions, the so-called perfect people will try to win all arguments to demonstrate that they are clever rather than getting the best solution for the organization, regardless of who takes the credit. When big egos are in the way, communication barriers arise, and it isn't easy to generate collaborative solutions to meet our customer's expectations. The flow of ideas is interrupted, and hierarchy and power take over, relegating the merit of the ideas to second place. Furthermore, striving for perfection runs counter to the necessary failure intrinsic to innovation, exploration, and creativity, jeopardizing the organization's ability to compete and win in today's business environment.

Instead of seeking perfection, I suggest organizations learn, improve, adapt, and set in motion a continuous process of discovery and experimentation to improve their work. The biology metaphor represents this type of thinking.

The most important feature of this metaphor is that the organization is never a finished product; it's always a work in progress. There is no predetermined state to reach; quite the opposite, the organization encourages continuous advancement and focuses on leveraging sound processes rather than achieving specific results. Managers praise effort and reward having good processes in place since it raises the probability of obtaining desired results consistently. Experimentation is welcomed and is recognized as an indispensable component for adapting to new and different business conditions.

By prioritizing adaptability and learning, the organization will be better positioned to navigate the challenges of an unpredictable environment and adapt more quickly to the new dynamics of the market. Furthermore, people will be more engaged in their work and willing to dare because the organization will provide the means to achieve their aspirations and drive personal growth.

The essential advantage of the biology metaphor, represented by the learning organization, over the machine metaphor, defined by perfectionism, is best summarized in Rick Rubin's phrase, "Perfectionism gets in the way of fun."

IV) Nurture a
"Rise to My Potential" Mindset

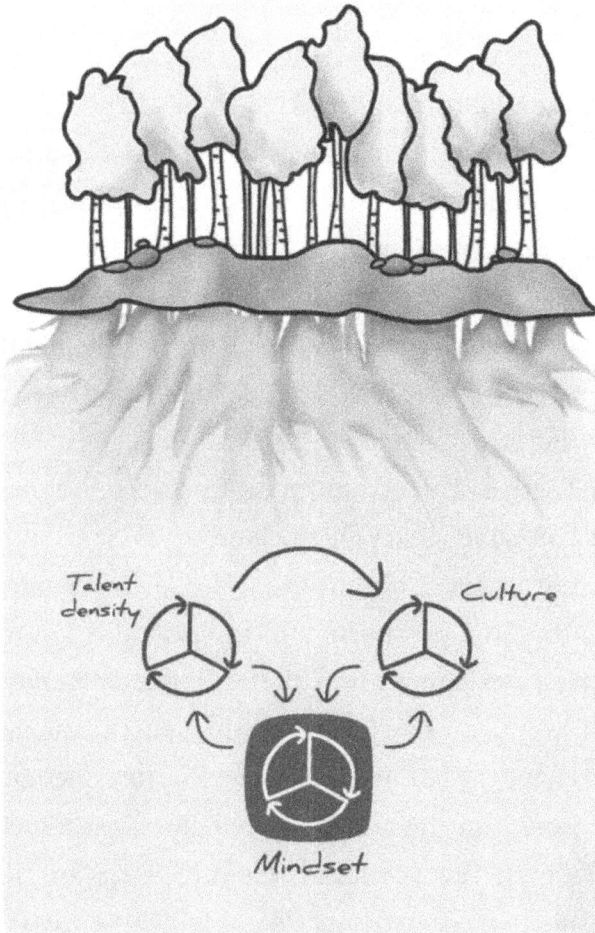

Let's quickly recap the steps we have followed up to this point. To set off a Regrowth journey, we must first acknowledge that the organization comprises human beings with aspirations, dreams, and needs, but most importantly, with the capacity to use their ingenuity to contribute to a larger purpose. Our people want to be developed and are on a journey to use their God-given talents to become all they can be. The essential principle of this step is to recognize that it is only through its people's humanity that the organization will regain its growth pattern; they are the source for envisioning possibilities and making things happen. Second, we need to chart the territories the organization aims to explore to gain knowledge that will give us an advantage in gaining customers' preferences. Simultaneously, in defining the knowledge space, we must assess if the organization can take us where we want to go. Even if we decide to play in the territories familiar to us, the organization will nevertheless be under stress to adapt to the new conditions, and this pressure will escalate as we move farther from our core activities. The commitment to rewire the organization to become a suitable vessel for the journey is inherent to gaining knowledge advantage. Third, those in leadership positions must embrace an organic perspective of the organization; instead of looking at it as a machine whose parts need to work perfectly, we should look at it as a biological entity that must adapt and learn as conditions change. From this view, the journey becomes a quest for learning and experimenting, where failure is accepted, and the goal is to get better every time. These three steps are the foundation that leads to the fourth and final step, where we will nurture a "rise-to-my-potential" mindset in the organization to advance the Regrowth journey. The steps must be addressed thoroughly, without skipping, because this communicates our commitment to our people and helps us structure a sound process.

Now, let us unpack the final step. The platform for nurturing a mindset is based on the biology metaphor; I propose using the Aspen Root Framework as a reference to guide our efforts. The Aspen Grove steers us to understand the organization as a single-rooted entity with diversified offspring. The threes can be conceived as departments, functions, or even individuals, operating under different conditions while being nurtured by the same root. The strong foundation represented by the root constitutes its source of life and scaffolds its journey to becoming all it can be. In this metaphor, three dimensions compose the system: Talent Density, Culture, and Mindset.

Talent Density demands having the best talent in charge of key positions in the organization, ensuring high performance in their respective areas, and setting a challenging, ambitious standard for all people to follow. It comprises three determinants: Conceptual Knowledge, Domain Knowledge, and Action Skills ("Rethinking Management Education: A View from Chicago," Harry L. Davis and Robin M. Hogarth, 1992). The Talent Density dimension steers the organization into developing the functional abilities and tools required to grow in a dynamic environment.

Culture sets the organization's interactions. It can be described as the shared assumptions, norms, values, attitudes, rituals, and attributes that distinguish one group from another. I like to think of it as the way the context and the rules of engagement in the organization create the conditions for people to do great work. Culture comprises three determinants: The Creed, Contextual Affect, and Stewardship. Culture is the invisible force that connects the whole.

Mindset is the mental setting that makes sense of the environment to envision possibilities and drive achievement. It is the nucleus for becoming all we can be and permeates the whole organization. It comprises three determinants: Identity, Perspective Taking, and Agency. Nurturing a "rise-to-my-potential" mindset is the main objective and constitutes the essence of the journey to Regrow. In this stage, the work must be performed in the whole organization, and congruence between what we say and do is paramount. It requires consistency, tolerance for frustration, and a long-term view of the organization since the outcome is far-reaching. Evaluating your progress is complex, but some signs will guide you and help you find the way when you are stuck.

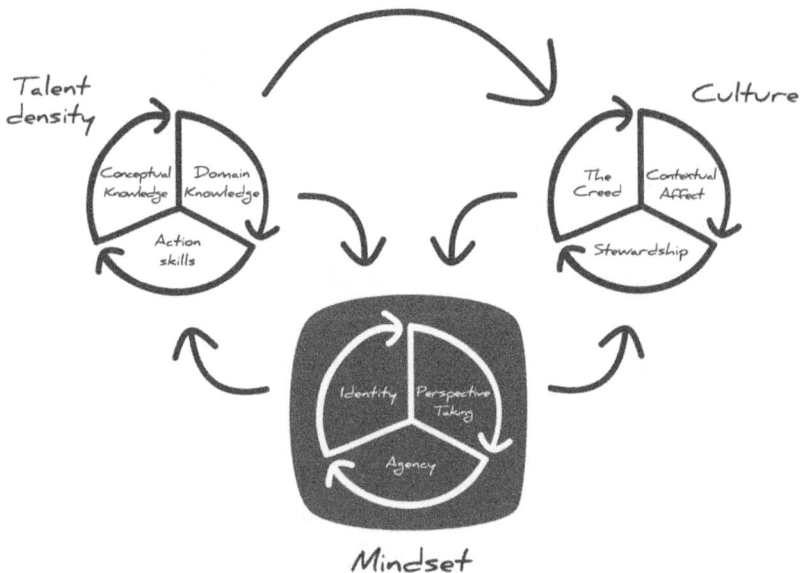

Talent density: adapted from Davis & Hogarth

The complete progression of the Regrowth Journey is the following:

The Regrowth Journey

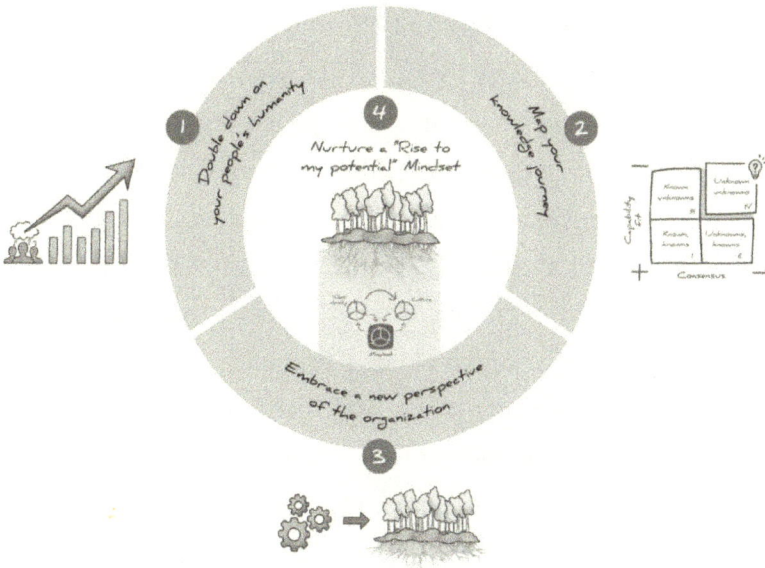

As a closure to this chapter, I would like to share some advice for those venturing into a Regrowth Journey; here are some ideas that I hope you will find helpful. They are meant to serve as principles to steer a successful process:

I) Be focused. It is key to focus on the few things that will make a difference and potentially move the needle. It is easy to get lost by attempting many things simultaneously.

II) Face the facts. Don't sugarcoat or mask your problems in making the Regrowth Journey a reality. Accept that frustration is an inevitable part of the process.

III) Be willing to relinquish control. Centralized control paralyzes the organization. The Regrowth journey demands distributive authority and autonomy in all leadership levels.

IV) Stay curious and have a beginner's mind. Our experience can be a blessing and a curse; don't let those preconceived ideas of how things should be get in the way. The Regrowth journey is uncharted territory, and learning and adjusting as we go is essential.

I would like to leave you with a quote from the late James March, a professor at Stanford University in the Graduate School of Business and best known for his research on organizations, whose insights are always valuable for many aspects of organizational work. The quote summarizes the balance necessary to make things happen in a Regrowth Journey: *"Leadership involves a delicate combination of plumbing and poetry."* Remember that both are important: plumbing, to fix what is not working, and poetry, to inspire and mobilize people towards a worthy goal, so don't yield to the temptation of doing one thing at the expense of the other. You must roll up your sleeves to do the nitty gritty work to scaffold the transformation and, at the same time, communicate a compelling vision to engage the organization and release the necessary energy to fuel the Regrowth journey.

CHAPTER 8

Self-Led Individual Regrowth

"Whenever anyone makes an important change,
it's because a switch has flipped."
—BERNARD ROTH

"Life is a series of collisions with the future; it is not the
sum of what we have been, but what we yearn to be."
—JOSÉ ORTEGA Y GASSET

"Above all, live with change and adapt to it. If the world
didn't change, I'd still have a 12 handicap."
— CHARLIE MUNGER

I n this book, I have advocated that for an organization to recover its growth trajectory when it stalls, it must generate a collective mindset shift to deal with a changing environment and support the development of the capabilities and products or services that meet customers' expectations. I introduced a comprehensive four-step process to attain a Regrowth Journey leading to a Talent Density, Culture, and Mindset system to generate the necessary impulse to secure the objective. I suggested that by working with these three dimensions, the organization would gain the capacity to learn and adapt to the environment's changing conditions and set in motion a positive reinforcing loop that would unlock its dormant potential. This refers to the macro aspects of the business, but I could not end this book without addressing the micro, that is, the dynamics of change at the individual level. Since individuals constitute organizations, looking at what unlocking potential means from a personal perspective is essential. In this chapter, I intend to probe into what needs to happen for individuals to become all they can be and explore its broader implications for their personal growth.

At some point, individuals, like organizations, get stuck; we all have been in situations where we are unsatisfied with how our lives go or our progress in accomplishing our goals. Our lives get naturally complicated without our intervention; entropy is inevitable, randomness presents unexpected challenges, and we face decline periods or crises that hinder our inner stability and happiness. Sometimes, the situation gets severe and escalates, and we halt; we feel overwhelmed. Getting out of a stall is difficult and orders of magnitude more complicated when facing strong headwinds.

When we encounter manageable challenges, we can usually solve minor problems with quick fixes and get back to our everyday lives without much trouble. However, when we face significant issues such as strained relationships, social isolation, discrimination, job loss, addiction, or depression, we often need to respond with substantial effort and draw strength from weakness. When we feel completely stuck and helpless, that is precisely the moment when we must tap into our potential, no matter how impossible it may seem. It is challenging to assemble ourselves and take over the situation when feeling shattered. It is much easier to blame external factors for our problems, play the victim, and complain that we were dealt a bad hand. But we must bite the bullet and accept the hard truth: things are what they are, not what we want them to be. We must take whatever challenges life presents and find a way to overcome our sense of helplessness when we are in a slump. We will never be able to reach our full potential if we see ourselves as victims. A major mental shift is needed for us to make a turnaround, which first entails acknowledging that we must change and then doing something about it.

The subject of personal change has always fascinated me. I have always believed that we all can change our reality by changing our thinking and behaviors, but I never quite figured out what needs to happen when the task implies going deep to change firmly rooted beliefs that are the backbone of our lives. When we face adversity and the world unravels before our eyes, our belief system will be tested, and very likely, we will have to upgrade or replace some old beliefs that are no longer useful to deal with the situation at hand. Changing our anchors, our fundamental truths, is far from easy; even when we accept that we must change them, the task appears inconceivable. These core beliefs have been our haven for a long time; we are so invested that getting rid of them seems out of the question. How can we do it? Lo and behold, I found a clue about changing deep-held beliefs when least expected and in one of the most unusual places.

Jorge Luis Borges's grave

A few years ago, I traveled to Europe with my family. My daughters were in their early twenties, and my wife and I wanted to spend quality time with them, knowing they would marry soon and start their own families. Among other cities, we spent a few days in Geneva, Switzerland's second most populous city. It was summer, and we had the opportunity to walk the city and its parks, having a wonderful time in the nice weather. As we were enjoying our last day in Geneva, I suddenly remembered that the late Argentinian novelist and poet Jorge Luis Borges was buried in a cemetery in the city. I have admired Borges for decades and read many of his novels and essays; he is one of my favorite writers, and it is fair to say that he and the Spanish philosopher Jose Ortega y Gasset have left an indelible mark on me and shaped my thinking into becoming the person I am today. Naturally, I wanted to visit his grave and pay my respects.

When I told my family I wanted to visit Borges's burial place, their response was lukewarm; they weren't happy about the idea. There were dozens of places they would rather be, and a cemetery seemed to be a terrible suggestion. Nevertheless, I managed to persuade them, and soon after, we arrived at the grounds called the Cemetery of Kings. Notwithstanding the grandiose name, the place was inconspicuous, and Borges's grave is modest. The cemetery is a peaceful lot with large trees; Borge's remains are placed in a small rectangle surrounded by green bushes. Resting at the head of the grave, there is a hand-carved gravestone with antique warriors in armor and an inscription that says, "And ne forhtedon na," which in Old English means "Be not afraid." I approached the grave solemnly and stood at the base, sizing the moment's significance. I spent a few minutes reflecting on how the person whose remains lay there had a powerful impact on people all over the world and, especially on me; in the meantime, my family was impatient and wanted to resume our tourist activities; they were constantly asking me if I was done with my hommage. Before leaving, I approached the heading of the tombstone to take a last look at the carvings, and I noticed a rectangular blue object lying on the ground in the small place left between the stone and the bushes. It was a book! I picked it up immediately, and I felt It was wet, but it was holding out pretty well; I could still turn the pages and noticed a postcard was sticking out, separating a page. The book's title was *Vent d'est Vent d'ouest* (East Wind, West Wind), and the author was Pearl S. Buck. I opened the page separated by the postcard; it was page number 80, and a phrase at the top stood out and immediately grabbed my attention: *"Les temps sont changés."* (Times have changed).

I was excited and curious about the serendipitous finding and filled with awe. Who put the book there, and why? After examining the book for a few minutes, I returned it to the ground, exactly where I found it. Whoever placed it there must have done it for a reason, and I wanted to honor that. I resumed my day with my family, but the experience and its meaning kept me thinking for several days. Finding a book at Borges' grave was a random event, but I fantasized that Borges was sending me a message, and it was for me to figure it out. I immediately ordered the book on Amazon and had it delivered to my house.

A few weeks later, after returning home, I read *East Wind, West Wind*, and I was dazzled by Pearl S. Buck's writing and her capacity to bring nuances in complex characters to life. The book tells the story of a traditional Chinese family in the early 20th century whose daughter, Kwei-lan, marries a non-traditional Chinese man. The narrative captures the clash between traditional Chinese values and the influence of Western ideas. Kwei-lan wants to uphold her family traditions in how she dresses, takes care of her husband, and obeys his wishes. Still, she soon finds herself rejected by her husband because he wants her to adopt modern ways, like dressing like a Westerner and not being submissive to him. Kwei-lan loves her husband, but her beliefs are firm, and she is reluctant to let go of them. She is troubled and seeks her mother's advice, who opposes her abandoning Chinese traditions. However, given the circumstances of her strained marriage, she counsels her in the following terms: "But you no longer belong to my family. You are your husband's. There is no choice left you save to be what he desires... Put forth once more every effort to beguile him... If he is still unmoved, then there is nothing left but bend yourself to his will. Unbind my feet? I whispered. My mother was silent a space.

Unbind your feet, she said wearily. The times are changed. You are dismissed. And she turned her face to the wall."[1]

Unbinding her feet was the ultimate test for Kwei-lan. She stood against doing it, but her love for her husband was overriding. She agreed to adopt Western traditions and rescue her marriage. I can only imagine how Kwei-lan was torn by the situation. She didn't want to change; she was raised in a tradition, and her whole life was anchored in deep, strong-held beliefs, but she loved her husband very much and, above all, wanted to make her marriage work. Love was the reason why she finally adopted a new perspective and changed.

East Wind and West Wind made me reflect on the dynamics involved in profound change, and the story produced four epiphanies for me about how to shift strong-held beliefs.

I) Deep Change needs mighty "Whys"

To change deeply held beliefs, we require a "Why" of significant or proportionate magnitude to the shift involved, and we must formulate it so that it becomes the anchor that steers our lives. Ordinary or general "Whys" will not do; we need robust, deeply personal reasons. The commonplace reasons for behaving as we do in our daily lives will lack the potency to move our pillars. "Give me a lever long enough and a fulcrum on which to place it, and I shall move the world," Archimedes said. To move our deeply rooted, entrenched beliefs that serve as mental anchors that guide our actions, we need a lever, not of any kind, but a mighty one that will allow us to do the job.

II) Conflicting beliefs must be resolved

Our beliefs need to be congruent to bring about change. Contradictory beliefs generate friction and can make change more complicated to achieve. However, reality shows us that even the most "rational" individuals may have conflicting beliefs. For instance, we may believe in religious tolerance and inclusivity yet still hold prejudices against those with different religious beliefs. The more coherent we are in our high-order beliefs, the better we will leverage their force to change our anchors. We will hold to these beliefs as if they are a rock to cling to during a storm, and we use them as a trampoline to weather difficult times. We must be clear in our beliefs and eliminate possible contradictions to embrace them with every ounce of our strength. This requires self-reflection to identify our contradictions and leverage the power of our beliefs to our benefit.

III) Profound transformations need partners

We are not the best advisors to ourselves and are often better off seeking counsel from others. We are not equipped to see our problems clearly; therefore, we need perspective and pointed, thought-provoking opinions from personal mentors or coaches to guide us when attempting to change deep-held beliefs. We must seek help from respected, trusted people who will help us see our blindspots and frame our situation to move ourselves forward.

Their assistance is not only valuable for accepting change but also for devising a plan for our future.

IV) Change is an act of love to self, to others, or to a cause greater than ourselves

Profound change is a victory of love over destructive emotions such as hatred, fear, or despair. We must pass a point of no return to be pulled by love. It is a personal decision; we must be willing to make the leap and surrender to love to redeem its power. Embracing a better version of ourselves requires unconditional love, which means letting go of our old selves. Love drives the process of rebirth, which is necessary to regrow when going through deep change.

Change Precursor

These four powerful epiphanies were instrumental in shaping my mental model for achieving profound change. They shed light on a complex phenomenon and advanced my thinking of how to begin approaching it. As I elaborated on the implications of these findings, another element became apparent. It is the most elusive yet essential factor that determines the difference between failure and success. It is the starting point that steers the journey.

Change is, first and foremost, a personal journey. As such, it requires a wholehearted commitment and the relentless desire to succeed as an individual. There is no transformation without first deciding to undertake it. This step is critical and, perhaps, the most difficult one. Accepting that we must change is less apparent than we might assume. A moment of truth and a mental switch-flipping must precede the endeavor. Let's double-click on this.

I credit the musician James Taylor with a very valuable insight into how commitment precedes profound transformations. Like many of my generation, I grew up hearing James Taylor's songs and have always enjoyed his music. I am always attentive to his public or T.V. appearances, so when I learned that he gave an interview on the Oprah Winfrey Network, I immediately set myself to watch it. The interview dates from 2015 and is named "James Taylor's Best Advice for Addicts: "Sweat It Out," Oprah's Master Class." In one segment, he talked about how he was able to overcome his drug addiction; it has informed my thinking on personal change ever since: "I finally got sober and serious about it and did what I had to do to clean up. You know, it is a self-diagnosed disease; the addict himself has to want to quit. To be in the position where you have to quit but you don't want to is much, much, worse than wanting to quit but you don't know how to."[2]

In my professional life, I have witnessed individuals display dysfunctional behaviors at work that affect their job performance. They are aware of their problem because they commonly receive abundant feedback about the negative impact of their actions on the work environment and team dynamics. As a result, they declare they want to change and openly commit to the task. Their commitment appears genuine and convincing; however, despite their initial assurances and occasional improved behavior, they revert to their destructive patterns a few weeks later. I always wondered why this happens; even though it is so apparent they must change, they don't. It is counterintuitive. When I heard James Taylor's interview, I realized that wanting to change and not knowing how to is not the same as knowing you have to change, but deep in your heart, not wanting to. For the average observer, it is not easy to distinguish one mentality from the other in stuck individuals. Watching this can be frustrating as it leads to wasted lives and unrealized potential. However, as Taylor points out, wanting something results from a choice we make, and moving from a state of not wanting to change to actively pursuing change is a less logical process than we imagine. Instead, I believe it is a journey that requires a heartfelt emotion to endure.

The truth is that we cannot force people to want to change; it can't be induced. It must come from within. Ultimately, the desire for change is an inside-out, not an outside-in undertaking. Conditions must be in place for the person to be able to change, and we can help there, but surpassing the threshold to embrace the "Why" of change and make it happen is entirely a personal decision.

The Transformative Power of Love

As I mentioned in the four epiphanies, profound change is driven by love. Love for oneself, love for others, or love for a cause greater than ourselves. In the process of profound change, we let the light of love in and embrace its redeeming force. Here is where the power of the Why is activated; it implies moving from an unwanted state into a desired one. Love is the medium to generate this shift, and we must be genuinely committed to making this leap and change. As I said, this desire must come from within; it cannot be imposed.

Sometimes, we cannot do it alone and need help. When we stall, pulling ourselves out of the problematic situation is hard, even when we are convinced and determined. To move forward, we often need the support of trusted mentors to help us navigate through challenges, make sense of it all, and resolve the natural contradictions that arise, where fundamental anchors must be shifted or strengthened to succeed. Love guides the way, and we should allow it to uplift us. At the same time, we need to be wise in using all the available resources to make progress, which may include seeking help from others when necessary. We must apply effort and be humble to hear the advice of those who can assist us.

When I realize how complex and personally profound change is, I cannot help but wonder why organizations often take it so lightly when attempting a challenging transformation. When the extent of the challenge in a transformation necessitates a connection with the human spirit of our people, we cannot rely on formulaic change management methods to achieve the desired outcome. We must be mindful of those situations where we must go further and dare to go deep into our people's internal makeup. This is a crucial step in developing a more comprehensive understanding of those around us and their challenges.

For those willing to cross the threshold of change, I suggest a few ideas to make it happen. I will probe the "wanting to change but not knowing how to" in Taylor's definition with a framework that, although I acknowledge that it comes short in explaining a complex phenomenon, I trust could shed some light on how to manage the process. I hope you will find it helpful.

The Individual Regrowth Framework

Opening the valves for Regrowth

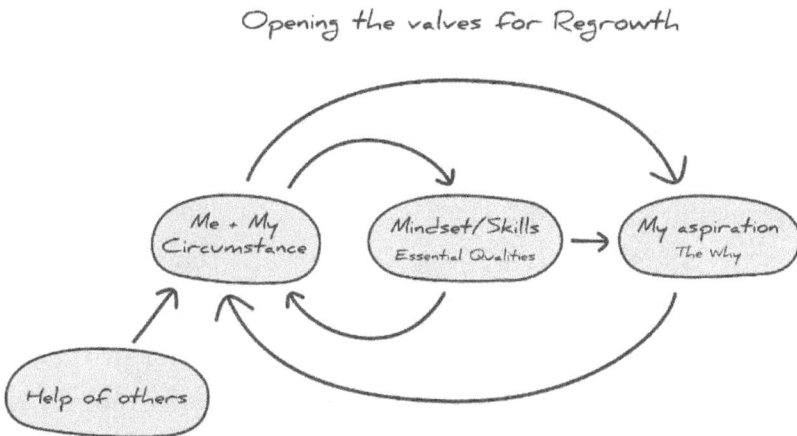

Me + My Circumstance

Mindset/Skills
Essential Qualities

My aspiration
The Why

Help of others

Undertaking a change journey demands acknowledging that we are in the driver's seat, making decisions, and taking actions that lead to Regrowth. This is why I named the framework "Opening the Valves for Regrowth" to emphasize the individual's active participation in its transformation adventure. We should operate and constantly monitor four "valves" in the Regrowth path: Me

+ My Circumstance, Mindset / Skills and Essential Qualities, My Aspiration, and Help from Others. We will explore each one and how they can help us advance our goals in the pages ahead. At this moment, I want to underscore the systemic nature of the model. All valves must be opened, but depending on the challenge, you may need to increase thrust on one valve more than another or even open two or three simultaneously to reach momentum or adjust the system as required. This is your Regrowth journey; you call the shots, and it's up to you to take control of it. No one else can do it for you. You must take responsibility for managing it and be willing to step into the unknown, trusting that things will somehow work out fine.

The "Opening the Valves for Regrowth" framework is based on three principles:

Principle I: Regrowth is an outcome. It is a sought-after consequence and the state we want to acheive to retake our growth trajectory when we hit a wall and stall. We cannot operate directly on Regrowth to attain it; instead, we must focus on the drivers that will help us achieve this outcome, which is described in the "valves."

Principle II: Unlocking potential is a necessary condition for attaining Regrowth. We will only Regrow if we first improve ourselves. By opening up the valves specified in the framework, we will move toward our potential frontier and, eventually, become the best version of ourselves. We must remember that the perception of our potential limits is just a reference on the horizon; it is not a set destination but a marker that moves forward as we approach it.

Principle III: Change must be embraced as an essential part of our lives. We must constantly let go of old beliefs and resources that no longer benefit us and adopt new ones that support us in overcoming obstacles and reaching our goals. We must seize change and accept it as an essential component of our identity.

Before we delve into the framework's components, I want to discuss the conventional wisdom around reaching our potential, particularly the concept of 'finding your passion.' I question the notion that to achieve peak performance, personal growth, and happiness, one must first 'find their passion.' While I acknowledge that those who have found their passion are on the path to realizing their goals, I have not seen enough compelling evidence to demonstrate that finding our passion is something everyone can do. For this to be general advice, it should apply to everyone, not just a select few. And I believe it does not. Let me elaborate.

In my over 40 years of professional career, I have been part of dozens of teams and provided mentorship and coaching to more than 50 individuals to assist them in attaining their goals. I have found that most people need more clarity about their passion, even with help and guidance. Discovering one's passion can be challenging for two main reasons. Firstly, people are seldom triggered by just one thing, and secondly, what was significant for them a few years ago may hold different importance today. Identifying the "burning platform" of passion to spearhead growth is not as straightforward as it appears.

Instead of "finding your passion," I believe it is more beneficial to focus on the simple activities people enjoy and keep them interested, regardless of their role or position. Once they are clear about this, they may start finding patterns or commonalities in those activities that reveal their essential traits. Those traits are the building blocks for achieving potential and growth.

I want to bring Michael Ray's work into the conversation to further reflect on this idea. He is a creativity, innovation, and marketing professor at Stanford University's Graduate School of Business. He describes the concept of connecting with our essence in his book *The Highest Goal*, where he presents the pursuit of our highest goal as the central piece in the transformation journey: "The highest goal is simply to be in this experience of connection to truth (no matter how you refer to it) all the time...If you live for the highest goal, you are living a life of the spirit—whether or not you consider yourself to be on a spiritual path."[3] His approach invites us to practice self-awareness on what is essential and valuable to us and what resonates with our inner core, taking small steps and gradually building from there (we will talk more about it when we discuss essential qualities).

At the individual level, our spirit yearns to be all it is meant to be, and we must diligently work to connect with it and realize the fullness of its possibilities. When I refer to connecting with our spirit, I am not talking about otherworldly matters but rather integrating our essence into day-to-day activities like work, personal relationships, community, etc. Venturing into a regrowth journey entails drawing from our essence and bringing it to the fore to perform; this will help us unlock our dormant potential. The qualities and abilities stemming from our essence are the tools that guide our path, so we must actively engage with them and use them as the foundation for our growth.

Returning to the "Opening the Valves for Regrowth" framework, we must view each of the components in the model as a scaffold to assist you at every step and bring you closer to your goals. The framework comprises an outer oval and an inner ring. The outer oval focuses on "Why am I doing this?" and "Where am I today?" The inner ring encourages you to consider, "What inner abilities and tools do I have at my disposal to succeed on this journey?" An input feeds into the system on the outer edge of the oval ring, representing the help we receive from others.

The development of the framework stems from my personal and professional experiences and all the significant transitions I have gone through in my life. Additionally, I incorporated insights from thinkers I admire and the practices I have seen that have worked for others in my orbit who have undergone multiple transformations. I selected the main elements anyone can leverage to overcome a stall.

To explain how the framework works and can be applied to real-life situations, I will share eight personal turning points that required unlocking my potential and led to my Regrowth. Many more critical situations have demanded personal change, but these represent significant pivotal moments in my trajectory. The first four entailed unlocking my potential in diverse projects I undertook, and the second four occurred within the business group I worked for carrying on different roles:

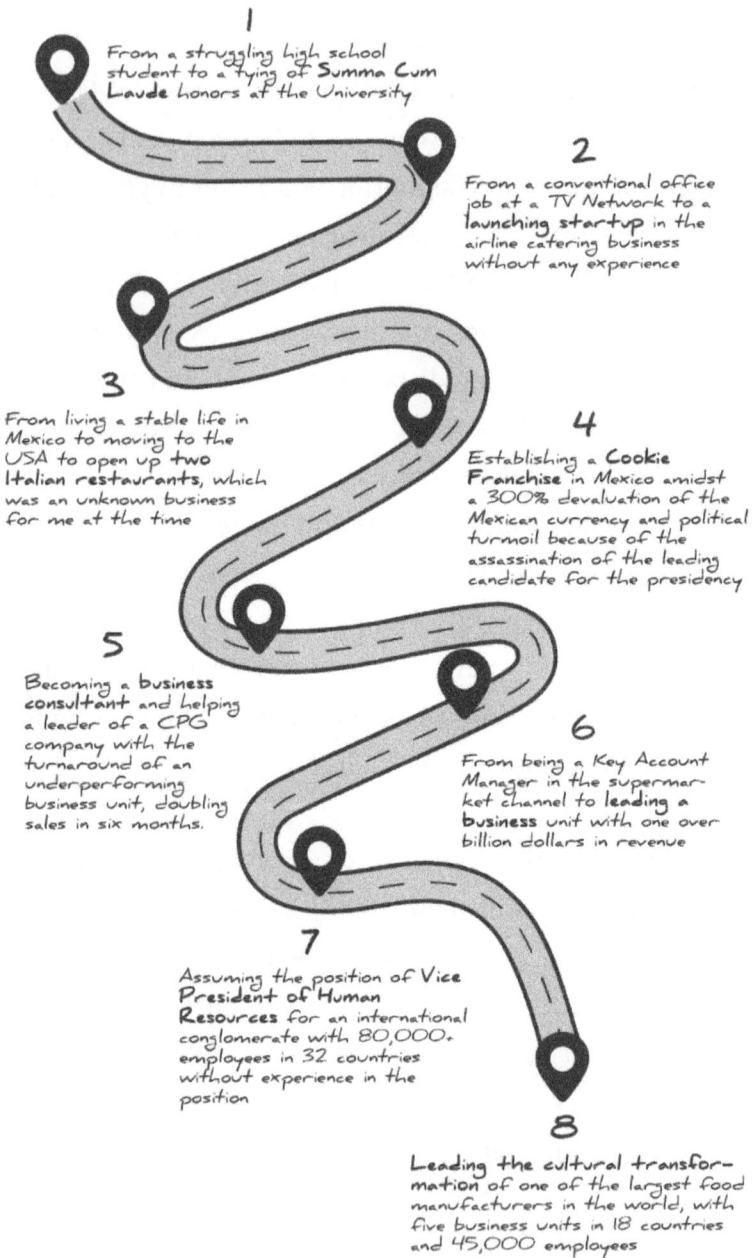

1
From a struggling high school student to a tying of **Summa Cum Laude** honors at the University

2
From a conventional office job at a TV Network to a **launching startup** in the airline catering business without any experience

3
From living a stable life in Mexico to moving to the USA to open up two **Italian restaurants**, which was an unknown business for me at the time

4
Establishing a **Cookie Franchise** in Mexico amidst a 300% devaluation of the Mexican currency and political turmoil because of the assassination of the leading candidate for the presidency

5
Becoming a **business consultant** and helping a leader of a CPG company with the turnaround of an underperforming business unit, doubling sales in six months.

6
From being a Key Account Manager in the supermarket channel to **leading a business** unit with one over billion dollars in revenue

7
Assuming the position of **Vice President of Human Resources** for an international conglomerate with 80,000+ employees in 32 countries without experience in the position

8
Leading the cultural transformation of one of the largest food manufacturers in the world, with five business units in 18 countries and 45,000 employees

- From a struggling high school student to achieving Summa Cum Laude honors at the University
- From a conventional office job at a TV Network to a launching startup in the airline catering business without any experience
- From living a stable life in Mexico to moving to the USA to open up two Italian restaurants, a business unknown to me at the time
- Establishing a cookie franchise in Mexico amidst a 300% devaluation of the Mexican currency and political turmoil because of the assassination of the leading candidate for the presidency
- Becoming a business consultant and helping a leader of a CPG company with the turnaround of an underperforming business unit, doubling sales in six months.
- From being a key account manager in the supermarket channel to leading a business unit with more than one billion dollars in revenue
- Assuming the position of vice president of human resources for an international conglomerate with 80,000+ employees in 32 countries without experience in the position
- Leading the cultural transformation of one of the largest food manufacturers in the world, with five business units in 18 countries and 45,000 employees

I do not proclaim myself to be a personal transformation guru, but I have faced the need to reinvent myself often enough to be able to suggest what has worked for me and hopefully could also work for you. Based on my experience, I can tell you that there is no off-the-shelf, step-by-step manual on self-managing a personal transformation; you cannot bottle the secret sauce for success that works in every situation. However, there are fundamental elements that you can regulate and tweak to unlock your potential and reinvent yourself.

As you read the explanation for each of the valves in the framework, you will find that, on occasions, certain components weigh more than others depending on the specifics of the particular challenge; this is to be expected since challenges come in different forms and will require distinctive approaches.

The First Valve:
My Aspiration, The Why

In the Culture chapter, we explored the concept of organizational purpose, highlighting the importance of aligning the company's and its people's purpose, which is the ideal scenario. The sweet spot of organizational purpose is when the individual's aspirations and the company's ethos are in harmony. However, such alignment is not always feasible; organizations have many constituents, and everyone has different perspectives and goals that may not align with the company's aims. This misalignment between the organization and the individual is not necessarily problematic. If there is room for our aspirations to coexist with the company's objectives, you can still flourish and grow personally and professionally. You may have personal goals unrelated to your organization, but they will still work perfectly as long as they don't collide. The most important thing for you is clearly defining your aspirations and clarifying why you want to achieve them.

When I addressed organizational purpose as the North Star guiding the company, I aimed to show the importance of understanding why it exists beyond making money. However, in the "Opening the Valves for Regrowth" framework, I deliberately chose to use the concept of "My aspiration," or why we do what we do, instead of using the "personal purpose" concept. The reason is that, in mentoring and coaching individuals for the last 20 years, I have witnessed that most have a blurry idea of their goals or the higher purpose they are meant to achieve (same as with "finding your passion"). They are unsure or fuzzy when describing the profound reason why they carry on their work. Maybe one out of 10 is clear about it, but most are not.

There is a difference in how companies and individuals approach defining their purpose. When companies define their purpose, they set a direction and pursue specific goals. On the other hand, individuals must embark on a journey of self-discovery to understand their higher life goals. This process requires deep self-reflection and self-awareness and can take years to accomplish. Defining a company's purpose is a design process while understanding personal purpose is an introspective journey of self-discovery.

If you are fortunate enough to know your purpose, congratulations! You should set your path and pursue it with all your might. However, don't give up hope if you are still figuring out your purpose. You can still set an aspiration that makes sense for you now and pursue it without having a well-defined personal purpose.

You can leverage your essential qualities, as we will discuss in the Third Valve segment in this chapter, to help you achieve your goals.

Aspirations release dormant energy

We know that our aspirations are an energy source that fuels our actions. In the Mindset chapter, we discussed loss aversion and righting a wrong as potent forces that can help you release the energy necessary for change. Using a negative idea we want to avoid as an energy source works well when addressing groups of people because it's easy to socialize a threat and find common ground around it. Perceived threats can be made personal with the proper framing and good communication and mobilize a substantial number of people.

However, while using a negative we want to avoid as an energy source also holds at the individual level, and righteous rage can be a mighty catalyst for our own behaviors, I suggest it is better to underscore a positive perspective when the individual, not the group, leverages energy to achieve their aspirations. It can be argued that the negative is the reverse side of the positive, so the negative we reject mirrors the positive we strive for. Be it as it may, I believe it is better to frame our aspirations positively, highlighting what we want to become instead of signaling the negative that inhibits us. The reason is that unlocking our potential uplifts us and brings the person we want to be to the forefront. It is inspirational and generates a constructive feeling that touches all aspects of our lives and those of others near us.

When setting aspirations, we must establish explicit goals; otherwise, it will be futile. Avoid generalizations as they are harder to translate into actionable items. The more we lay a path to convert our aspirations into actionable steps, the easier it will be to evaluate our progress and make the necessary adjustments. We must bring forth our aspirations and understand the underlying reasons to make them a reality. By going back and forth between our declared aspirations and why we want to achieve them, we can distill our thoughts and gain more clarity and certainty on what we truly want. You would be surprised to learn how understanding the rationale of your aspirations can increase their power and impact on your life.

My Story on Setting My Aspiration

The aspiration and its corresponding "Why" have played a key role in three of the eight personal transformations I previously shared:

- From a struggling high school student to a Summa Cum Laude honors graduate of my university
- Becoming a business consultant and helping a leader of a CPG company with the turnaround of an underperforming business unit, doubling sales in six months.
- Leading the cultural transformation of one of the largest food manufacturers in the world, with five business units in 18 countries and 45,000 employees.

I want to share how setting an aspiration fueled my way to becoming a Summa Cum Laude honors student at the university and became a consequential milestone in my personal life. Until high school, it is fair to say that I was an ordinary student with average grades and little interest in learning. I spent my time on sports and with friends and was content with that lifestyle. However, when it came time to choose a college and pick my courses, I realized I couldn't continue as I had been. It wasn't sustainable for the next chapter of my life. This was a crucial moment for me, a "make it or break it" moment. I realized that "getting by" in college was no longer an option. I had to hold myself to a new standard and take full advantage of the opportunity to learn and grow as much as possible, as the coming years had the potential to shape my life and define my future. So, I set my sights on absorbing as much knowledge as possible in college to create a foundation to propel my professional career.

It was clear that I could not waste this opportunity. I had to give it my best, even though I didn't know how to jump-start the process; I had never done it before! I focused on my studies with everything I had and made learning my top priority. I put my best effort 24-7 into learning and endured sleepless nights. I was not aiming for any particular accomplishment; I just wanted to give learning my best shot and take ownership of the process. It was not easy; I stumbled in the first and third semesters, but fortunately, I still got good grades; as soon as I achieved momentum, the results arrived, and my overall grades showed my commitment. With each accomplishment, my motivation grew, and I got into a virtuous cycle of progress; I felt very motivated and raised the bar for myself each semester.

Upon nearing graduation, I was notified by the university that I was tied with another student for the Suma Cum Laude award, which is one of the highest honors bestowed upon students upon graduation. This award signifies the highest level of distinction or excellence. While obtaining the award was not my original goal, I saw it as a good measure of my hard work and performance, and I was very grateful for the distinction.

The Second Valve:
Me and My Circumstance

The quote "I am me and my circumstance" was coined by José Ortega y Gasset and appeared in his first book, *Meditaciones del Quijote*, published in 1914. I have always found it very insightful to understand human performance and the dynamics of individuals as part of a context. The full Ortega y Gasset's quote is, "I am me and my circumstance, and if I don't save it, I don't save myself." The second portion of the citation is particularly helpful in showing how we must take ownership and assume responsibility for removing or overcoming the restrictions that hold our progress.

In Ortega y Gasset's view, a person cannot be defined in isolation. There is a dynamic interaction between what we are, our essence, and the context where we exist that shapes our identity and can either help or hinder our capacity to become what we are meant to be. In the first part of the quote, "I am me and my circumstance," Ortega y Gasset emphasizes that the environment surrounding us influences our actions, and it's important to acknowledge that conditions can impact our lives and our performance. In the second part of the quote, "and if I don't save it, I don't save myself," Ortega y Gasset highlights our responsibility to own and transform these limitations, as no one else will do it for us. He advocates that we are not passive actors in accepting what happens to us but active participants taking the necessary actions to overcome whatever life presents.

See the big picture with your "mind's eye."

To assess yourself and your circumstance and ultimately take action to save it (life matters, work, relationship, etc.), the first thing you must do is gain perspective and observe yourself as you perform in your day-to-day activities, not as the main protagonist of your life, but as if you were advising another person, a participant in a play that you are watching. Use your "mind's eye" to step out of your reality and see yourself and your context from an external viewpoint; you can gain valuable insights by stepping back and viewing your situation from an outsider's perspective. Ask yourself: What would I advise this person in this situation? Your insights will be more helpful in solving the problem than what you determine operating from the narrow perspective of the protagonist. The key is to detach yourself from the scene and be neutral as you observe the whole picture at a distance. Use your imagination to step outside the situation and try to look at it as a bystander. Doing so will change your perception of overcoming your challenges, and you could start devising a different way forward.

Having an outsider's view of yourself and your context will bring to the fore the barriers that are limiting you from rising to your potential. When assessing what it will take to be all we can be, we typically focus on our abilities and putting them to work to get us where we want to be. We allocate considerable weight to how skills can be leveraged to solve our problems, which we can agree is a necessary condition but, unfortunately, insufficient. We must also evaluate the contextual factors that may be stopping us from reaching our aspirations, such as social prejudices, ethnic biases, economic hardships, inadequate educational opportunities, family responsibilities, and unfair practices at work, to name a few, because if we can overcome those limitations, our struggle will yield a great return and will reduce friction in achieving our aspirations. At first, it may not be obvious to think about removing barriers to reach our potential. We are naturally inclined to jump into action with our skills, but I can assure you that it can be transformational; it's worth the effort to do it.

Removing barriers demands changing ourselves

The paradox of identifying and removing external barriers that hinder our progress is that, despite their external nature, it ultimately requires an internal effort on our part. The issue at hand may be external, located in the surrounding conditions, but the solution to address them is created internally, utilizing our creativity and inner resources. Removing barriers becomes a personal endeavor that requires us to reframe the situation and ourselves.

Removing barriers requires planning and attempting actions we have not taken before. We can't just keep doing what we've always done and expect this behavior will eventually solve our problems. We must assume a new perspective and be open to exploring new paths to break through the barriers restricting our potential, especially if they are significant. We must change our perception of the problem and see it with fresh eyes because our current perception keeps us stuck in our comfort zone.

But how do we change our perspective on a consequential challenge like the ones mentioned above? This is where the task becomes gnarly because we are so invested in seeing the world through our established point of view that imagining a new viewpoint appears contrived. And yet, there is no other way around it. Remember the quote from Anais Nin, "We don't see the world as it is; we see the world as we are"? It emphasizes that we never achieve an objective worldview; we filter reality according to who we are, the message being that if we want to see things differently, we have to change. We must transform how we filter reality to overcome significant obstacles, which requires a shift in our identity. We need to broaden the "see the world as we are" part of Nin's citation to solve our problems, and the only way to accomplish this task is by expanding our sense of self and letting go of the limitations holding us back.

The point is that you must reimagine who you are to overcome the barriers that limit your potential. It would be best if you did so informed by your aspiration and with a renewed view of yourself that will allow you to succeed. In the "Me and My Circumstance" characterization, the "Me" has to do the heavy lifting; the crux lies in enhancing our identity to succeed.

The greater the barrier, the more critical it is to broaden our perspective and identity. If we fail to expand our sense of self, we'll continue to repeat the same patterns that made us stumble in the first place. It's difficult to overcome our limitations; we know that it is often a lifelong endeavor, but if we want to see reality in a new light, there is no other way but to change ourselves and our identity. Your identity is shaped by how you perceive yourself and the internal dialogue that reinforces that self-image. To be the architect of your destiny, you have to be the architect of yourself first.

My Story on Me + My Circumstance

Evaluating myself and my circumstances and redefining my identity to remove barriers were key in my following transformations:

- Establishing a cookie franchise in Mexico amidst a 300% devaluation of the Mexican currency and political turmoil because of the assassination of the leading candidate for the presidency
- Becoming a business consultant and helping a leader of a CPG company with the turnaround of an underperforming business unit, doubling sales in six months.
- Assuming the position of vice president of human resources for an international conglomerate with 80,000+ employees in 32 countries without experience in the position

I want to share how assuming the position of vice president of human resources for a conglomerate with 80,000+ employees worldwide required a deep evaluation of "Me + My Circumstance" and how redefining my identity changed how I conducted my professional career.

In 2014, I was offered a vice president position in human resources. It was late in my professional trajectory, and the role represented a significant change compared to what I had been doing before. The group CEO thought it would be a good idea to bring somebody with operational experience to a senior staff position, someone who felt the pain of the trenches and had direct experience with the day-to-day needs of the business. It was a stretch, but the company gave me full support to bring me up to speed. I attended several human resources programs at top universities in the US and Europe and interacted with several hundred colleagues worldwide who worked in medium to large companies. After a few months on the job, I was thrilled with the challenge and passionate about taking the company to another level, but I felt I made a big mistake in accepting the role. My evaluation of the situation was that I did not belong to the Human Resources community, my profile was incompatible with the position's responsibilities, and I believed I was not the right person for the job.

On top of that, I had to navigate a challenging internal business environment. The Human Resources job entails a wide range of operational and strategic activities, and many decisions have no clear right or wrong approach. You can get stuck easily because there is no black-and-white solution, and the field is naturally intangible. My internal clients were business unit CEOs who were hard to please and questioned everything. Some were old-school and adamant about investing in their people's development. Additionally, economic conditions were adverse at the time, and they were reluctant to spend on anything that would not show in the bottom line in the short term. I encountered barriers on many fronts that demanded an uphill battle.

I was frustrated and hard-pressed to deliver results, but I did not want to quit despite the adverse conditions. I was fully committed to making it work. One afternoon, alone in my office, I was ruminating about my options. Should I reorganize and distribute some of my duties to my reports to free myself to focus on urgent and essential tasks? Maybe I could hire a consultant to help me devise a better strategy or benchmark what other companies were doing. Still, regardless of the options at hand, I felt uncomfortable in my Human Resources skin, and this was the most critical problem to solve. Everything else could be managed if I felt empowered to engage with my role and pursue my responsibilities to the fullest of my abilities. I thought I didn't have what it took to succeed. Suddenly, I had an epiphany: What if, instead of being the Human Resources guy at corporate, I assumed a different identity as the innovation guy in charge of Human Resources? What would this mean for me and my job? I felt a rush of energy going through my veins; bingo, this is who I wanted to be! Being the innovation guy in charge of Human Resources allowed me to be bold, experiment, and remove the traditional Human Resources clout to think differently. I could be creative and defy the status quo. I saw myself performing with this identity, and I was excited!

This was my Eureka moment. Becoming the innovation guy in charge of Human Resources was empowering and changed how I approached strategy and problem-solving at corporate. It helped me abandon stereotypes, unlock my potential, and transform the area under my responsibility. It was contagious, and soon, my team felt empowered to do the same.

The Third Valve: Mindset + Skills / Essential Qualities

As with the first two valves in the Regrowth framework, we already discussed two components of the third valve in previous chapters of the book: skills in the chapter devoted to talent and mindset in its own chapter. Still, I would like to briefly review these two elements from a different perspective and introduce a third element to shed light on how they constitute an important lever to unlocking potential at the individual level.

To explain the concept of the third valve, let's consider a thought experiment. Imagine you want to become an entrepreneur, grow your own business, and become economically independent. Upon acknowledging this aspiration, you assess yourself and confirm that you possess all the necessary traits to turn it into a reality: you are innovative, adaptable, and willing to take calculated risks. Additionally, you are inquisitive, resilient, disciplined, and have a growth mindset. You can adapt when circumstances change and are ready to do whatever it takes to succeed. In essence, you demonstrate a 100% positive mindset.

However, you lack the practical skills required to run a startup. You do not know about finance, management, operations, marketing, leadership, etc. In the trials before launching your product, you receive feedback from potential consumers stating that it has several pain points, and you do not have the slightest idea of how to solve them. You are clueless about managing a business. Under these circumstances, the likelihood of success is exceedingly low. While you might learn the necessary skills and get lucky, it's doubtful.

Let's consider the opposite scenario. Imagine possessing top-notch business management skills, scoring 100% in proficiency for all the mentioned skills. However, you lack the necessary beliefs, mental models, and confidence to implement your startup effectively. With this personal makeup, you will likely give up at the first sign of difficulty, scoring 0% in mindset. What would your chances of success be under these conditions? They would be very low.

Do you grasp the concept of the thought experiment? You must develop your mindset and skills to unlock your potential and achieve your goals. It's okay not to excel in every area or have a perfect balance because everyone has strengths and weaknesses. However, you must meet a minimum threshold in both mindset and skills to progress. Regardless of your starting point, you must activate the improvement process to reach your potential. Once you do that, mindset and skills will reinforce each other and create a virtuous cycle; the more they feed into each other, the more momentum you will gain.

The mindset and skills combo will give you the functional attributes and will be the launching pad for your improvement. Still, you need an additional lever, a personal trait, to boost your performance and achieve your goals. We will name this third element "Essential Qualities."

I will refer again to Michael Ray and his book *The Highest Goal* to elaborate on this concept: "A quality is a superior character-istic or property of something...a life quality represents a deep attribute that characterizes an important part of one's life. It is a distinguishing property of life."[4] The activities you like to do touch upon the essential qualities that give meaning to your life. When performing those activities, something resonates with who you are and what you want to become.

The process of identifying your essential qualities requires introspection. You must analyze the activities you enjoy to uncover the deeper traits they represent: "Some say that the very purpose of human existence is to get acquainted with your own essential qualities and express them in your daily activities. Whether it is the purpose of life or not, it is a fine definition of personal creativity: living every moment from your essence."[5]

When we go about our lives or work, we tend to engage in specific activities that bring us joy and a sense of meaning. Iden-tifying these activities is important as they connect us with our true selves. It may not be apparent initially, but exploring and embracing these activities to determine if they bring us happiness is crucial. Discovering our essential qualities is the key to living a fulfilling life: "If you know your qualities, you can stay right where you are and use them to make your work fulfilling... you can do what you love, and you can transform the things you have to do into activities you love."[6]

In his book, Michael Ray enumerates an array of essential qualities, including courage, friendship, harmony, communication, generosity, positiveness, excellence, humor, service, truth, freedom, gratitude, order, renewal, and wonder.

The main point of this section is about integrating our mindset and skills with essential qualities and incorporating them into our daily lives. Your Regrowth journey will be underway when your mindset, skills, and essential qualities are in harmony. Hitendra Wadhwa, a professor at Columbia Business School and the founder of the Mentora Institute, explains this concept as follows: "While you wait to find a vocation that fits your Purpose, you can mold your Purpose to fit your vocation."[7]

My story on Mindset + Skills / Essential Qualities

Mindset + Skills and Essential Qualities have been my preferred go-to "hack" for dealing with various challenges in my life. Specifically, I have often leveraged the Skill component, attempting to "outskill" every complex condition that has come my way. I realized the importance of incorporating the other two components later in my professional trajectory. Looking in hindsight, I identify three personal transformations where these attributes were instrumental to unlocking my potential.

- From a conventional office job at a TV Network to a launching startup in the airline catering business without any experience
- Becoming a business consultant and helping a leader of a CPG company with the turnaround of an underperforming business unit, doubling sales in six months.

- From being a key account manager in the supermarket channel to leading a business unit with more than one billion dollars in revenue

I want to share how my Mindset, Skills, and Essential Qualities were crucial to my consulting work journey and how I spread it to people I worked with, multiplying its impact. Here's the story: A leading CPG company requested my assistance with the turnaround of one of their business units; they needed to revamp it because it was not delivering the expected results. The CPG company is based in Monterrey, Mexico, and is the leader in processed meats, yogurt, and cheeses. They had heavily invested in a modern frozen food facility to venture into the prepared meals segment. They aimed to supply ready meals for home consumption and the food service channel of hotels, restaurants, theme parks, and other similar establishments. However, the frozen food unit failed to meet its sales and profitability targets. They requested my assistance in revamping their marketing strategy and product offerings to achieve profitability.

In my initial assessment of the business, I found out that, at the time, home consumers in Mexico were adamant about buying prepared meals for home consumption; to feed their families, they preferred to cook on their own. Betting on this segment to turn things around would be difficult, so I suggested focusing on restaurants, hotels, theme parks, etc., instead, where prepared meals could help solve safety-related problems, challenges in flavor consistency, labor costs, and difficulties in preparation. The company agreed with my assessment and offered me an "earn-out" agreement for my consulting services. In the agreement, I would commit to increasing sales by 100% in six months, and my compensation would depend on achieving this target. I was inspired by the challenge and trusted the business unit team's capacity to turn around the business under my guidance. I accepted the conditions, and corporate gave me complete freedom to do whatever I wanted, although I knew bureaucracy and slow decision-making could be problematic.

As the size of the undertaking sank in me, I evaluated my ability to succeed. I knew I had the right Mindset to pull it off. I have successfully executed many challenging projects, consider myself resilient, and believe in my ability to leverage internal resources to overcome hurdles. Regarding my skills and experience, I was already a seasoned executive who was comfortable dealing with business problems. I have also operated restaurants, catering, and food-to-go services. My background gave me confidence, but I was still wary. I knew I needed something more to succeed, which implied activating my left brain and surfacing my personal traits and essential qualities to boost my performance.

I have always been entrepreneurial; it is an essential quality near and dear to me, so I didn't have a problem bringing out my entrepreneurial juices to face the challenge immediately. Additionally, I could put forth other essential qualities to get the job done, like enthusiasm, communication, and creativity. I needed to leverage these to navigate uncharted territory and take smart risks along the way. The most crucial aspect was motivating the team towards the ambitious objective of doubling sales when they tried before and fell short. I needed to use my qualities to connect with others and bring everyone on board to undertake the challenge with a fresh perspective. While I was confident about my abilities, the question remained: Would it be sufficient to achieve the objective? Could I mobilize the team to make it happen?

As you can imagine, many functions, processes, and departments were involved in such an ambitious project. One thing was clear: I needed to unlock my potential and help others within the company unlock theirs to attain the goal. This was a team effort, and I needed a chain reaction to get the stalled business onto a Regrowth path.

To make a long story short, with the help of a great team of professionals, the business unit increased sales by 100% in 6 months. The company asked me to stay and offered me a permanent position to help move the unit forward. This experience led to a 23-year stint, heading many functions and businesses within the organization, significantly broadening my scope of influence and advancing my professional career.

Leveraging your mindset, skills, and essential qualities is critical to reaching your potential. When you can spread this positive energy to others to help them rise to their potential, magic happens.

The Fourth Valve: Help From Others

Throughout this book, I have stressed the importance of exploring our blind spots, confronting the negative aspects of our ego, cultivating psychological safety, expanding our perspectives, adopting a more holistic approach, and more. These themes revolve around our capacity to integrate diverse perspectives and leverage valuable insights to better ourselves. It is essential to listen to the perspectives of others attentively, get feedback about our performance, and learn to achieve this goal. Doing so is vital to unlocking our potential and paving the way for growth and transformation. This thinking leads to the framework's last valve: Getting Help From Others. I cannot emphasize more how opening this valve will help us jumpstart our Regrowth journey.

In the "Opening the Valves for Regrowth" framework, "Getting Help from Others" is placed outside the system as input. In contrast, all other elements are located inside the system and are a function of our thinking. This component represents external sources available to us that we can tap into to obtain information that we can leverage to our benefit. Usually, we seek help only when we are stuck or need assistance figuring out what to do, but this doesn't have to be the case. Seeking other's advice habitually allows us to be aware of our shortcomings and enhance our performance.

We usually seek advice from those we trust and who know us well. We may also seek guidance from individuals who are knowledgeable in our areas of interest and can act as mentors, coaches, and guides to help steer our growth. Regardless, the most crucial part to remember is to ensure that the information they provide us is transparent and honest, even if it's painful or hard to hear. They are valuable resources for identifying our blind spots and acting as soundingboards to correct them. Do not fall into the trap of thinking that once you reach a certain level of performance, you no longer need help from others. Many accomplished individuals who have triumphed in their respective fields use this resource consistently; this is precisely what allows them to continue delivering their best performance. For example, one might assume that a renowned football quarterback like Tom Brady wouldn't require any further assistance once he reached the top. However, he continually sought feedback to enhance his game. He said, "You must understand yourself, and that what you know is limited and what you don't know is infinite. Every day, you have the opportunity to surround yourself with individuals who can assist you in your growth."[8]

There are other sources that one can utilize to obtain relevant help, as well. They can be pretty valuable, especially when you know your areas to improve. Such sources include books, journals, podcasts, interviews, specialized publications, conferences, and industry networks. By leveraging them, you can obtain a wealth of knowledge and valuable insights that can be instrumental in your development.

Knowing what to ask makes the difference

Whether we seek help through personal interactions or other means, the key to obtaining the information we need to improve lies in the questions we ask. If we have access to knowledgeable individuals but fail to ask the right questions, the interaction will not yield the desired benefits. Thoughtfully crafted questions enhance our understanding of the issues and lead to insightful discussions. By asking the right questions, we take control of our learning process and significantly improve our chances of receiving valuable advice.

If the quality of the answers we receive depends on our ability to ask the right questions, how can we ensure we are asking questions correctly? What are the characteristics of a good question? Warren Berger's perspective on creating good questions is valuable. His book *A More Beautiful Question* (Bloomsbury, 2014) describes a good question as a "beautiful question." He defines it as "an ambitious yet actionable question that can begin to shift the way we perceive or think about something—and that might serve as a catalyst to bring about change." He adds, "The focus here is on questions that can be acted upon, questions that can lead to tangible results and change."[9]

I believe that the ability to ask good questions is a combination of science and art. You can learn a method that will help you improve, but there is a creative component to it that is difficult to bottle. Exploring the process of asking good questions is beyond the scope of this book, but there are excellent sources you can access if you are interested. I recommend books like *Humble Inquiry* (Berret-Koehler Publishers, 2013) by Edgar H. Schein, *Questions are the Answer* (Harper Business, 2018) by Hal Gregersen, and Warren Berger's *A Beautiful Question*. Moreover, remember that practice and reflection on your questioning skills are essential to advance in this area.

I found an interesting approach to asking questions that Elon Musk shared during a Lex Friedman podcast on December 28, 2021. Elon Musk talked about his process for asking the right questions about the meaning and purpose of the universe, which I found very revealing: "What Douglas Adams was saying in *The Hitchhiker's Guide to the Galaxy* is that the universe is the answer, and what we really need to figure out are what questions to ask about the answer that is the universe...if you can properly frame the question, then the answer, relatively speaking, is easy. There-fore, if you want to understand what questions to ask about the universe, you want to understand the meaning of life, we need to expand the scope and scale of consciousness so that we're better able to understand the nature of the universe and understand the meaning of life and, ultimately, the most important part would be to ask the right question".[10]

Elon Musk introduced a clever way of asking a question on a complex subject; instead of asking, "What is the purpose of the universe?" and probably getting lost in a conceptual, never-ending discussion, he reversed the thought process. He asked, "What are the questions to ask for which the universe is the answer?" This approach allows us to understand the universe's purpose by identifying the questions that lead to the universe as an answer. In the context of this book, I would like to follow Elon Musk's thinking and ask, "If the answer is unlocking our full potential, what questions must we ask?"

I would urge you to think about it. If the answer is unlocking your potential, what questions would you ask?

Let me share the questions I would ask:

- What essence is in me that wants to be expressed?
- What is the distinctive impact that I believe can make?
- What do I stand for? What activities bring me joy?
- What is holding me back from becoming who I aspire to be?
- What mindset will help me attain my goal? What beliefs must I hold?
- What do I need to know? What new topics should I learn and be good at?

- How do I manage my daily activities so I can invest the necessary time and effort in achieving my goals?
- How do I assess my progress?
- How can I achieve a compound effect on developing my talent and skills?
- What type of people do I need to associate with?
- What external sources should I access to help me guide the process?
- How can I adapt better to a changing world?

As you can tell, the topics we covered in the "Opening the Valves for Regrowth" framework touch on many of these questions. Still, I encourage you to pause and reflect on the questions you would ask to unlock your potential. This way, you can devise your own approach and set a path to realize your potential and become the person you want to be.

My Story on Getting Help From Others

"Getting help from others" was crucial in achieving my objectives in the eight personal transformations I shared, so selecting a few was difficult. I will forever be grateful to the many individuals who kindly helped me by answering my questions and guiding my way forward with their insights. There is one instance, though, that I would like to highlight because the help I obtained from that encounter continues to inspire my thinking to this day. I will refer to the transformation episode I explained in the "Me + My Circumstance" section, but I will indulge in going at it again.

- Assuming the position of Vice President of Human Resources for an international conglomerate with 80,000+ employees in 32 countries without experience in the position

As I mentioned, overcoming the challenge of holding this new position was difficult; my knowledge was limited since I had no experience in this field. Immediately after my assignment, I researched training programs, experts, consultants, etc, that could assist me in my endeavor. I mentioned how, thanks to my company's support, I attended several executive education programs and connected with renowned faculty of top universities. One of the universities I attended and later developed a close relationship with was Massachusetts Institute of Technology's Sloan School of Management. MIT was a precious source of knowledge in many ways. My friends there helped me arrange a conversation (that, fortunately, led to a few more encounters) with Peter Senge, one of my most admired thinkers and guru of organizational transformation.

I became familiar with his thinking when I read *The Fifth Discipline, The Art & Practice of the Learning Organization* (Crown Business, 1990). I prepared to make the most of the one-hour meeting he graciously offered. On the meeting day, he asked me about the company and my goals and listened to my explanation kindly and attentively. I presented my challenge and bombarded him with many ideas, training options, methods, and how I would use technology to scale the company's transformation as quickly as possible. By the time I finished my monologue, I asked his opinion. He calmly replied that I should experiment with alternatives to determine what could work best. However, he pointed out that the sense of community that people developed in a transformation and how the collective leadership in the organization embeds change in their daily work is what matters most. He closed his comment with a remark that sparked a revelation that to this day stays with me: "You know, technology is not the frontier; people are."

This insight is a powerful one. I was attempting change at scale by implementing all the tools and methods in the toolbox that would arguably produce the desired outcome in the organization. This "outside-in" approach tried to push change into the people, but I lost sight that change is an "inside-out" undertaking that a perspective shift must elicit. To handle the people frontier, I needed to bring our people together into the cause and jumpstart a movement I could support with team practices. So, I pursued a transformation journey with the "inside-out" approach, which led to initiatives and development programs where the individual was at the center and helped mobilize the organization.

After my conversation with Peter, I have come to appreciate the concept of human beings being the ultimate frontier even more. This idea has helped me understand the organizational transformation phenomena and make better decisions to help it unlock its potential and Regrow. With the increasing attention on artificial intelligence, this concept is more important than ever. It reminds us that the organization should not be managed as a function of artificial intelligence algorithms but rather vice versa. In other words, while AI undoubtedly offers transformative capabilities, it is crucial to emphasize a human-centered approach to inspire and lead the organization's overarching goals.

The Faith Factor

In the mindset chapter, I discussed how faith is an anchor in our minds, strengthening our belief system and feeding the energy required to move forward and face our challenges. I presented some examples of leaders such as Winston Churchill, Steve Jobs, Tom Brady, and Ben Horowitz to illustrate its impact. Since faith is such an essential component of performance, you may wonder why I did not explicitly include it in the "Opening the Valves of Regrowth" framework.

I did not include it because having faith is a personal decision, and I wanted to discuss the actionable items anyone can use to attain their goals. Even if you feel low on faith, you can still progress by following my outlined system. Nevertheless, I firmly believe that having faith is crucial for achieving our goals. It's essential to have faith in something that inspires you —whether it's God, ideals, family, community, or yourself— and use that faith to become all you can be. Out of your love for the things that give meaning to your life will come the faith in yourself to undertake your goals.

Faith that you will succeed and keep going until the end is not just an additional component in our journey to unlock potential; it's the platform we can leverage to transition toward significant achievements. I urge you to hang on to faith and trust that, in the end, everything will fall into place, and your journey will be worth every step. Faith paves the way for becoming all we can be, and we must use it as a lever to guide our path to Regrowth.

Final Thoughts

As I conclude this book, I want to highlight that the "Opening the Valves for Regrowth" framework is a flywheel that gains momentum with each turn. Once we set it in motion and make progress, it is critical to reflect on what is working and what is not so we can adjust accordingly. Unlocking our essence and abilities and reaching our potential is not a one-time endeavor but a permanent adventure renewed by our will to improve. As we move forward with the flywheel, we will expand the horizon of what we thought was possible since our perceived limits are targets that move as we go. Anders Ericsson illustrates this point beautifully: "In this new world, it no longer makes sense to think of people as born with fixed reserves of potential; instead, potential is an expandable vessel, shaped by various things we do throughout our lives. Learning isn't a means to reaching one's potential but rather a way of developing it. We can create our own potential."[11]

I wish you the best in your Regrowth journey. I hope these concepts will be helpful and shed light on how to take action. Before finishing, I would like to leave you with an idea I shared earlier in this chapter that I believe is essential for your success and must guide your way forward: Profound change is an act of love, a victory of the love we hold for ourselves, others, or a cause greater than ourselves over limiting or harmful conditions. Love is the vital force that drives our lives; when attempting to change, love is the springboard that helps us move from the darkness of an undesired state into the light of becoming what we are meant to be. Be well.

Afterword

My main goal of this book was to deliver the message that for organizations to overcome stalling and Regrow, they need to establish an adaptive internal system leveraging talent density, culture, and mindset to address their customers' constantly changing needs. This inside job must be supported by unlocking their people's potential to generate distinctive knowledge and the corresponding actions to succeed in the market.

When we think about unlocking our team's potential, our initial instinct is often to focus on developing functional, learnable skills that can be easily integrated within teams—and there's merit in that approach. Focusing on the operational aspects can indeed yield benefits for organizations. However, we must move beyond the operational to truly unlock our organization's potential. This requires fostering a large-scale 'soul-searching' process with our people, aligning their insights with the company's goals. By encouraging collective introspection—where individuals connect with their aspirations, inner qualities, and essence—we enable them to grow personally while contributing to the organization's success. Massive growth becomes possible when people connect deeply with their true selves and embody who they are meant to be, empowering them to achieve their highest potential and conquer the seemingly impossible.

Given the significant time we invest in work, organizations have a unique opportunity to ignite this transformation, creating immense value for their customers and the world. We should embrace a new perspective of the organization as a place of personal and spiritual growth. In supporting their people in reaching their full potential, organizations must be committed to nurturing the spiritual side of their people, as I explained. Still, we must be careful not to confuse this effort with advocating religious beliefs, as they are distinct and belong to a personal domain.

As the book found its voice and I approached the completion of my writing, I felt compelled to convey an additional message: While organizations can help us connect with our true selves and realize our unique talents, personal renewal depends on understanding our inner qualities and harnessing the power of love. Love is the foundation for overcoming stagnation and Regrowing ourselves. To support this journey, I introduced a 'valves' framework, symbolizing the adjustments we can make to navigate our paths with greater clarity and purpose. Our personal journey requires constant calibration and reflection to overcome life's challenges.

We must understand ourselves deeply before we can truly grow, whether as individuals or organizations. We don't grow and then discover who we are; instead, we first look inside to embrace our full potential, and then we can grow. Nurturing our true essence is vital for real evolution.

Acknowledgments

Writing this book has been the most daunting challenge of my life. My thinking on how organizations can unlock people's potential has undergone a transformative and unpredictable journey over the past six years, from the first spark of ideas to the final manuscript. I crafted countless outlines and indexes to shape the book's structure, but the real challenge was putting my thoughts in black and white. In your mind, ideas make sense and work together "seamlessly," but once you attempt to put them into a narrative, you realize how difficult it is to distill a coherent message that leads to action. While writing can offer moments of joy, for me, it was a demanding struggle to reconcile words and ideas. This experience has deepened my respect for writers and their craft; creating a book is a solitary and intense endeavor where you must always be at the top of your game. Despite being exacting, I am thrilled that I could accomplish the task.

This book also allowed me to set an example for my family and friends. I intend to show you can achieve anything you wish despite limitations or challenging circumstances. With a compelling aspiration accompanied by creativity and determination, our possibilities are limitless. What more significant legacy could I leave to my family than this book? It is a tangible testament that we can reinvent ourselves at any stage or age.

I was lucky to have Elaine Pofeldt as my editor when developing the book. She is an outstanding professional and also a great person. She tells it as it is directly, without sugarcoating, but graciously. Her smile is contagious, and she can drive you to perform better. Jane Tabachnick helped me give the book its final form and its look and feel. She is a master of her craft and a highly structured person; I was fortunate to have her on my team. Denisse Prado helped me with the cover design and the illustrations. She is a very talented and super-creative designer. She can read your mind and represent your ideas better than you imagine. My daughter, Fernanda Gomez, is an exceptionally talented photographer, and I genuinely believe no one could have captured my photos better than she did. Fernanda has built a highly successful international photography firm (EFEGE); I cannot recommend her enough. While you might think I'm biased, I assure you that her work speaks for itself. She consistently delivers outstanding results.

My family has been my rock, and I am deeply grateful to them. My wife, Thelma, has been a constant source of support throughout my life and during the development of this book. I can't imagine accomplishing what I have without her. Andrea, Fernanda, and Cordelia are the most wonderful daughters I could ever ask for, and they bring me happiness like no one else. I am truly fortunate to have them in my life. My sons-in-law, Andrés, Juan Pablo, and Joaquín, are valuable additions to my family. They are inquisitive and not afraid to challenge my thinking. My granddaughters, Mariel, Raquel, and Lorenza, bring me immense joy. They have given my life new meaning, and I eagerly look forward to watching them grow.

I've always believed I am a work in progress, constantly evolving and striving to improve. Most of what I have accomplished is due to the trust and confidence that others have placed in me throughout my life. I owe much of my success to those who have provided me with invaluable opportunities, guidance, and encouragement. Many mentors and colleagues come to mind, and I want to extend my heartfelt thanks to each of you.

References

Introduction

1. *The Founder's Mentality: How to Overcome the Predictable Crises of Growth*, by Chris Zook and James Allen, Harvard Business Review Press, 2016.
2. *Change by Design.* Brown, Tim, New York, Harper Collins, 2009.
3. *The Founder's Mentality: How to Overcome the Predictable Crises of Growth*, by Chris Zook and James Allen, Harvard Business Review Press, 2016.
4. Ibidem
5. Ibidem

Chapter 1

1. *Zero to IPO: Over $1 Trillion Worth of Advice from the World's Most Successful Entrepreneurs*, Frederic Kerrest, McGraw-Hill Education, 2022
2. *Digital Disruption: Unleashing the Next Wave of Innovation*, James McQuivey, Forrester Research, Incorporated, 2013
3. *Winning the Right Game: How to Disrupt, Defend, and Deliver in a Changing World*, Ron Adner, MIT Press, 2021
4. *The Structure of Scientific Revolutions: 50th Anniversary Edition*, Thomas S. Kuhn, University of Chicago Press, 2012

5. *More than you know: finding financial wisdom in unconventional places,* Michael J. Mauboussin, Columbia Business School Pub., 2008

6. *Only the paranoid survive: how to exploit the crisis points that challenge every company and career,* Andrew S. Grove, Crown, 1996

7. Ibidem

8. *CEO Excellence: The Six Mindsets That Distinguish the Best Leaders from the Rest.* Carolyn Dewar, Scott Keller, and Vikram Malhotra, Scribner, 2022

9. *The Practice of Management,* Peter F. Drucker, HarperCollins, 1993

10. *Management: Tasks, Responsibilities, Practices,* Peter F. Drucker, Harper & Row, 1985

11. *Competing Against Luck: The Story of Innovation and Customer Choice,* Clayton M. Christensen, Taddy Hall, Karen Dillon, and David S. Duncan, HarperCollins, 2016

12. Ibidem

13. *Digital Disruption: Unleashing the Next Wave of Innovation,* James McQuivey, Forrester Research, Incorporated, 2013

14. *Only the paranoid survive: how to exploit the crisis points that challenge every company and career,* Andrew S. Grove, Crown, 1996

15. *Hit Refresh: The Quest to Rediscover Microsoft's Soul and Imagine a Better Future for Everyone,* Satya Nadella, Greg Shaw, and Jill Tracie Nichols, HarperCollins, 2017

Chapter 2

1. *Competing Against Luck: The Story of Innovation and Customer Choice*, Clayton M. Christensen, Taddy Hall, Karen Dillon, and David S. Duncan, HarperCollins, 2016

2. *The Heart of Business with Hubert Jolly,* Gary Hammel, and Michele Zanini, June 16, 2022 https://www.youtube.com/watch?v=C2vujGFTeRI

3. *Customer Experience First,* Steve Jobs, February 10, 2019, https://www.youtube.com/watch?v=d8n5hCLvuzc

4. *Measure what Matters: How Google, Bono, and the Gates Foundation Rock the World with OKRs,* John Doerr, Portfolio/Penguin, 2018

5. *Invent and Wander: The Collected Writings of Jeff Bezos, with an Introduction by Walter Isaacson,* Jeff Bezos, Harvard Business Review Press, 2020

6. *Winning Investors Over: Surprising Truths about Honesty, Earnings Guidance, and Other Ways to Boost Your Stock Price,* Baruch Lev, Harvard Business Review Press, 2012

7. *The 4 Stages of Psychological Safety: Defining the Path to Inclusion and Innovation,* Timothy R. Clark, Berrett-Koehler Publishers, 2020

8. *Value Creation Thinking,* Bartley J. Madden, LearningWhat-Works, 2016

9. *Rumsfeld / Knowns,* Donald Rumsfeld, February 12, 2002 https://www.youtube.com/watch?v=REWeBzGuzCc

10. *Breaking Down Barriers to Innovation,* Paul Cobban, Rahul Nair and Natalie Painchaud, Harvard Business Review, 2019

11. *Creativity, Inc.: Overcoming the Unseen Forces That Stand in the Way of True Inspiration*, Ed Catmull and Amy Wallace, Random House Publishing Group, 2014

12. *The Disruption Dilemma*, Joshua Gans, MIT Press, 2016

13. Ibidem

14. *Lead and Disrupt: How to Solve the Innovator's Dilemma*, Charles A. O'Reilly and Michael Tushman, Stanford University Press, 2021

15. Ibidem

16. Ibidem

17. *Exploration and Exploitation in Organizational Learning*, Organization Science, Vol. 2, No. 1, Special Issue: Organizational Learning: Papers in Honor of (and by) James G. March (1991)

18. *Invitation to Read James G. March: Reflections on the Processes of Decision Making, Learning and Change in Organizations*, Thierry Weil, Mines ParisTech-PSL, 2022

19. *An interview with Professor James G. March*, September 2013, https://www.youtube.com/watch?v=PwgOiE4DAzA

20. *That Will Never Work: The Birth of Netflix and the Amazing Life of an Idea*, Marc Randolph, Little, Brown, 2019

21. Ibidem

22. *Ballmer Laughs at iPhone*, September 18, 2007,https://www.youtube.com/watch?v=eywi0h_Y5_U

23. *Creativity, Inc.: Overcoming the Unseen Forces That Stand in the Way of True Inspiration*, Ed Catmull and Amy Wallace, Random House Publishing Group, 2014

24. Ibidem

Chapter 3

1. *Masters of Scale: Surprising Truths from the World's Successful Entrepreneurs*, Reid Hoffman, June Cohen, and Deron Triff, Crown, 2021

2. *Simply Managing: What Managers Do—and Can Do Better*, Henry Mintzberg, Berrett-Koehler Publishers, 2013

3. *Superforecasting: The Art and Science of Prediction*, Philip E. Tetlock and Dan Gardner, Crown, 2015

4. *Creating Great Choices: A Leader's Guide to Integrative Thinking*, Jennifer Riel and Roger L. Martin, Harvard Business Review Press, 2017

5. *When More is Not Better: Overcoming America's Obsession with Economic Efficiency*, Roger L. Martin, Harvard Business Review Press, 2020

6. *The Score Takes Care of Itself: My Philosophy of Leadership*, Bill Walsh, Steve Jamison, and Craig Walsh, Penguin Publishing Group, 2010

7. *The Number One Killer of Successful Organizations: How To Avoid Being Its Next Victim*, Fred Koffman, Linkedin, July 21, 2014

8. *When More is Not Better: Overcoming America's Obsession with Economic Efficiency*, Roger L. Martin, Harvard Business Review Press, 2020

9. *Presence: Human Purpose and the Field of the Future*, Peter M. Senge, C. Otto Scharmer, Joseph Jaworski, and Betty Sue Flowers, Crown, 2008

10. *Clonal Colonies in the Forest*, Jeff Schmerker, Integrated DNA Technologies, July 16, 2020 https://www.idtdna.com/pages/community/blog/post/clonal-colonies-in-the-forest

Chapter 4

1. *Noise: A Flaw in Human Judgment*, Daniel Kahneman, Olivier Sibony, and Cass R. Sunstein, Little, Brown Spark, 2021
2. *Good to Great: Why Some Companies Make the Leap...and Others Don't*, James Charles Collins, HarperCollins, 2001
3. Ibidem
4. *That Will Never Work: The Birth of Netflix and the Amazing Life of an Idea*, Marc Randolph, Little, Brown, 2019
5. *CEO Excellence: The Six Mindsets That Distinguish the Best Leaders from the Rest*, Carolyn Dewar, Scott Keller, and Vikram Malhotra, Scribner, 2022
6. *Great People Decisions: Why They Matter So Much, Why They are So Hard, and How You Can Master Them*, Claudio Fernández-Aráoz, Wiley, 2007
7. *CEO Excellence: The Six Mindsets That Distinguish the Best Leaders from the Rest*, Carolyn Dewar, Scott Keller, and Vikram Malhotra, Scribner, 2022
8. *It's Not the How or the What But the Who: Succeed by Surrounding Yourself with the Best*, Claudio Fernandez Araoz, Harvard Business Review Press, 2014
9. *The State of Organizations 2023: Ten shifts transforming organizations, Patrick Guggenberger*, Dana Maor, Michael Park, and Patrick Simon, April 26, 2023
10. *Steve Jobs on Hiring Truly Gifted People*, August 9, 2017, https://www.youtube.com/watch?v=a7mS9ZdU6k4
11. *Time, Talent, Energy: Overcome Organizational Drag and Unleash Your Team's Productive Power*, Michael C. Mankins and Eric Garton, Harvard Business Review Press, 2017

12. *The State of Organizations 2023: Ten shifts transforming organizations*, Patrick Guggenberger, Dana Maor, Michael Park, and Patrick Simon, April 26, 2023

13. *Working Backwards: Insights, Stories, and Secrets from Inside Amazon*, Colin Bryar and Bill Carr, St. Martin's Publishing Group, 2021

14. *Inner Mastery, Outer Impact: How Your Five Core Energies Hold the Key to Success*, Hitendra Wadhwa, Hachette Books, 2022

15. *Good to Great: Why Some Companies Make the Leap...and Others Don't*, James Charles Collins, HarperCollins, 2001

16. *Time, Talent, Energy: Overcome Organizational Drag and Unleash Your Team's Productive Power*, Michael C. Mankins and Eric Garton, Harvard Business Review Press, 2017

17. *Invent and Wander: The Collected Writings of Jeff Bezos, with an Introduction by Walter Isaacson*, Jeff Bezos, Harvard Business Review Press, 2020

18. *Working Backwards: Insights, Stories, and Secrets from Inside Amazon*, Colin Bryar and Bill Carr, St. Martin's Publishing Group, 2021

19. *The Hard Thing About Hard Things*, Ben Horowitz, HarperCollins, 2014

20. *Working Backwards: Insights, Stories, and Secrets from Inside Amazon*, Colin Bryar and Bill Carr, St. Martin's Publishing Group, 2021

21. *Chasing Stars: The Myth of Talent and the Portability of Performance*, Boris Groysberg, Princeton University Press, 2012

22. *Meditations on Quixote*, José Ortega y Gasset, University of Illinois Press, 2000

23. *It's Not the How or the What But the Who: Succeed by Surrounding Yourself with the Best,* Claudio Fernandez Araoz, Harvard Business Review Press, 2014

24. *Chasing Stars: The Myth of Talent and the Portability of Performance,* Boris Groysberg, Princeton University Press, 2012

25. *Trillion Dollar Coach: The Leadership Playbook of Silicon Valley's Bill Campbell,* Eric Schmidt, Jonathan Rosenberg, and Alan Eagle, HarperCollins, 2019

26. *Masters of Scale: Surprising Truths from the World's Most Successful Entrepreneurs,* Reid Hoffman, June Cohen, and Deron Triff, Crown, 2021

27. *The Score Takes Care of Itself: My Philosophy of Leadership,* Bill Walsh, Steve Jamison, and Craig Walsh, Penguin Publishing Group, 2010

28. Ibidem

29. Ibidem

30. *Creativity, Inc.: Overcoming the Unseen Forces That Stand in the Way of True Inspiration,* Ed Catmull and Amy Wallace, Random House Publishing Group, 2014

31. Ibidem

32. *No Rules Rules: Netflix and the Culture of Reinvention,* Reed Hastings and Erin Meyer, Penguin Publishing Group, 2020

33. *That Will Never Work: The Birth of Netflix and the Amazing Life of an Idea,* Marc Randolph, Little, Brown, 2019

34. *No Rules Rules: Netflix and the Culture of Reinvention,* Reed Hastings and Erin Meyer, Penguin Publishing Group, 2020

35. *Rethinking Management Education: A View from Chicago"*, Harry L. Davis and Robin M. Hogarth, The University of Chicago, Booth School of Business,1992

36. Ibidem

37. Ibidem

38. Ibidem

39. *Understanding Ignorance: The Surprising Impact of What We Don't Know,* Daniel R. DeNicola, MIT Press, 2017

40. *Rethinking Management Education: A View from Chicago"*, Harry L. Davis and Robin M. Hogarth, The University of Chicago, Booth School of Business,1992

41. Ibidem

Chapter 5

1. *Hit Refresh: The Quest to Rediscover Microsoft's Soul and Imagine a Better Future for Everyone,* Satya Nadella, Greg Shaw, and Jill Tracie Nichols, HarperCollins, 2017

2. *Trillion Dollar Coach: The Leadership Playbook of Silicon Valley's Bill Campbell,* Eric Schmidt, Jonathan Rosenberg, and Alan Eagle, HarperCollins, 2019

3. Ibidem

4. *Intangibles: Management, Measurement, and Reporting,* Baruch Lev, Brookings Institution Press, 2001

5. *Capitalism Without Capital: The Rise of the Intangible Economy,* Jonathan Haskel and Stian Westlake, Princeton University Press, 2018

6. *How and Where Diversity Drives Financial Performance*, Rocio Lorenzo and Martin Reeves, Harvard Business Review, January 30, 2018

7. *The End of Accounting and the Path Forward for Investors and Managers*, Baruch Lev and Feng Gu, Wiley, 2016

8. *Creating a Culture of Unconditional Love*, Claudio Fernández-Aráoz, Harvard Business Review, January 08, 2014

9. *Peter Drucker never said, "Culture eats strategy for breakfast"*, Dean Foust, March 4, 2024 https://www.linkedin.com/pulse/peter-drucker-never-said-culture-eats-strategy-breakfast-dean-foust-kilfe/?trk=public_post_main-feed-card_feed-article-content

10. *What You Do Is Who You Are: How to Create Your Business Culture*, Ben Horowitz, HarperCollins, 2019

11. *Playing to Win: How Strategy Really Works*, Alan G. Lafley and Roger L. Martin, Harvard Business Review Press, 2013

12. *What You Do Is Who You Are: How to Create Your Business Culture*, Ben Horowitz, HarperCollins, 2019

13. *Heroic Leadership: Best Practices from a 450-year-old Company that Changed the World*, Chris Lowney, Loyola Press, 2003

14. *What You Do Is Who You Are: How to Create Your Business Culture*, Ben Horowitz, HarperCollins, 2019

15. *When it comes to culture, does your company Walk the Talk*, Donald Sull, Stefano Turconi, and Charles Sull, MIT Sloan Management Review, July 21, 2020

16. Ibidem

17. Ibidem

18. Ibidem

19. *That Will Never Work: The Birth of Netflix and the Amazing Life of an Idea*, Marc Randolph, Little, Brown, 2019

20. *The Score Takes Care of Itself: My Philosophy of Leadership,* Bill Walsh, Steve Jamison, and Craig Walsh, Penguin Publishing Group, 2010

21. *Danny Meyer, Founder of Shake Shack — How to Win, The 4 Quadrants of Performance, and More,* The Tim Ferris Show, April 6, 2023 https://www.youtube.com/watch?v=9-QoxpY4TeE

22. *The Knowledge Project Ep. #68: Daniel Kahneman: Putting Your Intuition on Ice.*The Knowledge Project with Shane Parrish, October 15, 2019

23. *When it comes to culture, does your company Walk the Talk,* Donald Sull ,Stefano Turconi, and Charles Sull, MIT Sloan Management Review, July 21, 2020

24. Ibidem

25. *Creativity, Inc.: Overcoming the Unseen Forces That Stand in the Way of True Inspiration,* Ed Catmull and Amy Wallace, Random House Publishing Group, 2014

26. https://www.aboutamazon.com/about-us/leadership-principles

27. *The Heart of Business: Leadership Principles for the Next Era of Capitalism,* Hubert Joly and Caroline Lambert, Harvard Business Review Press, 2021

28. *Uncommon Sense, Common Nonsense: Why Some Organisations Consistently Outperform Others,* Jules Goddard and Tony Eccles, Profile Books Limited, 2013

29. *The Heart of Business: Leadership Principles for the Next Era of Capitalism*, Hubert Joly and Caroline Lambert, Harvard Business Review Press, 2021

30. *The Smell of the Place - Prof Sumantra Ghoshal*, https://www.youtube.com/watch?v=EvWL1HcDYSQ

31. *Creativity, Inc.: Overcoming the Unseen Forces That Stand in the Way of True Inspiration*, Ed Catmull and Amy Wallace, Random House Publishing Group, 2014

32. *How a door became a desk, and a symbol of Amazon*, Neal Karlinsky and Jordan Stead, Amazon News, April 17, 2018, https://www.aboutamazon.eu/news/working-at-amazon/how-a-door-became-a-desk-and-a-symbol-of-amazon

33. *Working Backwards: Insights, Stories, and Secrets from Inside Amazon*, Colin Bryar and Bill Carr, St. Martin's Publishing Group, 2021

34. *Check-in Check-Out*, Fred Kofman, The Systems Thinker, https://thesystemsthinker.com/check-in-check-out/

35. Ibidem

36. *Steve Jobs's Rock Tumbler Metaphor*, July 30, 2030, https://www.youtube.com/watch?v=njYciFC7mR8

37. *Man's Search For Meaning*, Viktor E. Frankl, Pocket Books, 1985

38. *The Last Dance Series 1 Episode IV*, ESPN and Netflix, 2020

39. *Radical Candor: Fully Revised & Updated Edition: Be a Kick-Ass Boss Without Losing Your Humanity*, Kim Scott, St. Martin's Publishing Group, 2019

40. *Principles: Life and Work, Ray Dalio, Avid Reader Press / Simon & Schuster, 2017*

41. *The 4 Stages of Psychological Safety: Defining the Path to Inclusion and Innovation*, Timothy R. Clark, Berrett-Koehler Publishers, 2020

42. *The Fearless Organization: Creating Psychological Safety in the Workplace for Learning, Innovation, and Growth*, Amy C. Edmondson, Wiley, 2018

Chapter 6

1. *Loss aversion— everything you need to know,* Michelle Klotz, Inside BE https://insidebe.com/articles/loss-aversion/
2. *The Dynasty,* Jeff Benedict, Avid Reader Press / Simon & Schuster, 2020
3. *The Hard Thing About Hard Things,* Ben Horowitz, Harper-Collins, 2014
4. *The Fifth Discipline: The Art & Practice of The Learning Organization,* Peter M. Senge, Crown, 2006
5. Ibidem
6. *The Crux: How Leaders Become Strategists,* Richard P. Rumelt, PublicAffairs, 2022
7. Ibidem
8. *Mindset: The New Psychology of Success,* Carol S. Dweck, Random House Publishing Group, 2006
9. Ibidem
10. Ibidem
11. *Superforecasting: The Art and Science of Prediction,* Philip E. Tetlock and Dan Gardner, Crown, 2015
12. Ibidem

13. *A More Beautiful Question: The Power of Inquiry to Spark Breakthrough Ideas,* Warren Berger, Bloomsbury USA, 2016

14. *Presence: Human Purpose and the Field of the Future,* Peter M. Senge, C. Otto Scharmer, Joseph Jaworski, and Betty Sue Flowers, Crown, 2008

15. *Self-Efficacy: The Exercise of Control,* Albert Bandura, Worth Publishers, 1997

16. Ibidem

17. *Peak: Secrets from the New Science of Expertise,* Anders Ericsson, Houghton Mifflin Harcourt, 2016

18. Ibidem

19. Ibidem

20. Ibidem

21. *Atomic Habits: An Easy & Proven Way to Build Good Habits & Break Bad Ones,* James Clear, Penguin Publishing Group, 2018

22. Ibidem

Chapter 8

1. *Viento del este, viento del oeste,* Pearl Sydenstricker Buck, DEBOLSILLO, 2003

2. James Taylor's Best Advice for Addicts: "Sweat It Out," Oprah's Master Class, 2015 (https://www.youtube.com/watch?v=58CP-qi1JDjA)

3. *The Highest Goal: The Secret That Sustains You in Every Moment,* Michael Ray, Berrett-Koehler Publishers, 2005

4. Ibidem

5. Ibidem

6. Ibidem

7. Inner Mastery, Outer Impact: How Your Five Core Energies Hold the Key to Success, Hitendra Wadhwa, Hachette Books, 2022

8. *Tom Brady Opens Up - 7th Ring Motivation MJ or Belichick | Enemies | Style of Leadership*, Patrick Bet-David, September 20th, 2023 https://www.youtube.com/watch?v=liz8rZx1NJ8)

9. *A More Beautiful Question: The Power of Inquiry to Spark Breakthrough Ideas*, Warren Berger, Bloomsbury USA, 2016

10. *Elon Musk: Meaning of Life* | Lex Fridman Podcast Clips, Dec 28, 2021 https://www.youtube.com/watch?v=QtDJ5Fxwh9Q

11. *Peak: Secrets from the New Science of Expertise*, Anders Ericsson, Houghton Mifflin Harcourt, 2016

Index

Recommended Readings

Great People Decisions: Why They Matter So Much, Why They are So Hard, and How You Can Master Them, Claudio Fernández-Aráoz, Wiley, 2007

Meditations, Marcus Aurelius, Martin Hammond, Penguin Publishing Group, 2006

Switch: How to Change Things When Change Is Hard, Chip Heath and Dan Heath, Crown, 2010

Good Strategy Bad Strategy: The Difference and Why It Matters, Richard Rumelt, Crown, 2011

The Crux: How Leaders Become Strategists, Richard P. Rumelt, Public Affairs, 2022

The Design of Business: Why Design Thinking is the Next Competitive Advantage, Roger L. Martin, Harvard Business Press, 2009

Playing to Win: How Strategy Really Works, Alan G. Lafley and Roger L. Martin, Harvard Business Review Press, 2013

American Icon: Alan Mulally and the Fight to Save Ford Motor Company, Bryce G. Hoffman, Crown, 2013

Zero to One: Notes on Startups, Or How to Build the Future, Peter Thiel and Blake Masters, Crown, 2014

Heroic Leadership: Best Practices from a 450-year-old Company that Changed the World, Chris Lowney, Loyola Press, 2003

The Hard Thing About Hard Things, Ben Horowitz, Harper Business, 2014

That Will Never Work: The Birth of Netflix and the Amazing Life of an Idea, Marc Randolph, Little, Brown, 2019

A Curious Mind: The Secret to a Bigger Life, Brian Grazer and Charles Fishman, Simon & Schuster, 2015

Zen in the art of archery, Eugen Herrigel, Vintage Books, 1989

The Ambiguities of Experience, James G. March, Cornell University Press, 2010

Man's Search For Meaning, Viktor E. Frankl, Pocket Books, 1985

Winning the Right Game: How to Disrupt, Defend, and Deliver in a Changing World, Ron Adner, MIT Press, 2021

Mindset: The New Psychology of Success, Carol S. Dweck, Random House Publishing Group, 2006

Zero to IPO: Over $1 Trillion Worth of Advice from the World's Most Successful Entrepreneurs, Frederic Kerrest, McGraw-Hill Education, 2022

Disciplined Entrepreneurship: 24 Steps to a Successful Startup, Expanded & Updated, Bill Aulet, Wiley, 2024

The Heart of Business: Leadership Principles for the Next Era of Capitalism, Hubert Joly and Caroline Lambert, Harvard Business Review Press, 2021

Competing Against Luck: The Story of Innovation and Customer Choice, Clayton M. Christensen, Taddy Hall, Karen Dillon, and David S. Duncan, HarperCollins, 2016

Inner Mastery, Outer Impact: How Your Five Core Energies Hold the Key to Success, Hitendra Wadhwa, Hachette Books, 2022

The Creative Act: A Way of Being, Rick Rubin, Penguin Publishing Group, 2023

The Highest Goal: The Secret that Sustains You in Every Moment, Michael L. Ray, Berrett-Koehler, 2004

Creativity, Inc.: Overcoming the Unseen Forces That Stand in the Way of True Inspiration, Ed Catmull and Amy Wallace, Random House Publishing Group, 2014

Ignorance: How It Drives Science, Stuart Firestein, Oxford University Press, USA, 2012

More than you know: finding financial wisdom in unconventional places, Michael J. Mauboussin, Columbia Business School Pub., 2008

The Success Equation: Untangling Skill and Luck in Business, Sports, and Investing, Michael J. Mauboussin, Harvard Business Review Press, 2012

On the Shortness of Life, Lucius Annaeus Seneca and Seneca, Penguin Publishing Group, 2005

Uncommon Sense, Common Nonsense: Why Some Organisations Consistently Outperform Others, Jules Goddard and Tony Eccles, Profile Books Limited, 2013

Trillion Dollar Coach: The Leadership Playbook of Silicon Valley's Bill Campbell, Eric Schmidt, Jonathan Rosenberg, and Alan Eagle, HarperCollins, 2019

On Becoming A Leader, Warren G. Bennis, Basic Books, 1989

High Output Management, Andrew S. Grove, Knopf Doubleday Publishing Group, 1995

The Almanack of Naval Ravikant: A Guide to Wealth and Happiness, Eric Jorgenson, Magrathea Publishing, 2020

About the author

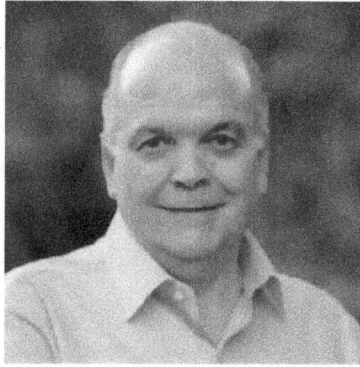

Ernesto Gomez is a seasoned executive with over 30 years of experience, having built and led successful ventures across the food service industry in both the US and Mexico. Transitioning from a dynamic serial entrepreneur to a high-level corporate leader, he served as VP of Human Capital at Grupo Alfa, a major Mexican conglomerate with 83,000 employees, before becoming Chief Human Resources Officer at Sigma Alimentos, a global consumer packaged goods company with 43,000 employees. In these roles, he spearheaded global talent and cultural initiatives, playing a pivotal role in organizational transformation.

Ernesto is a lifelong learner. He studied social communications and has completed executive programs at leading institutions, including Stanford GSB, MIT Sloan School of Management, Wharton

Business School, Kellogg School of Management, Chicago Booth, London Business School, and IMD Business School. He is the founder and CEO of **Aspen Mindset1**, a consulting firm dedicated to helping organizations and individuals reach peak performance. In 2024, Ernesto was invited as a guest speaker in the "Lead through Ambiguity" course at MIT Sloan School of Management.

Outside of his professional life, Ernesto is a devoted family man, celebrating 36 years of marriage. He is the proud father of three daughters and the doting grandfather of two granddaughters, with a third grandchild on the way. In his free time, he enjoys watching soccer and exploring new books, always eager to find the next great read.

Visit Aspenmindset1.com

www.ingramcontent.com/pod-product-compliance
Lightning Source LLC
Chambersburg PA
CBHW031839200326
41597CB00012B/199